WHITE LINE
FEVER

lemmy kilmister

WHITE LINE FEVER

THE AUTOBIOGRAPHY

WITH JANISS GARZA

CITADEL PRESS
Kensington Publishing Corp.
www.kensingtonbooks.com

PICTURE CREDITS
The publishers have used their best endeavours to contact all copyright holders.
They will be glad to hear from anyone who recognises their photographs.

Cover photograph of Lemmy by Nicola Rübenberg ©; Hawkwind photograph
by Michael Odis Archives © Referns; Motorcycle Irene, Phil Taylor and
Lemmy photograph by Ray Stevenson © Retna Pictures Ltd; Motörhead at
Bloomsfield Terrace © Redferns; Motörhead photograph by Fin Costello
© Referns; Motörhead photograph © Corbis; Motörhead photograph by Paul
Slattery © Retna Pictures Ltd; Motörhead photograph by Fin Costello
© Redferns; Bishop Lemmy photograph by Fin Costello © Redferns;
Motörhead photograph by Glenn Laferman ©; Motörhead's 10 year anniversary
party photograph by Tony Mottram ©; Lemmy photograph by Mick Hutson
© Redferns; Lemmy photograph by Mitran Kaul © Redferns

CITADEL PRESS BOOKS are published by

Kensington Publishing Corp.
119 West 40th Street
New York, NY 10018

Copyright © 2002, 2016 Ian Fraser Kilmister and Janiss Garza

First published in Great Britain by Simon & Schuster UK Ltd, 2002

All Kensington titles, imprints, and distributed lines are available at
special quantity discounts for bulk purchases for sales promotions,
premiums, fund-raising, educational, or institutional use. Special book
excerpts or customized printings can also be created to fit specific needs.
For details, write or phone the office of the Kensington sales manager:
Kensington Publishing Corp., 119 West 40th Street, NY 10018,
attn: Sales Department, phone 1-800-221-2647.

CITADEL PRESS and the Citadel logo are Reg. U.S. Pat. & TM Off.

ISBN-13: 978-0-8065-4118-1
ISBN-10: 0-8065-4118-0

First printing: January 2004
Twentieth printing (updated edition): June 2021

28 27 26 25 24 23 22 21 20

Printed in the United States of America

Electronic edition:

ISBN-13: 978-0-8065-3832-7 (e-book)
ISBN-10: 0-8065-3832-5 (e-book)

This book is dedicated to Susan Bennett,
who might have been the one.

CONTENTS

	Prologue	1
1	Capricorn	5
2	Fast and Loose	19
3	Jailbait	37
4	Metropolis	53
5	Speedfreak	69
6	Built for Speed	97
7	Beer Drinkers and Hell Raisers	123
8	Keep Us on the Road	147
9	Back at the Funny Farm	171
10	(Don't Let 'Em) Grind Ya Down	193
11	Angel City	221
12	We Are Motörhead	257
13	Brave New World	289
	Epilogue	293
	The Final Successful Years	297
	Index	323

PROLOGUE

I was born Ian Fraser Kilmister on Christmas Eve, 1945, some five weeks premature, with beautiful golden hair which, to the delight of my quirky mother, fell out five days later. No fingernails, no eyebrows, and I was bright red. My earliest memory is shouting: at what and for what reason, I don't know. Probably a tantrum; or I may have been rehearsing. I was always an early starter.

My father was not pleased. I suppose you could say me and my father didn't hit it off – he left three months later. Perhaps it was the hair falling out; perhaps he thought I was already taking after him.

My father had been a padre in the RAF during the war, and my mother was a very pretty young librarian with no idea of the duplicity of the clergy – I mean, you teach people that the Messiah was the offspring of a vagabond's wife (who is a *virgin*) and a *ghost*? And *this* is a basis for a worldwide religion? I'm not so sure. I figured if Joseph believed *that* one, he deserved to sleep in stables!

So anyway, I didn't really miss my father, 'cause I didn't even remember him. And on top of that, my mum and my gran spoiled me rotten.

I met him twenty-five years later, in a pizza place on Earls Court Road, since he had apparently worked himself into a frenzy of remorse and wanted to 'help me'. My mum and I figured, 'Maybe we can get some loot out of the son-of-a-bitch!' So I meandered off up there to meet the sorry blighter – I thought it was iffy, and I was right.

I recognized him right away – he looked smaller, but I was bigger, right? He was a crouched little wretch with glasses and a bald spot all over his head.

I suppose it was awkward for him – having walked out on someone for whom you were supposed to be the breadwinner, and then not a word for twenty-five years ... awkward, sure. But it had been bloody awkward for my mum, bringing me up on her own and providing for my gran as well!

So he said, 'I'd like to help you in your career, to try and make up for not being a proper father to you.' Ha!

I said, 'Look, I'll make it easy for you. I'm in a rock 'n' roll band and I need some equipment' – amp on the fritz again! – 'so if you can buy me an amplifier and a couple of cabinets we'll call it quits, okay?'

There was a pause. 'Ah,' he said.

I could tell he wasn't a hundred per cent into this scenario.

'The music business is awfully precarious,' he said. (He'd apparently been an excellent concert pianist in his day. But his day was gone.)

'Yeah,' I said, 'I know, but I'm earning my living at it.' (Lie . . . at least at the time!)

'Well,' he said, 'what I had in mind was paying for some lessons – driving lessons, and sales technique. I thought you might become a sales rep or . . .' He trailed off.

It was my turn to be unenthusiastic.

'Bugger off,' I said, and rose from the table. He was pretty lucky the vast reunion pizza hadn't arrived, or it would have become his new hat. I strode back into the fatherless street. It was clean out there – and that was the Earls Court Road!

Talking of two-faced bastards – my band, Motörhead, got nominated for a Grammy in 1991. The music industry doing us yet another favour, you know. So I got on the plane in Los Angeles – New York's a long walk. I had a pint of Jack Daniels in my pocket: I always find it helps with the sobering up. As we taxied elegantly out on to the sun-drenched tarmac, I took a sip and mused pleasantly on this and that.

A voice: 'Give me that bottle!'

I looked up; a stewardess with concrete hair and a mouth like an asshole repeated herself, as history will – 'Give me that bottle!'

Well, I don't know what you might have done, honoured reader, but the fucking thing was bought and paid for. No chance. I volunteered this information. The reply: 'If you don't give me that bottle, I shall put you off the plane!'

This was becoming interesting; we were about fifth in the queue for take-off, were already late, and this boneheaded bitch was going to take us out of the line for one pint of Jack Daniels?

'Fair enough,' I said. 'Put my ass off this fucking plane right now,' or words to that effect. And can you believe it, the stupid cretin did it! AHAHAHAHAHAHAHA!! She made all those people late and miss their connections in New York, all for a pint of the amber pick-me-up . . . So what? Fuck her! And the horse she rode in on! Come to think of it, perhaps she *was* the horse she rode in on! I got another flight an hour and a half later.

It was an inauspicious start to the festivities, and it carried on like it began. When we got to the fabled Radio City (Home of the Stars!), everyone was dressed in hired penguin tuxedos, trying to look as much as possible like the motherfuckers who were stealing their money! I don't wear tuxes – I don't think it's really me, you know? And I don't think the ushers liked the Iron Cross.

Anyway, having been nominated for a Grammy for our first album for Sony, I had foolishly entertained the idea that the company might be pleased. I don't think they even noticed! I have still, to this day, not been lucky enough to gaze, enthralled, upon the splendour that is Tommy Mottola – that night, I think he was probably too busy chasing Mariah Carey around her dressing room. I'm not an overly ambitious man: 'Hello' or just 'Glad to have you aboard' or even 'Hey, dude' would have sufficed. Nothing. *Nada*. Fuck all. So I went to Sire's party. Better. Got laid.

So fuck 'em. And the horse they rode in on!

CHAPTER ONE

capricorn

I started life in Stoke-on-Trent, in the West Midlands of England. Stoke consists of about six towns clustered together. Burslem was the nastiest, so it's only fitting that I was born there. The area is called the Potteries, and the countryside used to be black with slag from the coal used in the kilns that produced all kinds of pottery, including the famous Wedgwood. The ugly slagheaps stretched over the landscape wherever you looked, and the air was dirty with the chimneys' smoke.

By the time my wayward father took off, we had moved to Newcastle, my mum, my gran and I – Newcastle-under-Lyme, that is, which is not too far from Stoke. We lived there until I was six months old, and then we moved to Madeley, a village nearby that was really nice. We lived opposite a big pond – nearly a lake – where there were swans. It was beautiful, but definitely amongst the hoi polloi.

My mum had it rough, trying to support us on her own. The

first job she had was as a TB nurse, which was rotten fucking work, because in those days it was like being on a terminal cancer ward – so she was more or less just seeing the patients on their way. And she saw TB babies being born – apparently there were some real horrors. TB does something weird to the chromosomes: she saw newborn babies with rudimentary feathers on 'em, and another one born with scales. Eventually she left that job and worked for a time as a librarian but then she stopped working for a while. I didn't quite understand the pressures she was under and I figured we'd be all right. Later on, she was a bartender, but that was after she married my stepfather.

I had problems at school right from the start. The teachers and I didn't see eye-to-eye: they wanted me to learn, and I didn't want to. I was always like a fuckin' black hole when it came to maths. You might as well have spoken Swahili to me as try to teach me algebra, so I gave up on it early. I figured I wasn't going to be a mathematician so I might as well fuck off. I played truant constantly, and that was it from day one, really.

The first episode in my difficult schooling that I remember clearly was at primary school. This stupid woman wanted to teach the boys knitting; she was probably a feminist, right? I must have been about seven, so really it was a bit pointless. And this woman was a real brute, too – she quite enjoyed hitting kids. I wouldn't knit because it was sissy. In those days, we still had sissies, see. They weren't running the country, like they are now. I told her I couldn't do it, and she hit me. Then I said I couldn't do it again, and after a while she stopped hitting me.

Honestly though, I think hitting a kid's good for him if he's a bad kid – not if he gets hit indiscriminately, but when he does something wrong. It'll stop him from being bad early if he's fucking terrified of a teacher. I used to get it regular: I got the board rule, the T-square that hung near the blackboard. The teacher would stand behind us and he'd whop it in the back of your head. Later on, the physics teacher would hit us with the leg of a chemistry stool. That was a good one but I never got it 'cause I was pretty good at physics. That is, until I left school, by mutual agreement.

If you get a good smack around the ear so it rings and sings for about half an hour, you're not going to do that shit again in class; you're going to listen to what you're being told. That's how it worked, but now it's gone. It worked for me and it worked for my generation pretty well, because as far as I can see, we're smarter than this generation's shaping up to be.

Anyhow, my mum remarried when I was ten. His name was George Willis, and she met him through my Uncle Colin, who was her only brother. I think the two of them were friends in the army (Colin and George, that is . . .). He had played professional football for Bolton Wanderers, and as he told it, he was a self-made man with his own factory, which made plastic shoe stands for shop windows. That went bust about three months after my mum married him. He was too much. He was fucking funny as shit: he kept getting busted for selling purloined washing machines and fridges off the back of lorries, but he wouldn't tell us about it. He used to say he was off on a business trip; you know, 'I'll be gone about a month, darling,' and he'd go and do thirty days in jail. We didn't find out about this for a while but he turned out all right in the end.

With him, of course, came his two children from his previous marriage – Patricia and Tony. I was the youngest of the three and was constantly being bullied by these huge, newly acquired siblings. And I had a very fraught relationship with my stepfather, because I was an only child, as far as my mother was concerned. She used to fight like a fucking bantam for me, so he'd get a terrible hard time. Patricia's lofty ambition was to work at the Treasury, of all things, and eventually all her dreams came true. Tony lives in Melbourne, Australia, head of some plastics division (*I didn't know plastic was hereditary*!). He went in the Merchant Navy for about ten years and didn't write to us for nearly twenty. My stepfather thought he was dead.

When my mum and stepfather married, we moved to his house in Benllech, a seaside resort on Anglesey. It was about this time that I began to be known as Lemmy – it was a Welsh thing, I believe. I was in a very bad school, being the only English kid among about seven hundred Welsh – that was made for fun and profit, right? So I've been known as Lemmy since I was around ten. I didn't always have the moustache . . . I've only had that since I was eleven.

But I did manage to entertain myself. By stealing some gelignite and rearranging the coastline of Anglesey. There was this construction company redoing all the drains in the village. They could only work in the summer because after that the weather got too cold. So they used to pack up around September or October and they would stash all their supplies in these PortaKabins. And around the end of October, beginning of November, me and some friends would break into them. I mean, Jesus Christ, if you're a boy of about ten or eleven, it was like finding buried treasure! We found caps and overalls, gelignite and detonators and fuses, all kinds of wonderful shit. We would bite the detonator on to the fuse and shove it into the gelignite. Then we'd dig a hole in the sand on the beach, shove the contraption down it, twill the fuse out and cover it up. We'd finish up by putting a big rock on top, lighting the fuse and running like bloody fuck. And BOOM! – the stone would fly fifty feet in the air. It was great! Later, I'd find crowds of people standing there in the rain, looking at the damage and muttering, 'What do you think?', 'I don't know – aliens?' I have no idea what the village copper thought was going on, 'cause he'd hear all these terrifying bangs and he'd come out to the beach and half the cliff had slid into the sea. About two miles of coastline was different when we were finished with it. Just innocent fun, right? Schoolkids get up to all kinds of shit, and after all, why not? That's their job, isn't it – to piss off their elders and give them a cross to bear; otherwise, what use are they?

Of course, these were mere diversions compared to my growing interest in the opposite sex. You have to realize that in those days, the fifties, there wasn't *Playboy* or *Penthouse*. The kicks then were those magazines that featured things like nudists playing tennis – *Health and Efficiency* and shit. That's what an awful world the fifties were. And people call it the age of innocence. Fuck that – you try living in it!

My sexual education began when I was very young. My mother brought home about three uncles before we decided on one being Dad. But that was always fine with me – I figured she was lonely and she was working all day to feed me and my granny, so I didn't mind going to bed a bit early. And growing up in a rural area, one would find people goin' at it in the fields. Plus there were always cars, of course, with the windows steamed up – you could always get a good look at a bared leg or breast as the couple crawled from the front into the back seat. In those days, the fashion was those skirts with the two petticoats underneath, which you whizzed around dancing the jive – so I used to dance a lot. I gave up dancing when the twist came in because it offended me – you couldn't touch the woman any more! Who wants that when you've just discovered adolescent lust? I needed to get close and warm; tactile, hands-on, experiencing, giving and receiving and counter-groping and stuff like that, you know!

But it was when I was fourteen and working at the riding school that I really discovered my lust and desire for women of all shapes, sizes, ages, colours and creeds. And political persuasions. The whole of Manchester and Liverpool would come down to our little seaside resort town every summer. College students on holiday would take out the rides at this school. And the Girl Guides would come every year, en masse – the whole troupe, with their tents and gear. And there were all of two Guide mistresses to look after them – ha! Who were they kidding? We were going to get to those chicks if we had to don wetsuits! And the girls obviously felt the same way. They were eager to learn and we were eager to learn and between us, we learned it. Believe me, we learned every fucking note.

I got a job at the riding school because I loved horses. I still do. We had a good time there because horses make women horny. There's a sexual power to a horse. Women would rather ride a horse bareback, and it's not for the obvious reasons. I think it's to feel the animal's body next to the skin. Through a saddle, you can't, especially an English saddle. And then there's the fact that they're fucking strong too. A horse can do anything it wants with you, really, but it doesn't because, except for a small minority, they aren't temperamental animals. They give in to you. I think that's what women like about horses – a being so strong that gives in without fighting back, or at least trying to assert its rights. It won't do the washing up, but that's a small price to pay.

I was in love with Ann. She was five years older than me, which at that age is an impossible gulf to cross. But I can still recall how she looked – very tall, mostly legs, sort of a broken nose on her but she was well attractive. She went out with this really ugly geezer, though. I couldn't understand that. I caught them fucking once in a barn and I tiptoed out, going, 'Jesus Christ.' But the funniest story regarding those Girl Guides involved a friend of mine called Tommy Lee.

Tommy only had one arm – he was an electrician and one time he put his finger on the wrong wire and the shock literally burned his arm off up to the bicep. They had to remove the rest of it and stitch up his shoulder. He was never quite the same after that – he used to listen a lot to things that only he could hear. But anyway, he had this false arm with a black glove on it, which he would hook on to his belt or put in his pocket. So one night, the two of us sneaked over to the Girl Guides. We crawled under the hedge and through the gorse . . . but when you're fourteen, you don't care, do you? You'll do anything for a piece. We finally got there and I went into this one tent with my bird and Tommy went in the other tent with his. Then it all went quiet, you know, apart from the sound of bed springs. Afterwards, I dozed off for a bit, like people do, because it all just felt so nice (that's why I keep doing it!). Then I was startled awake.

'[*Whack*] Ow! [*Whack*] Ow! [*Whack*] Ow! [*Whack*] Ow!'

So I peeked under the tent-flap and there was Tommy, stark naked with his clothes under his one arm, running like a maniac. Following closely behind was a furious Guide mistress beating him on the head with his own arm! I laughed so hard, they caught me! I couldn't move, I couldn't run, I was just helpless. That was one of the funniest fucking things I'd ever seen in my life.

My initial discovery of sex came before rock 'n' roll, because you have to realize that for the first ten years of my life, rock 'n' roll didn't even exist. It was all Frank Sinatra and Rosemary Clooney, and 'How Much Is that Doggie in the Window?' – that one was on the top of the charts for months! I experienced the birth of rock 'n' roll firsthand. I heard Bill Haley first – 'Razzle Dazzle' I think it was. Then there was 'Rock Around the Clock' and 'See You Later Alligator'. The Comets were a very poor band, actually, but they were the only ones at the time. Plus, it was tough up in Wales – you could get Radio Luxembourg, but that was patchy. It would fade in and out and you had to keep on twiddling the knob to get any kind of reception. Then you'd never find out what they were playing because they announced it once at the beginning and if you came in five or eight bars into the song, they'd never mention the guy's name again. It took me months to find out the name of 'What Do You Want to Make Those Eyes at Me For?' by Emile Ford and the Checkmates. (There's a geezer who just vanished. Emile Ford and the Checkmates had five hits in England. He was huge and then there was a scandal – he was caught charging a kid money for an autograph, and that's what killed him. The Checkmates went out on their own for a while after that but it was no good.)

Then if you wanted a record, you had to order it and wait a month for it to arrive. The first 78 I ever bought was by Tommy Steele, the British answer to Elvis Presley, and then I got 'Peggy Sue' by Buddy Holly. My first full album was *The Buddy Holly Story*, which I got right after he died. Actually, I saw him perform at New Brighton Tower. See, that fuckin' shows your age – I saw Buddy Holly live! Nevertheless, I must say, my street cred is impeccable!

It was a long time before I bought an Elvis Presley record – the first I purchased was 'Don't Be Cruel', I believe. His style, his look was great, he really was a one-off, but I thought he was inferior to Buddy Holly and Little Richard. The problem was he had really naff B-sides. See, albums in those days were different: an album could be a collection of the last six hit singles and the B-sides. So half of Elvis's albums were crap. He only started making good B-sides when he did 'I Beg of You'. Buddy Holly never did a bad track, as far as I could hear. Eddie Cochran, too, was an idol of mine. He used to work at a studio in Hollywood and if somebody finished an hour ahead of time, he'd dash in and make a record. And he used to write and produce all his own stuff. He was the first one ever to do that – a very inventive guy. I was supposed to see him on the second leg of his tour through Britain, but that was when he was in the accident out by Bristol that killed him. I remember being dismayed. That was a great tragedy for rock 'n' roll. He and Holly were the ones who inspired me to play guitar.

I decided to pick up the guitar partly for the music, but girls were at least sixty per cent of the reason I wanted to play. I discovered what an incredible pussy magnet guitars were at the end of the school year. You get shunted in the classroom for a week after the exams with nothing to do, and this one kid brought in a guitar. He couldn't play it, but he was surrounded by women immediately. I thought, 'Ah, now, that looks like fun!' My mum had an old Hawaiian guitar hanging on a wall in our house – she used to play it when she was a kid, and her brother would play banjo. Hawaiian guitar had been very popular not long before: they were lap steels with a flat neck and upraised frets. Hers was very smart, covered with mother-of-pearl inlay. So that was a stroke of luck – not many people had a guitar lying around the house in 1957.

So I dragged the fuckin' thing into class. I couldn't play it, either, but sure enough I was surrounded by women straight away. It actually worked, instantly! That's the only thing that ever worked so immediately in my life. And I never looked back. Eventually, I got the idea that the girls expected me to play the thing, so I taught myself, which was pretty excruciating on that Hawaiian guitar with the strings raised up.

When I was fifteen, we went on a school trip to Paris and I'd learned 'Rock Around the Clock'. So I played that for three hours one night, even though I'd just nearly cut my forefinger off with a flick-knife that refused to do what it was told. I bled on my guitar, and the chicks thought that was absolutely cool. You know – sort of the equivalent of a Sioux warrior going out into the tall grass and killing a bear with his own hands, I suppose. Bleeding for 'em!

Back home my mother and stepdad knew exactly what I was up to. It was quite obvious – they saw the constant procession of chicks. The garage had been converted into living quarters, which I had to myself, and I'd take the girls there. My stepfather used to come in and catch me going at it. He caught me so many times, it was fucking silly; I think he was a voyeur.

'Do you know you're on top of that girl?' he'd shout.

'Yes, I know I'm on top of the bloody girl!' I'd say. 'How do you do it?'

It wasn't long after that Paris trip that I was expelled from school. I played truant with two of my friends. We went on a train to the other side of the island for the afternoon and came back in time for the bus home. But as luck would have it, some bastards from another class saw us on the platform and turned us in. There's always a snitch, isn't there? So I was taken up before the headmaster. He was a real moron, a do-nothing. I think he became headmaster because he was too old to be a magistrate. For two fucking weeks, he had me in his office every day during break and lunchtime, trying to break me down.

'You were seen by two Holyhead boys, when the train turned around,' he told me.

'It wasn't me, sir,' I'd insist. 'I was never there.'

That's when I learned to lie. Another thing discipline teaches you is lying, because if you don't lie, you're in the shit. Anyway, to cut a long story in half the length it would have been, he was going to give me the cane, two on each hand. This was right after my accident with the flick-knife in Paris, remember. It had taken ages for that to start healing. I mean, you might know how you bleed from a cut like that – every time your heart beats, *ber-doom*, blood straight across the fucking room! I must have lost a pint at the time. So I asked the headmaster, 'Could I have four on one hand because of my finger?'

But no, that wouldn't do for him. He stood there impassive, urging my hand up and – *whap*! Fucking blood all over the place. And as if nothing had happened, he said, 'Put your other hand up.'

'You bastard!' I thought. So when the cane came down on my hand, I grabbed it from him and whacked him around the head with it.

'I think you'll find that we don't need your presence here anymore,' he glowered.

'I wasn't coming back anyway,' I told him, and with that, I was out the door.

But he was right, I stayed away and they never came after me for truancy. There were only six months left to go anyway. I didn't tell my parents about it: I would leave like I was going to school every morning and then come back every night. I just used to go up to the riding school and work up there on the beach with the horses but eventually I got a couple of jobs. One was as a house painter with this gay guy, Mr Brownsword (what a name for a queer, absolutely perfect!). All the same, he never hit on me. He was after my good-looking friend, Colin Purvis, which I was quite pleased about. I left him to it, you know – 'Colin will paint in here, Mr Brownsword. I'll go upstairs, shall I?' And Colin would be muttering 'Bastard!' under his breath.

Then we moved off the island to a farm in Conwy, along the Wales coast, right up in the mountains. That's where I learned to be alone and not mind it. I used to wander around the fields with the sheepdogs. I really don't mind being alone now. People think it's weird, but I think it's great.

About that time, my stepfather got me into a factory that made Hotpoint washing machines. Everyone worked on just one piece of them. I was one of the first in line: I had to take four small brass nuts and bolt them on this thing and then a machine came down and knocked a ridge across the sides of them. Then you took the pieces off and threw them in a huge box. There were 15,000 of them to do, and when you were done with that batch, and really garnered a sense of achievement, they'd come and steal them and give you an empty basket. You can't be smart and do that job, man. It's impossible because it would fucking drive you out of your mind. I don't know how those people did it. I suppose they submerged their intelligence because they had responsibilities.

Everybody I knew who left home in search of something better wound up coming back. I had other plans for my life. So I grew my hair till the factory fired me. And I stayed out. I would rather fucking starve to death than go back to that. I'm very lucky and privileged that I escaped.

CHAPTER TWO

fast and loose

I needed a companion, and one was right there – a guy called Ming, after the emperor in *Flash Gordon*. Ming had long hair and that kind of a long, droopy moustache. We began to hang out in coffee bars and dancehalls and pull other blokes' birds and generally appal everybody!

After a bit of this it seemed to us that we should take drugs (not that we knew what the fuck they were), so we got in touch with a friend of mine from when I lived in Anglesey, Robbie Watson of Beaumaris (famous also for its well-preserved castle). Robbie had lived in Manchester and had very long hair, which we thought was a Very Big Thing. We started smoking a bit of dope and then one night, in the Venezia Coffee Bar in Llandudno, Rob gave me an ampoule of speed – methyl amphetamine hydrochloride – with a little skull and crossbones on it. You were supposed to shoot it into your arm.

I never fancied fixing anything, and I never have, even to this day. You get into the ritual. I've seen people do weird shit around needles: shooting water just to have an excuse for getting the needle in their arms. That's what Rob was doing, and he thoroughly recommended that I should try it, too. But I put it in a cup of something – chocolate, I think – and drank it.

There was a poor little girl behind the counter at this coffee bar, and I talked to her non-stop for about four or five hours. I kept saying to Robbie how it was having no effect on me, and then back I went to this poor devil who was in a kind of alphabetic shock from my babbling – but I felt great, you know, King of the World! Trouble is, it wears off. (By the way Robbie Watson, who was my best friend for a long time and had a brilliant dry, ironic sense of humour, has been dead these twenty years – one needle too many. Any questions?) But back to me and Ming – or the Ming and I!

I was sixteen when Ming and I left Wales and headed east to Manchester. Actually, we were chasing after a couple of girls, whom we'd met while they were on holiday in Colwyn Bay. We were going to marry them and all kinds of shit. But of course, it ended up just being sex, as usual. They are much better off than if we had married them, I assure you of that.

I don't remember Ming's girl's name, but mine was called Cathy. She was a great girl, all of fifteen years old, and a curious, enthusiastic fifteen at that. So when they went back to Stockport, Ming and I followed them. We got a flat in Heaton Moor Road and we kept meeting people, and they would have nowhere to stay, so we'd let them sleep on the floor, or the sofa or somewhere, and within a month there were thirty-six of us in one room! The only one I remember was Moses (whom he resembled very closely, if all those Charlton Heston films are to be believed).

Then Cathy got pregnant . . . I mean, she was wonderful, but she was also fifteen – visions of prison bars! Her father was writing letters to my stepfather calling me an exiled Welsh beatnik. The two of them worked out one of those 'convenient' solutions and the baby, Sean, was adopted at birth. I remember Cathy was taking her O-levels at the maternity home and I used to go and visit her. She got really big and I used to fall off the bus, laughing – 'Hello, porky!' and she'd crack up laughing, too. She was a great girl, my first love. I didn't see Cathy again, I don't know why. Funnily enough, she got back in touch with me two or three years ago, just in time for this book . . . She said she'd found Sean, but I won't go into it here – let him have his life.

As for my living situation, we (the thirty-six roommates) obviously got flung out pretty quick – the landlord probably wondered why the gas bill was for £200,000. Since Ming the Fearless Adventurer had gone back to Wales (eventually to become a clerk at a social security office – and you tell me there's a grand pattern and a meaning to life . . .), I was alone again.

During the time I knew Cathy, and for a couple of years after, I was a 'dosser', which then was a particular occupation among kids in the country. We all used to wear US Army jackets, the waterproof ones with a double lining. You could get them really cheap secondhand, and the thing was to get everyone that you knew to write their names on your jacket in felt-tip pen, so you were covered in these weird autographs. And we'd hitchhike around the country, staying with girls or staying in parked railway carriages or caves or whatever, just visiting women of local persuasion. In those days, it was a great thing to be 'on the road'. It was the time of Bob Dylan, with the guitar on the back and the bedroll. A lot of girls like the transient thing. It's a tradition, if you think about it: the circus, the Army, pirates, rock bands on tour – the girls always find them. I think women see something romantic in a geezer's being here today and gone tomorrow. I like it too – but being a geezer, I would like it, wouldn't I? Those days in the early sixties were great. We'd grow our hair down to our assholes and just bum around and live off women wherever we found ourselves. Chicks used to steal food out of the fridge from their parents to feed us and shit – kind of like bringing a meal to the convicted prisoner on the run. They liked the drama of it, and we liked the food.

It wasn't all fun and good times, however. Sometimes, when I was hitchhiking, guys would stop their trucks to come and beat me up. Or you would wind up getting a lift with some huge, homosexual trucker.

'Hello, son. How far are you going?'

'Manchester.'

'Manchester, right. I'd like to suck your dick.'

'I'll get out here, then.'

The flat in Heaton Moor was like a forerunner to the commune, I guess. If one of you had a chick, it was murder. You'd be surrounded by very big eyes in the darkness, and you knew their night vision was getting better all the time! Sex was a lot more fun then – there weren't dire things attached to it like there are now. And sex should be fun, instead of all this stigma – 'Oh, you only want one thing!' Well, of course I do, don't you?! When it stops being fun, then don't do it any more, for Christ's sake.

All of us used to go out begging on Mersey Square and if you got anything, you'd come back and share it. I think we lived mainly on Ambrosia Creamed Rice. You used to have a beer can puncher and you'd sort of suck it out of the can. It was a great delicacy at the time, much better cold. I believe that is when I acquired my taste for cold food, which I have to this day – I can eat cold steak, cold spaghetti, even cold french fries, and that takes some doing! But if you've got enough salt on them, they're all right.

Manchester is not many miles from Liverpool, and there was incredible music coming out of both towns during the early sixties. Through both cities runs the River Mersey and so the music scene of that area took the name Merseybeat. There was even a very well-known band from those days called the Merseybeats, as well as the Mersey Squares, named after the place we went begging. There were hundreds of bands coming out of Manchester and Liverpool, and they all played the same twenty songs – 'Some Other Guy', 'Fortune Teller', 'Ain't Nothing Shaking but the Leaves on the Trees', 'Shake Sherry Shake', 'Do You Love Me' . . . All the bands from 1961 to 1963 were cover bands, including the Beatles.

There was this terrible one-upmanship rivalry going on, concerning whether you knew the original artist or not. Like the support band would say, 'We're gonna play "Fortune Teller" now by the Merseybeats,' but then the Merseybeats would come on and say, 'We'd like to do "Fortune Teller" now by Benny Spellman.' Of course, that never lasted very long, 'cause they just told the whole audience who the original artist was, right? Another thing that bands would do was take an old standard and rock it up. Rory Storm and the Hurricanes really did a number on 'Beautiful Dreamer', I recall, and the Big Three had a go at 'Zip-A-Dee-Doo-Dah'!

It was a unique time with some truly incredible bands. One of them was Johnny Kidd and the Pirates. Johnny Kidd used to wear an eyepatch and a striped shirt and pirate boots. Sometimes he'd wear a white shirt with bouffant sleeves – great get-up. The Pirates had the first strobe light I ever saw, created by the simple expedient of the roadie getting his hands on the club's main switches and turning them all on and off very fast. Their guitar player was Mick Green, who was excellent – I used to carry his guitars to get into their shows for free. Years later, I made a record with Mick. Loners like him never made a reputation then. Eric Clapton got lucky – being an isolationist worked for him, because people sought him out. All the other isolationists, people didn't bother with 'em!

Another great band was the Birds – nothing like the American Byrds who were happening around the same time. This Birds had Ronnie Wood, who later joined the Rolling Stones, playing guitar. The Birds were magic, fucking excellent, far ahead of their time. They only had three singles and they were gone. I used to follow them all over the place, even slept in their van. The band I was in at the time – the Motown Sect, of whom you will hear more in a bit – had the honour of doing a gig with them. I still remember the Birds' line-up: Ali McKenzie singing, Ron and Tony Munroe on guitar, Pete McDaniels on drums and Kim Gardner on bass. Kim now has a pub/restaurant in Hollywood called Cat and the Fiddle. He was a great bassist, but he hardly plays any more. A very good-looking band, the Birds were and Ronnie especially in those days was a very charismatic boy. He used to wear a brown herringbone tweed suit, two-tone shoes and he had a white Telecaster – that was very cool. They were like Mods with long hair, which I liked, 'cause I would never have my hair cut.

See, England has always been very fashion-oriented. Fads came and went very fast. The Mods were a very odd sort, as least in my estimation. They had very short hair, combed over to one side – kind of like John Kennedy but with a rooster-tail-like swatch at the back. And they wore trousers made of this very thin cord material with these bright print, tropical-style jackets, and two-tone shoes. The nearest American equivalent would be the Beach Boys, but we didn't have the surf thing – it was really more in-town, as far as England was concerned. And the Mods used to wear eye make-up too, especially the boys. The crowd of people I was in disliked them, but in retrospect, it was no worse than what we were doing. I mean, we thought they were sissies, and they thought we were yobs – and you know, we were both right.

I got to meet a lot of great musicians at the start of our careers. Jon Lord was one. Jon Lord was, and is, a consummate musician.

He later on played with Deep Purple, Whitesnake and Rainbow, but when I met him, he was playing for the Artwoods who, funnily enough, were fronted by Art Wood! Even funnier, Art Wood was Ron Wood's brother, but hold on a moment.

There was this huge, great palace of a boozer called the Washington on the seafront at Llandudno, and they had rock shows in the upstairs ballroom. Then they started having jazz and blues nights. They had Graham Bond, with Ginger Baker and Dick Heckstall–Smith; they had the Downliners Sect, jazzman Alan Skidmore and them one night, the Artwoods.

So I was lounging about the place, staring at the exotic equipment, and I watched them play – pretty good, I thought, from my lofty critic's perch in north Wales! Anyway, I was talking to Jon Lord after the show, and he and the band offered me a lift back to Colwyn Bay. I'm sure Jon's regretted that ever since! The poor fool gave me his address in West Drayton, near London, and about three weeks later, off I went. I mean, this Impossibly Huge Star would probably have a huge mansion, and he would probably let me sleep in the servants' quarters and introduce me to other Impossibly Huge Stars with whom I would seek my fortune, etc.

Alas for dreams. The address turned out to be a house on a council estate. I arrived at about three in the morning and rang the knocker and banged on the bell.

A sweet little old lady opened the door – 'Yes, who is it?'

'It's me,' I said, 'er, Lemmy from north Wales.'

'Eh?'

'Jon Lord will remember me. He gave me this address.'

'Oh, no, dear, he's on tour in Denmark!'

Why hadn't I considered this possibility? I was young and dumb, that's why.

'Ah . . .' I said.

She looked at me. I looked at her.

'Er,' I said. Silence grew between us.

Then she said something for which I will be eternally grateful, star turn that she was. 'Oh well, never mind dear, you can sleep on the couch and we'll see in the morning.' You don't get much of that in our brave new world!

So I awoke to find Ron Wood, with three of his mates, hanging over me, going, 'Oi, wot you a-doing on my mum's sofa, eh?' So she was Mrs Wood, mother of Ron and Art, and Jon was living there. Coincidence, eh? I got to go to a Birds gig that night, and then I went to Sunbury-on-Thames – but more of that later.

Back in those days, the most impressive band, hands down, was the Beatles. They were the best band in the world. There will never be anything like the Beatles, and you really had to be there to understand what I've just said. Nowadays younger people think the Beatles were just a band, but they weren't. They were a huge phenomenon all over the world. Everybody changed because of the Beatles, even politicians. The *Daily Mirror* in London ran a page every day about what they were doing. Imagine: a big, national fucking newspaper devoting a page each day to a band? They were more than huge.

The Beatles revolutionized rock 'n' roll, and they also changed the way everyone looked. It seems ludicrous now, but for those days, they had very long hair. I remember thinking, 'Wow! How can any guy have hair that long?' Really, it was just combed forward, with a slight fringe over the collar. We all had quiffs then – before the Beatles, it had been ducktails and Elvis.

I was lucky enough to see them play the Cavern club in Liverpool, back at the beginning. They were really fun, eating cheese rolls while singing, and they used to tell a lot of jokes. They were hilarious. They could have been a comedy team. And they had weird guitars that none of us had ever seen. John had his Rickenbacker and Paul had that violin-shaped bass. All the rest of us had Stratocasters; I mean, a Strat was the ultimate you could wish for, Gibsons weren't even around. And George, I believe, was playing a Hofner Futurama, God help him. Later on, he got a series of Gretsch's. It was like, *what*? These weird guys with long hair and these funny guitars and they're posing in their shirt sleeves with their ties pulled out! Everybody else was wearing these horrible, rigid suits, encased in these terrible, ten-button, suffocating Italian jackets. So that was quite a revelation.

And the Beatles were hard men, too. Brian Epstein cleaned them up for mass consumption, but they were anything but sissies. They were from Liverpool, which is like Hamburg or Norfolk, Virginia–a hard, sea-farin' town, all these dockers and sailors around all the time that'd beat the piss out of you if you so much as winked at them. Ringo's from the Dingle, which is like the fucking Bronx. The Rolling Stones were the mummy's boys –

they were all college students from the outskirts of London. They went to starve in London, but it was by choice, to give themselves some sort of aura of disrespectability. I did like the Stones, but they were never anywhere near the Beatles – not for humour, not for originality, not for songs, not for presentation. All they had was Mick Jagger dancing about. Fair enough, the Stones made great records, but they were always shit on stage, whereas the Beatles were the gear.

I remember one gig the Beatles had at the Cavern. It was just after they got Brian Epstein as their manager. Everyone in Liverpool knew that Epstein was gay, and some kid in the audience screamed, 'John Lennon's a fucking queer!' And John – who never wore his glasses on stage – put his guitar down and went into the crowd, shouting, 'Who said that?' So this kid says, 'I fucking did.' John went after him and BAM, gave him the Liverpool kiss, sticking the nut on him – twice! And the kid went down in a mass of blood, snot and teeth. Then John got back on the stage.

'Anybody else?' he asked. Silence. 'All right then. "Some Other Guy".'

The Beatles opened the door for all the bands that came out of that area. It was like Seattle became in the early nineties – the record labels came up and signed everything that moved. Oriole Records held an audition session in a ballroom that lasted for three days. They set up some equipment and seventy-something bands went through and played one song each and the label signed about half of them.

Epstein had other bands besides the Beatles. One of the few he had that didn't make it was called the Big Three. Johnny Gustafson, who later was in Quatermass, Andromeda, and then the Merseybeats, played bass. The band had a fantastic guitar player, Brian 'Griff' Griffiths who had this old, beat-up Hofner Colorama – a horrible fucking guitar with a neck like a tree trunk, but he played unbelievably. And the drummer, Johnny Hutchinson, did all the singing, which was unheard of then – a drummer singing? They were an excellent R&B band, but they got emasculated by the business. The band put out one record that they were happy with, but it didn't make it, so after that they were stuck with two Mitch Murray titles – he wrote a lot of those saccharin-sweet pop songs (one of them was 'How Do You Do It?' for Gerry and the Pacemakers). Those didn't go anywhere, either, so Epstein dropped them. It was a shame 'cause they were a great band.

I suppose you could say that these bands were my peer group, a few years older than me, maybe. And I was in bands myself all this time, of course. You were no doubt wondering when I would get around to that. I already had been through the usual local band thing back in Wales, but in those days, putting together a group wasn't easy. You couldn't get equipment for a start. Whether a guy was going to play bass for you rested mainly on if he had a bass or not, not if he was a good player. And if he had an amp you could all plug into, he was definitely in. It was primitive shit. I was lucky to have my Hofner Club 50 guitar. I saw it hanging in this music store, Wagstaff's, in Llandudno.

Old man Wagstaff – he was about 107 and he was an all right guy. He ran an old-fashioned store that would let you take things on spec – put a few quid down and he'd hold it for you for ever. Needless to say, he went out of business. His son took over and immediately sold the fucking store! I think it became a ladies' lingerie shop.

It was after seeing *Oh Boy* (possibly the best rock show ever) and *6–5 Special* (which wasn't!) I was driven to be a guitar slinger. There weren't many players around in Wales. You'd hear about somebody three villages up who had a guitar and you'd go and interview him. I met Maldwyn Hughes somewhere in Conwy when I was living there – he was a drummer (or, he had a drum kit!). He played in a dance-band style – brushes and riveted cymbal – but he was okay for then. We got a guy he knew, Dave (his last name escapes me, but he came to a Motörhead gig last year!), who was a good guitarist, but a horrendous person. He had green teeth, and his father, a failed comedian on the dinner club circuit, was always around cracking these rotten jokes. Dave, however, thought his old man was hilarious and would quote him when he wasn't there. At first we called our band the Sundowners, then our second name was the DeeJays.

My first show in front of people was in a basement caff in Llandudno. My big moment was singing 'Travelin' Man', a song by Ricky Nelson who, incidentally, was a real good singer, and as handsome as few thousand motherfuckers. Otherwise, we did a lot of instrumentals by people like the Shadows, the Ventures, Duane Eddy, stuff like that. Around the same time I was also playing with this guy Tempy. He was an extraordinary person who taught me a lot about sarcasm, and was a most difficult person to get along with. He played bass – I mean, he really played bass, and for about one and a half hours we hooked up with the local moody guitarist, Tudor, but what with Tempy's scornful sarcasm, my amiable insults and Tudor's eggshell ego, it was no surprise that, although we played together beautifully, that one rehearsal was it. Shows how good it could have been if I remember it forty years later. That sort of petered out, so back to the DeeJays!

We got a singer, Brian Groves, who was a dark, heartthrob sort of guy, a bit like Johnny Gentle, if anyone remembers him. And finally we found a large bass player called John, who was a remarkable rarity in that he had a Fender bass and an amplifier – so he was sort of the Bill Wyman of north Wales, I suppose. My God, we thought, we're made now! But amazingly, we weren't! We played a lot of factory dances and weddings and stuff, and then I got the itch – I knew that wasn't it. Then we kept losing members until it was finally just me and Dave, two guitarists and nobody else, so we played instrumentals for a while. That was the DeeJays. I joined another local band called the Sapphires but they had this terrible hyperventilating guitar player who I couldn't put up with. Between that and the Hotpoint factory, you can see why I left Wales.

When I arrived in Manchester, I had an Eko in my hand. What a horrible guitar that was! It looked like Liberace's fucking stage jacket made into a guitar – all silver glitter and black. And it had ten push buttons on it and only two of them worked. The others were just for show – I took the panel off and they weren't connected to anything. But I swapped it soon enough for a Harmony Meteor (which I should have kept), then traded that in for a Gibson 330, which was a cheap version of the 335. And I changed bands about as often as I changed guitars. First, the Rainmakers: I don't recall how I got with them but by the time I'd joined them, they were already past their prime, and I wasn't in them for very long. After that, I was with another band for about three weeks. I don't even remember what they were called – that shows how impressive they were. Then I joined the Motown Sect, where I would stay for about three years.

I met the guitarist, Stewart Steele, and his bass player Les just from hanging around in Manchester. They had a drummer called Kevin Smith (who lived next door to Ian Brady and Myra Hindley), and I joined up as a guitarist and did most of the singing too. I didn't like singing much – I still don't, but I've gotten used to it by now, obviously. After about two years Les left and we got this bass player whom I knew, name of Glyn, but we called him Glun – who knows why? Glun was a very strange individual. He only ever had one girlfriend, and they got into weird sex immediately when they met. She was this chick who used to walk around the sand dunes in Wales and she always wore this white bikini made out of chamois leather – very thin, clingy material. And she would never talk to anybody. Nobody knew who she was, but everybody wanted to know her! Then she showed up one day with Glun, who was going bald already at the age of twenty.

He was a good-looking guy, though. He looked a little like Dennis Quaid, the actor who played Jerry Lee Lewis in *Great Balls of Fire*, except he had a mass of blond, frizzy hair.

Anyway, the Motown Sect were a kickass R&B band. Stewart was a very good guitarist, well ahead of his time. He had a Gibson Stereo 345, which to everyone else was very big news. And he had a treble-boosted Vox amp, too, which was also a big deal. The Sect played exactly the kind of music that I wanted to play, so I fitted right in. We only called ourselves the Motown Sect because Motown was very big then and it got us gigs. But we didn't play any Motown songs at all, not one. We all had long hair, dressed in striped T-shirts and we would play harmonica and sing blues. We did some great covers of Pretty Things tunes, and the Yardbirds. On stage, we used to say, 'Here's one for all the James Brown fans!' And the audience would go, 'Yaaayyyy!' Then we'd say, 'It's by Chuck Berry and it's called –' Some of the crowd would go for it, because they'd never heard it before. Some of them would really hate it, but what the fuck could they do? We were on stage, you know, fait accompli.

We really had no equipment, no one did in those days. I remember we played at Halifax town hall, supporting the Pretty Things, and we had one 30-watt amplifier. Can you imagine that? The two stacks I've got now are 100 watts each – back then, it was everyone, bass, two guitars and vocal, hooked into one 30-watter about the size of a practice amp. It seems to me like I've always played at the same earblasting volume, but obviously that's not the case. I suppose back in those days we were taking more care with what we were playing, because you could hear every note. And we always used the house PA. Everybody did, even Hendrix years later. Hendrix used the house PA all through his career in England. Some of the places we played had two 10-inch floor speakers on each side of the stage with a little metal amp with handles on the back. Hopeless. How we ever did it, I'll never know. But you never know how you did anything when you were twenty. You look back and you think, 'Fuck me! What was I doing! I didn't do that, surely.'

Members of the band started to leave eventually. Stewart, as talented as he was, wound up going nowhere, sacrificed himself to his nagging mother and his marriage. Anyhow, I wanted to get out of Manchester, because the band was obviously going nowhere. When I saw the Rocking Vicars for the first time, I knew they were my ticket.

CHAPTER THREE

jailbait

I first saw Reverend Black and the Rocking Vicars at Manchester's Oasis club. The Oasis was where all the bigger rock bands played. I took to the Vicars straight away. The drummer's kit had double bass drums – the first time I'd ever seen that – and he sat at the front. And they wore the Finnish national costume: reindeer-skin boots, white trousers with lace-up flies, these smocks from Lapland and vicars' collars. I thought that was very big, you know. They were extremely loud and smashed up all their equipment, just bashed everything to bits. That was very cool, too. And they had long hair.

See, the drummer in the Motown Sect was hassling for us all to get our hair cut short. We had gone to see the Who one night at the Oasis and he was going on about, 'Oh, they look great with that short hair, don't they?' Fuck that! I wasn't gonna cut my hair. In fact, I was the last one in the band with long hair. Everybody else did cut theirs. Just in general, I was getting more and more pissed off with the guys in the band. Finally, I saw the Rocking Vicars at the Oasis again, and they were fucking excellent, so I made sort of tentative inquiries. I learned that the guitar player was not reckoned a good long-term investment, so I followed them doggedly.

The night I auditioned for the Rocking Vicars, I smashed my first guitar. I never could play lead guitar, you see – still can't play lead guitar as we speak. But I fooled them by turning it up and moving my hands very fast all over the guitar. Then at the end, I jumped on the piano. It collapsed and I rode it into the ground and smashed up all my equipment. There's a lot to be said for that, you know. A lot of times over the years, I should have smashed a lot of guitars, but I didn't because it was the only guitar I had. But you know that if I had smashed it, I would have gotten another one somehow. I would have been better off.

The Vicars hired me immediately, and I was with them for over two years, from 1965 till 1967. The band owned a guitar that sort of came with the gig, a Fender Jazzmaster. I had a Telecaster – I'd just recently traded in my Gibson 330 for it – so I put the Tele's neck onto the body of the Jazz. That was a wonderful guitar and I played it right through my time with the Vicars. When I left, I had to give them the Jazz's body back – but after all, who am I to judge?

The Vicars' lead singer, Harry Feeney, was known as Reverend Black. He looked very much like Peter Noone from Herman's Hermits. When he sang, he used to do the 'windshield wipers' – you know, forefingers in the air, waving them back and forth. But he was a good frontman, and the chicks used to adore him.

Pete the bass player would soon leave, so we ended up with Steve Morris, or Moggsy. He was a very miserly person, a trait he got from his father. I remember going over to his house once. I went up to the toilet, and his father shouted up the stairs after me, 'Only use four sheets!' Scrooge comes to your town, you know.

We had a guitar player for a while called Ken, who had this Mini Cooper, a racing model, that was the apple of his eye. But he couldn't get the wire wheels, which were very hard to come by. He was driving down the road once when this other Mini Cooper overtook him like a bat out of hell. As he came to the next roundabout, he saw it upside down, all smashed up with the wheels still spinning, the guy hanging out of it, unconscious, covered in blood. And Ken thought, 'Ooo! Fuckin' unconscious, is he?' Took the fucking wheels off it, drove them back to a farm and hid them in a haystack. Then he called the police and ran back to the roundabout, and this cop was standing there, saying, 'Look at that – some bastard stole his fucking wheels!' Ken nodded and said, 'Ay, there's some cunts around.' That's the sort of people the Rocking Vicars were, in a nutshell.

Then there was Ciggy (short for Cyril), the drummer. He was the leader of the band, and he was one of them people who, everything he did, he was best at. Swimming – you'd do four lengths, he'd do six. If you went climbing, he would be up the tree and down again before you started on the second branch. Shooting pool – he'd have all the balls down and be on the eight-ball and you were still wondering how the fuck he did it. A driven man, but an excellent drummer. He was sort of like Keith Moon.

Remember, he always had his drum kit right up at the front of the stage, which tells you a lot about his personality.

Ciggy was a right tyrant. We had this roadie, Nod, who used to stay with him. Nod was, and is, mentally unstable but a truly wondrous man, really, all round. He's a very successful business-man now on the Isle of Man, where he's from. He got the job of bass player with the Vicars when Moggsy left, but he only lasted one night – he got so excited smashing everything up that he nearly fucking killed himself. Before he roadied for the Vicars, Nod was the first DJ ever to broadcast on Radio Caroline, the first pirate radio station in the world. That kind of thing doesn't exist any more, but back in the mid-sixties, people would anchor a ship three miles off the coast of England, so they could evade its radio laws and play what the ordinary radio stations wouldn't. There were a bunch of them around, and Nod was with the first one. But he left that to be Ciggy's servant because he saw the Rocking Vicars and was immediately gone over them.

Ciggy had this huge bed in his bedroom, while Nod had a campbed a couple of feet away.

'Do you know what I'm doing now, Nodder?' Ciggy would ask.

'No, Cig.'

'I'm stretching out and my arms don't even reach the edges of the bed, it's so big. And you're in that campbed, Nodder.'

'Yes, I know.'

'Say "sir" when you speak to me!'

'Yes, sir, I know!'

Then, in the morning, Ciggy would snap his fingers and Nod would be out there with a frying pan, cooking his breakfast. There had to be some sort of latent gay thing going on there. They weren't fucking each other, because Ciggy was sleeping with this bird, I think her name was Jane. And Nodder used to go with girls, too. So I don't think they were really aware of it. It was some weird, subconscious thing.

There was this one time Nodder was driving our van along the promenade in Douglas, on the Isle of Man – a big van, with a gold cross on the roof and covered in lipstick-written messages like, 'I love men with long hair'. That was the thing in those days, lipstick on the van: the more covered it was, the more successful you were – the one-upmanship thing again. Ciggy looked over at the rest of us.

'I don't think you boys realize how devoted Nodder is to me,' he said.

'Yeah we do,' we told him.

'No you don't. Stop the van, Nodder.'

Nodder stopped the van.

'Everybody get out,' Cig declared.

So we all got out of the back of the van. Ciggy slammed the door shut, opened the window and spoke to Nod.

'Nodder, drive this van through that window.' He pointed at a wedding store, with a large display showing.

'Certainly, sir.'

VROOOOM! BROOOUUUMMM!!! Straight through it. Wedding dresses all over the van.

The guys in the Vicars were a strange lot, but I had a lot of fun playing with them. We toured all over the north of England and we'd fucking bring the place down wherever we went. And I would always do a piano. A lot of places we played had a grand piano, usually painted white, and I would leap on the end with the outermost leg and ride it down into the crowd. We were a hell of a band, loud and exciting, kind of like the Who with long hair. We never did any original material, however. It was all covers, like 'Skinny Minnie' by Bill Haley, or the Beach Boys. We did 'Here Today', from the *Pet Sounds* album, which was quite innovative in those days.

We used to do something of a cabaret act. Pete, the bass player before Moggsy, would drop his trousers during our show, and he had these big, theatrical underpants on. That's always good for a laugh in England. So Pete would stand there like that, and I'd hit him with a custard pie. I'd go right to the audience, pie in hand, asking, 'Shall I? Shall I?' And they'd reply, 'YEAAAHHH! Hit him!' – they always do, don't they? Nothing as funny as a guy getting pied, you know. Every night – boof! Pete would get the pie, everybody would laugh, and we'd finish the song and pack up. The roadies used to make the pie out of flour and water, just mush the stuff around on a paper plate, and set it up behind the amplifier every night, and I never really checked on it. But there was one night where I went back to pick it up and it was in a tin plate – a thick tin plate at that, like an ex-Army tin plate. So I went over to Ciggy, playing away, and I said, 'It's a tin plate!'

'Hit him!' he hissed.

'But I'll fuckin' – it's a tin plate! Look!'

'The act – hit him!'

'All right, then.'

So I went over to Pete and – WHAP! You could hear a muffled scream of 'FUCKIN' HELL!' I broke his nose in two places and there was blood and snot everywhere. The kids thought it was excellent though, thought it was part of the show. We used to have a good laugh with the Rocking Vicars.

We had this terrible manager, Jack Venet, a Jewish crockery salesman. He had a shop full of wholesale crockery in Salford, north Manchester, near to the Jewish neighbourhood of Cheetham Hill. He got us this apartment there, and all the Jews really hated us because we were lying on the lawn on towels with chicks doing our nails and our hair. You know, all the Orthodoxes walking by, glaring at the girls and shit. They didn't like us at all. The wrong side of the tracks, we were. But we got away with murder there because they were nice people, most of them. It was just the militant ones that wanted to give us trouble – but aren't there militants of every race, creed and political persuasion who want to ruin it for everyone else? And we were fairly militant too, I guess, so fuck 'em.

So we had our nice, big flat in Cheetham Hill, and I fell in love with a French girl while we were living there. It was wonderful – I was smitten completely. Anne-Marie, her name was. She looked just like Brigitte Bardot. She was a dentist's daughter from near Limoges, and she came on holiday to my house in Wales. After two days, I left her sitting there totally on her own while I went out with the lads. I don't know why I did that. She obviously wasn't the right one. I never found the right one. I thought I'd found the right one a few years later, but she died. But then, it'll always be the right one who died because you'll never know – she didn't have a chance to become the wrong one.

Come to think of it, my next unintentional foray into parenthood happened while I was in the Rocking Vicars. There were these two girls who were singers in a band that used to tour the American air bases in Europe. I forget what their group was called – the Rock Girls or the Rock Birds or some sort of birds (it was always 'birds' around Liverpool). Anyway, Tracy and her friend used to come around. I really wanted her friend, but Harry got her. Tracy was cute too, and she had bigger tits anyway, so I was quite keen. The two of them came back to our apartment in Manchester and stayed for a weekend. Then after that, they would come and stay with us now and again. And then Tracy showed up one morning around six o'clock and woke me up.

'I'm pregnant,' she said, standing by my bed.

'Eh, what? Pregnant?' I groggily inquired. I mean, who's conscious at six in the morning?

She took this as a terrible affront, that I wasn't immediately awake and at attention.

'Right then!' she snapped and walked out.

That was it. She went away and had the kid, Paul, and brought him up on her own. I met him when he was six, on a coke deal. I went to buy some cocaine from these Brazilian guys in Warwick

Road, Earls Court. We were all, you know, waiting for the man, and I was in the kitchen making a piece of toast. Then in walked this little blond kid.

'You're my daddy,' he told me. 'Mummy's in the other room.'

I walked in there, and sure enough, it was Tracy. I know why I was there, but how the fuck did she come to be there? I'll never know. So I got her a fridge, 'cause she didn't have one. Dragged it up four flights of stairs for her. Fucking terrible job, really, with only me and another guy doing it.

Anyway, this kid was a great kid. He still is. I remember one time he came to see me. He was about twenty-three at the time.

'Dad?'

'Yeah?'

'I have a problem.'

'How much is it, Paul?'

'It's the landlord, Dad.'

'How much is it, Paul?'

'He said he was going to throw us out on the street with all our stuff and he's going to take my guitar—'

'*How-much-is-it-Paul*?'

'Well, it's quite a lot.'

'Fuck it. How much is it?'

'It's £200, actually.'

So I gave him the £200 and he went away. The next day, he showed up in a secondhand Lincoln Continental, the little fucker. He pulled up outside of the house saying, 'Come and look at my new car!'

'Good con, Paul,' I told him, 'but don't ever ask me for rent again 'cause you ain't gonna get it.'

An excellent scam, though. And then he stole one of my chicks off me. But I got him back – I stole one off of him. In fact, we swapped girls one night, at Stringfellows in London. You'd be amazed how many women want to fuck the old man and the son as well.

Paul came over to the States a couple of years ago. He went over to my place and stayed for one day. The next day, two chicks called for him in a car and he was gone. He went up into the hills with them and I didn't see him again. He went back home without even calling and saying goodbye. I remember he was asking me for advice and I was giving it to him. He's always done the exact opposite of what I've said, which I think is fundamentally sound. Chip off the old block, wouldn't you say? But as usual, I digress.

The Rocking Vicars recorded three singles while I was with them, two for CBS and one for Decca in Finland. One of the songs was called 'It's All Right', which Ciggy claimed he wrote, but it was mainly a bastardized version of the Who's 'The Kids Are All Right'. Our other song was the Kinks' 'Dandy', and we actually got all the way up to No. 46 in the charts with that one. We even wound up getting the Who and the Kinks' producer, Shel Talmy. He was an American who was living in London. His office was above a Chinese food store on Greek Street in Soho, London – quite a multinational happening. But that Chinese store with all the ginger and shit in jars stunk really bad. When we had to go and see Shel, we would hold our noses and dash across the street and up the stairs until we got into the office.

Shel was blind as a bat. He did have some sight but it was pretty thin. He used to come into the studio saying 'Hi guys!' and immediately blunder into the drum kit. He was always walking into walls and doors and shit. He had minders lifting him up out of the debris everywhere, but he'd never admit that he couldn't see – he just had friends who 'happened to be there' picking him up like it was an accident. His face was a constant mass of scar tissue about the eyebrows. But he was all right. He got the job done.

We never had a hit, but we were huge on the circuit in the north. South of Birmingham, nobody had ever heard of us, but we used to pull thousands in places like Bolton. There was this one place we played in Bolton which had a circular stage that would spin around, and we'd all be torn off stage by our fans before we were able to make the first rotation. The chicks would pull us down and tear all our clothes off us – the Beatlemania thing, you know. Sounds like fun, doesn't it? Ha! Have you ever had a pair of jeans *ripped* off you? The seams split against the inside of your leg. It's fucking agony, believe me. And the scissors. It was all the go then to get 'locks' of hair from your fave combo! If you've never seen forty serious, grim-lipped birds, all holding scissors, rushing at you . . .

At another gig, Harry went running out to grab the mic, like he always did to start the show, and these chicks had hold of the cord and they pulled on it. Well, he went running out and he never came back, just went over this seven-foot-high stage straight into the crowd. Later on, he told us that as he was going down, a split-second thought ran through his head: 'Ah, great! We're really famous and I'm really popular and I'm gonna fall into all these chicks and they love me and it's gonna be a sea of tits and legs and pussy.' But these chicks parted like the Red Sea – he could see the nails in the floor planks coming up very fast. He also broke his nose in two places. And some girls broke his finger once, pulling his gold ring off. Another time, they took the boots off Ciggy while he was playing the drums! Ciggy ran through the hall bare-foot, screaming, 'Get that fucking chick! I haven't got any spares!'

All this adulation sometimes went to Ciggy's head. Once we were scheduled to play with the Hollies at Manchester University, and Ciggy insisted that we go on last. The Hollies were fucking huge at the time – they'd just done something like six No. 1 records in a row. And here was Ciggy – 'We go on last, the Rocking Vicars,' and the rest of it. And the guy running the show said, 'I can't tell the Hollies that! They're the top of the bill! Don't be unreasonable.'

'Fuckin' tell them the Rocking Vicars go on last and that's it,' Ciggy insisted.

So the guy went to the Hollies and they didn't give a fuck – 'Yeah! Go home early!' So they went on first and when we came on, the hall was empty – after all, everybody came to see the Hollies, right? So we go out to the stage, which was actually in two parts, pushed together and locked. And the night before,

Ciggy had complained to Nod that the bass drums had been moving forward – 'If those bass drums move tomorrow, Nodder, you know what'll happen, boy.' So Nodder freaked out about that, and he put the spurs for the bass drum right in the join between the two parts of the stage. The only problem was that someone had unlocked them. So we come on and Ciggy calls, 'Ah one, two, three, four!' Boom – WHAP! The whole fuckin' stage separated and all his drums fell in the hole. There he was, left sitting on his stool with his sticks in the air. That was the end of the show. It was probably a good thing no one was there!

As if all this wasn't surreal enough, I saw a UFO while I was with the Rocking Vicars. We were in our Zephyr, going home to Manchester from Nelson in Lancashire, across the moors, and this thing came over the horizon. It was a bright pink colour and shaped like a ball. It went *zhoom* and stopped dead. I don't give a fuck what you tell me – a cloud of seagulls, a fuckin' air balloon, forget it. It wasn't any of them things. This object went *whuuum* like a bat out of hell and stopped like that. So we got out of the car and we were all looking at it. It hung there and it seemed to be pulsing, but that was probably the effect of the atmosphere, just like the stars appear to pulse. Then suddenly, *bang*, and it went right over our heads, from standing still to about a hundred miles a second. *Phoom*! And it was over the horizon within two seconds of starting off. Nothing we make can even produce a facsimile of that performance, right? Therefore, when you've eliminated all the possibilities, it was a UFO, however improbable that may seem. I'm sure it wasn't looking at us. It was probably more interested in America – it was probably there by the time we were back in the car!

A couple of times the Rocking Vicars got to play outside of England. One trip was to Finland (I never went back there again until I had Motörhead). The Vicars had a No. 1 record there – of course, you only had to sell about 30,000 45s to be No. 1.

The Vicars were the first British band to play behind the Iron Curtain. I'm not sure how that got set up – our manager was an enterprising geezer, despite the crockery. We played in Yugoslavia, which was sort of the crossover country of the Eastern Bloc. That area doesn't have much going for it, really, other than that. Basically, its crops are rocks and scrub, and everybody's poor. We played in Ljubljana, now the capital of Slovenia. Then we went down into Montenegro and Bosnia. And everyone would be bitching about everyone else. I mean bitching like these people really wanted to kill each other, apparently for historical reasons that have faded from their memory. It's ingrained in the children from the time they're a year old, it'll take a miracle to ever stop them. The Serbs hating the Croats – that's all you ever heard then, and it's still the same now. Of course, I figured they all were the bad guys because the Communists were doing shit that I wouldn't do to people. I didn't know my own people were doing the same shit to them. I can't say that Yugoslavian trip was particularly enlightening. We only got to see the good bits – you get the tour guide, you know, but in a Communist country, he's the Tour Guide, right? If he says we don't go down there, we damn well don't go down there!

Finally, in early 1967, I left the Rocking Vicars. They were still going until seven or eight years ago, as a sort of cabaret act. But I had bigger plans for myself, see. Conquering the north of England wasn't good enough for me any more. I wanted London.

CHAPTER FOUR

metropolis

I left the Rocking Vicars, thinking I was going to be a star in my own right immediately. Everything was going to be wonderful and huge women would get a hold of me and do things to me with raw carrots – you know, shit like that. Of course, it didn't happen quite that way.

The first time I went to London I lasted there for about a month – after waking up on Ron Woods' mum's sofa. I stayed with a friend of mine called Murphy, whom I knew from when he was living in Blackpool. He was a little Irish folk singer, fellow dosser. Nice character. We used to know these two gay tailors who would make all our clothes – they'd measure the inside of your leg four or five times. They liked Murph and Murph would go hang out with them now and again. He wasn't fucking them, though – at least I don't think so. But they made him a Batman suit, with a hood and batwings that went from the arms to the waist. He was going to fly off Blackpool Tower, see – publicity stunt, like.

Blackpool Tower is a scale model of the Eiffel Tower – it's about a quarter the size! Still too tall to fly off it if you don't make it, really. But Murph got all dressed up in his batsuit and we all went with him to the Tower and headed straight for the geezer at the ticket stand.

'Hello!' Murph announced. 'I am Murph the Bat Man! Let me in!'

'Why?' the ticket-selling geezer phlegmatically inquired.

'I'm going to fly off the top!' Murph declared.

'No you're not.'

'I am!' Murph insisted.

'No you're not.'

'Out of my way!' demanded the five-foot-five batperson.

'I'll tell you what, mate,' the guy told him. 'You give me the money and then fly up there, and if you make it you can come back down and I'll give you your money back. How's that?'

He took the glory away from poor Murph, his fleeting chance of a claim to fame. Anyhow, Murph had already gone to London when I decided to head down there myself. He had this terrible rat-hole flat in Sunbury-on-Thames. Well, it wasn't that bad a flat, except there were about twenty of us dossers living in its four or five rooms and there was no hot water. No grub and no money either. We were getting a band together, me and Murph and Roger, this drummer – he had no drums, but he played on cushions! I ran out of patience after a short while, so I went up north. I woke up one morning, sitting on a beach in South Shields eating cold baked beans out of a can with my comb. I thought, 'There's got to be more to life than this.' So I went back home and got fed for a bit. I didn't see Murph again for about thirty years, and when I did I was pleasantly surprised to find that he'd weathered the years with his mind relatively intact (at least what was left of it after the sixties). He's now an author; when I saw him he gave me a novel he'd written. When I get around to reading it, I'll let you know how it is!

Not long after I'd returned home, the Birds were playing up in Northwich, near Manchester, so I got a ride down with them back to London. When I got there, I phoned the only number I knew in London (apart from John Lord!) – Neville Chesters. He had been a roadie for the Who and the Merseybeats. I asked if I could doss on his floor and he told me to come on over. At that time, Neville was working for the Jimi Hendrix Experience and he was sharing the flat with Noel Redding, Hendrix's bass player. They needed a spare set of hands, so about three weeks after I landed at Neville's, I got a job working for them.

Jimi Hendrix was huge in England at the time – he'd just had two No. 1 records – but no one in America had heard of him yet. I worked for his band for about a year on all the TV shows and the tours through England. I didn't get to go to any of the foreign gigs, unfortunately, because I was only a fetcher and a lifter. Still, it was an amazing experience. Hendrix was the most startling guitarist ever, no doubt about that. Everything about him was great – his playing was truly astounding, plus he had a great stage act. He was like a cat, a snake! When he performed, he would drive the chicks fucking nuts. I've seen him go in his bedroom with five chicks – and they'd all come out smiling too. And of course, the road crew got the spin-offs. A stud, Hendrix was; and I'm crass enough to think that's quite a good thing. I don't know what's wrong with being a stud – it's more fun than *not* being a stud, that's for sure! Unfortunately I didn't get to mix with him offstage much – I wasn't part of his private life. I was just working for him. I do recall that he was a very gentle, very nice guy. But most people were nicer in those days. It was one of those ages of innocence, you know. Nobody had started dying yet.

I liked the other two guys in the Experience, too. Noel Redding was all right, only he used to wear a nightshirt to bed, and Aladdin-type shoes with the curly toes and a nightcap with a tassel. That was quite a sight. Mitch was nuts, as he still is today, in fact. One time I was standing on a traffic island in the middle of Oxford Street and Mitch bounced up to me, wearing a white fur coat, white trousers, white shirt, shoes and socks – complete vision, you know. 'Hello, I don't know who I am!' he said and ran off again. I don't think he knew who I was, either!

This period of time, the late sixties, was brilliant for rock 'n' roll in Britain. There hasn't been such a wealth of talent in one era since. The Beatles, the Stones, the Hollies, the Who, Small Faces, Downliners Sect, Yardbirds had all come out of the same three-year period. The 'British Invasion' had changed the face of rock music for all time, so in London we were sitting on top of the world. There was a lot of blues going on: Savoy Brown (which was much bigger in the States than in England) and Foghat started off as blues bands, and the jazz–blues thing came in for a little while. There were people like Graham Bond, who had Jack Bruce in his band, and Ginger Baker, both of whom went on to be in Cream. The Beatles had just come out with *Sergeant Pepper*, so they were certainly flavour of the fucking month! Two of them had just gotten busted, too, so they could do no wrong – John Lennon as icon–martyr, and Yoko looking violated at his side.

Everywhere you looked, there were good bands coming up. It's depressing nowadays because you have to dig to find a really great band, and there seem to be thousands of awful ones. There were thousands of bands then, too, but really, at least half of them were great. Just to give you an example, I was along for Hendrix's second UK tour, which ran from 14 November 1967 until 5 December. Co-headlining were the Move, who'd also just had two No. 1s in a row; then Pink Floyd with Syd Barrett – his last tour; Amen Corner, who were then at No. 2; the Nice, featuring a young organ player called Keith Emerson; and the Eire Apparent, later to become the Grease Band backing Joe Cocker. All for an entrance fee of 7 shillings and sixpence (70 cents American). And that was normal for the era.

You didn't think I'd get to talking about sixties London without mentioning drugs, did you? Oh no, not I. Our whole crew was on acid during the entire tour. And we all got the job done just fine. Orgasms on acid, by the way, are fucking excellent, really unbelievable, so I was doing plenty of that, too. As a matter of fact, acid was still legal back then. There weren't any laws against it until the end of '67. And as for marijuana – well, you could have passed by the average copper on the beat, smoking a joint, and he wouldn't have known what it was. In fact, a friend of mine once told a cop it was a herbal cigarette, and the guy went for it. It just seemed like all of London was out of their heads back then. We used to get high and go down to the park and talk to the trees – sometimes the trees would win the argument. We were told that acid didn't work on two consecutive days, but we found that if you double the dose, it does!

There were some great clubs in London, like the Electric Garden and Middle Earth. You'd go there and *everybody* would be tripping. There was a chick who used to stand in the doorway of Middle Earth, by the cash register, handing out acid. She'd give one to each person as he or she walked in, free. One thing we used to do was get a crystal of acid, which had a hundred trips in it, and dissolve it into a hundred drops of distilled water in a bottle. Then we'd take a dropper and lay the mixture out in rows on a sheet of newspaper. Then when it was dry, we'd put the page back in the paper, go out, rip off the corners and sell them to people for a quid. Sometimes, if you were lucky, you'd get a piece of the treated newspaper that had two trips in it; other times, a soggy bit of paper!

Real acid tripping, in those days, wasn't all groovy-like, peaceful shit. The first trip I took lasted for eighteen hours, and I couldn't really see. All I saw were visions, not what was actually around me. Everything, every sound – you could snap your fingers and it would be like a kaleidoscope – doomph! Your eyes would just turn into noise-activated, coloured strobes. And all the time your mind felt like you were on a rollercoaster, sometimes slow at the approach to the top of each drop and then – *wheeee!* Your teeth would kind of sizzle, and if you started laughing, it was incredibly hard to stop. You could say I liked acid. But acid is a dangerous drug – that is, if you're complacent because it will wake your ass up! If you were a little uneasy about yourself, you would either be catalyzed by it or you wouldn't show up again – you know, they'd take your tie and shoelaces away, and your belt, and put you in a room with no windows in it and a lot of soft walls. A lot of people I knew went to the basket-weavers' hotel on acid.

Everybody was taking pills, too. Uppers, like Blues, Black Beauties and Dexedrine. It was all pills – I never took powder for years and years. Really, if you're in a band, or especially if you're a roadie, you need to take them things because otherwise you can't keep up with the pace. You can't go on a three-month tour without being on something. I don't give a fuck what they say – keep fit, eat your greens, drink juice – fuck off! It's not true! I don't care if you eat two hundred artichokes, you still won't last through a three-month tour, doing a gig a day.

Everybody did downers as well. We were doing Mandrax (the same as Quaaludes in the States). Once we bought a canister of a thousand Mandrax, but when we opened it, they had all melted – they must have got wet somehow. There was just this mushy mess of Mandrax at the bottom of this thing. So we laid it all out on the breadboard, rolled it down with a rolling pin and put it under the grill and we wound up with this white sheet of Mandrax, and we'd snap a corner off and eat it. Sometimes you just got a mouthful of chalk (the binding) and sometimes you'd get three Mandrax – sort of opiate Russian Roulette! I had a prescription for Dexedrine and Mandrax. In those days, there were a lot of doctors who'd prescribe you anything if you gave them the money. Harley Street doctors at that. And the doctor I went to took me off Mandrax, because a law had just been passed against it, and put me on Tuinol as a substitute. They were horrifying, really. Fuckin' Tuinol was seven or eight times worse than Mandrax. Mandrax is a little baby boy compared to Tuinol! That was dumb as shit. As usual.

But back to the rock 'n' roll part of my story, as opposed to the drugs (or the sex) parts. Eventually, I did start playing in some bands around London. At first, I got a job playing guitar for P.P. Arnold. She used to be one of the Ikettes, and she had a couple of hits in England. I was in her band for about two weeks, until she discovered I couldn't play lead. So I lost that job. Then in '68, I wound up singing for Sam Gopal. He was half-Burmese, half-Nepalese or something like that – I forget now. But he played tablas, which are impossible to amplify. They're too boomy, see – at least they were for the equipment of the time. He'd had a band previously called the Sam Gopal Dream, which had been on a show called 'Christmas on Earth' with Hendrix in December of '67. Some people think I played that gig, but I didn't. By the time I met up with Sam, he'd dropped the 'Dream' and was just going on as Sam Gopal, in suitably modest fashion!

I was introduced to Sam by a friend of mine called Roger D'Elia. He played guitar and his grandmother was Mary Clare, a very famous English actress, a long time ago. I was living at Roger's house and he told me he was forming a band with Sam

Gopal and this bassist Phil Duke, and they needed a geezer who could sing. The music was sort of a blend of psychedelia, blues and Middle Eastern rhythms meets the Damned! We recorded one album, did one tour through Germany and played a gig at the Speakeasy in London. That show at the Speak was standing-ovation time, so we thought we were gonna be stars, but it was actually all downhill from there on in!

Sam was determined to be a star. That's what he really wanted. He was a real fucking poseur, but I didn't mind that at all. I mean, *I'm* a poseur – what are you doing in this business if you're not a poseur, right? So Sam was all right. He had his own ideas and all, but he let me write anything I wanted to. I wrote nearly all the songs that wound up on our only album. Back then, I was still using my stepfather's name, so I'm listed as 'Ian (Lemmy) Willis'. I credited 'group' on a few of the songs, but the truth is I stayed up and wrote them in one night. That was when I had first discovered this wonderful drug called Methedrine. The only two I didn't do on the record were 'Angry Faces', which was written by Leo Davidson, and a Donovan song, 'Season of the Witch' – we did a fair version of it, actually.

The album, *Escalator*, was put out by this record company called Stable. That was a joke. It was run by these two Indian geezers who had no idea whatsoever how to run a record label. I don't know how that whole deal came together. It was one of Sam's projects – he knew the producer and all. *Escalator* wound up doing nothing, zero. Stable was too indie of a label, even for the indies. Eventually, it dawned on us that the band was going nowhere, so we just gave it up. Funny enough, I ran into Sam Gopal in 1991, just before I left England to move to America. It was very strange, because he was just walking up the street, right around where I lived, and I hadn't seen him for ten years. We chatted for a bit and he told me he was getting a band together – you know, all that fun stuff. Still!

After Sam Gopal, I spent about a year with my guitar hanging on the wall, and I just tripped out and dossed around, living in squats. It's easy to do when you're young, and I was twenty-three. It was around this time that I learned to hate heroin. It was always around, of course, but not very much at first – it started to be a real problem around 1970. I knew this guy, Preston Dave – he wasn't even a junkie. He was getting there, but not quite. And a bunch of us were sitting with him at a Wimpy Bar, the early English attempt at, say, Burger King. It was in Earls Court Road and was open all night. Preston was shaking and shit, so he went off to Piccadilly – where you went to score heroin. So he came back and went to the toilet. A few minutes later, he came lurching out backwards. His face was black and his tongue was sticking out. Somebody had sold him rat poison – took his money, smiled at him and sold him certain death. I thought, 'Hell, if that's the kind of people who are hanging around with heroin, you can fucking have it.' And I also saw people doing horrible fixes with old, blunt needles that would really fucking mess their arms up. You'd see people with embolisms in their arms the size of a cricket ball. And they'd be selling their asses for a fucking shot. It always looked like misery to me. No fun at all.

I've had so many fucking friends die from heroin, but the worst of it was that the girl I was the most in love with in my life died of the stuff, too. Her name was Sue and she was the first girl I ever lived with. She was all of fifteen when we first got together – most embarrassing if caught by the police, but there you go. I was just twenty-one when we met in 1967 anyway, so I wasn't exactly some randy old geezer. More like two randy young ones! The big deal – at least to everyone else – was that she was black. We were ostracized completely. All our friends left us – hers *and* mine. And this was supposed to be the era of peace and love, you know! Everybody was listening to black music for the first time and all. Ha! It just proved how hypocritical they all were. Nobody knew how to deal with us. My friends left because I was associating with a nigger, which I thought was very bad news all around – fuckin' assholes. Her black friends thought I was the oppressor, stealing a young black girl and making her my plaything and shit. Bollocks! I pointed out to them that when I left the house, I didn't hold her by the wrist – she could come with me if she wanted and stay if she wanted. But Sue and I didn't care, really. Hell, if you lose friends like that, they ain't your friends anyway. Besides, we were in love, so no one else mattered anyhow.

Sue and I used to fight like cat and dog, though. She was a triple Gemini, so you never knew which personality you were talking to. We never had enough money, and then she started working at the Speakeasy. She kept getting offers from people – she was young and had only just discovered she was beautiful, so people took her for a ride. While she was working at the Speak, we split up – one of the four or five times during the course of our relationship – and then she screwed Mick Jagger. I asked her afterwards, 'What was he like?' And she said, 'Well, he was good, but he wasn't as good as Jagger, you know,' which was perfect! She meant, of course, that Jagger couldn't live up to his own reputation. No way he could, even if he swung in, pole-vaulted into the room on his – well, you catch my drift.

Anyway, Sue eventually got a job in the Lebanon, dancing in Beirut. That was before it got demolished, and it was still a playground of the Western world. She returned with a staggering heroin habit, and it was never quite the same after that. I'd just gone back with her and she went up to her granny's. While she was there, she got one of her friends to come around with some smack. So she went in the bathroom and shut the door. Did the shit, drew herself a bath and then she passed out and drowned in her own bathwater. She was all of nineteen.

I was in London when she died – I had joined Hawkwind by this time – but I didn't go to the funeral. I mean, who wants to see them dead? I liked them alive. She had a sister, Kay. She was as pretty as Sue. I don't know what happened to her but if she's reading this, get in touch – we'll talk about Sue a bit. Yes?

So I knew from personal experience that heroin was the most awful drug to get involved with, but that doesn't mean I didn't go through a few harrowing experiences involving the search for my own substance of choice. One time, about '69 or '70, I really came unstuck. A bunch of us were sitting around, waiting for the speed to arrive. This guy was going out with a nurse, see, who worked at a dispensary, so he bribed her into getting us some amphetamine sulphate. Finally, she came in with a mason jar with what looked like amphetamine sulphate written on it. And we, greedy bastards that we were, dug in immediately. But it wasn't amphetamine, it was atropine sulphate – belladonna. Poison. We'd all done about a teaspoonful of it, which is like 200 times the overdose, and we went berserk, the whole lot of us.

I was walking around with a TV under my arm, talking to it. Somebody else was trying to feed the trees outside his window. It was really interesting for a while, actually. Then we all passed out and somebody called Release, the firm with the free drug rescue van, and they loaded us all in the back like bundles of wood and took us to the hospital. I woke up in this bed and I could see through my hand. I could see the wrinkles in the sheet under it. Then I saw the institution walls. 'Fuck me!' I thought. I was convinced I'd landed in the loony bin. Then I realized it was a normal hospital because the sleeves on the jacket weren't long enough. And I saw, across from me, my friend Jeff, just waking up.

'Psst! Jeff!'

'What?'

'We're in hospital.'

'Wow.'

'We've got to get out of here. Are you okay?'

'Yeah.'

'Be quiet!'

So we got out of bed and I was just pulling up the jockeys when:

'AAAAARGHH! THEY'RE ALL OVER THE FLOOR!'

And he was leaping and screaming, eyes like organ stops, 'Worms and grubs and ants – WAAARGH!'

I got back in bed.

Eventually the doctor showed up. 'If we'd got to you in another hour, you would have been dead.'

I was thinking, 'I bet you're sorry, you miserable bugger.'

He said we'd had the antidote, and that it would take a while to wear off. Well, it took two weeks and it was a really strange time. I mean, I would be sitting, reading a book, and I'd turn to page 42 – but there was no book. Or I'd walk down the street, thinking I was carrying a case and suddenly – oops! I'd have nothing in my hand. Weird . . . but interesting. Not interesting enough to do it again, though!

Finally, after dossing around for some months, I wound up in another band, Opal Butterfly. I met their drummer, Simon King, at a place called the Drug Store in Chelsea. The Drug Store was a big flash gaff, about three floors high. There was a restaurant at the top and a boozer on the ground floor and a record store in the basement. All these boutiques and other stores, too. It was one of the first mall-type places. It was rather expensive, but it was an all-right place. The guys in Opal Butterfly used to hang out there to drink, and I hooked up with Simon and just sort of drifted into the band. I don't really know why I was hanging out with him – I never got along with him all that well. But you will be hearing more about Simon later.

Anyhow, Opal Butterfly was a good band, but they never went

anywhere. They'd been around for years when I got in and it was only a few months after that that they gave it up. One of the guys, Ray Major, went on to be in Mott the Hoople. The break-up turned out to be rather timely, because it was only a couple of months later that I wound up in Hawkwind.

CHAPTER FIVE

speedfreak

My association with Hawkwind began with Dikmik. The 'instrument' he played in the band was a small box with two knobs that sat on a card table. It was called a ring modulator, but it was actually an audio generator that went out of human hearing at both high and low end. If it went up, you would lose your balance and fall down and vomit; if it went down, you shit your pants. You could make people have epileptic fits with this contraption. On stage, Dikmik could pick out the audience members who were susceptible. When we were playing in Hawkwind together, I'd go up to him and say, 'Any good 'uns?' He'd say, 'Yeah, that guy there. See that?' And he'd twist the knob – *hrum-mmmm* – and the guy would start flopping about. Amazing things you can do with sound. But of course, we could never tell for sure if it was the audio generator or if it was because we'd spiked all the food with acid before the gig. But as usual, I'm getting ahead of myself.

Anyway, it was Dikmik who got me in Hawkwind. He was running around, looking for speed and of course he found me eventually. I was living with this girl in a squat on Gloucester Road in London, and she ran into him. 'Oh, I've got a friend at home who takes pills,' she said. So he came round and we discovered that we had a mutual interest in discovering how long the human body can be made to jump about without stopping. We went on something of a binge that lasted about three weeks, during which we had about two hours' sleep. He had decided he was going to India to find the Sufic secret or some fucking mystical shit like that. But he only got as far as Gloucester Road, which is in the wrong direction anyway, and then he gave up. He'd found me anyhow, and that was fine with him because he was the only speed freak in Hawkwind – the rest of them were acidheads – and he wanted some company.

I'd seen Hawkwind before – not at the beginning, when they were known as Group X, though. The entire audience looked like they were having an epileptic fit, all six hundred of 'em doing the same move. I remember thinking, 'Well, I have to join them – I can't watch them!' I wanted to get a spot playing guitar. Their lead guitarist, Huw Lloyd Langton, had just left the band – disappeared, really. They had been doing a gig at the Isle of Wight festival. They weren't really playing at the festival, though; they played outside of the festival – how's that for being alternative? Anyway, a bunch of them were sitting around a campfire and Huw had done something like eight tabs of acid. 'I'm going for a walk, lads,' he told the others, went over a hill and nobody saw him again for something like five years! That's the way things were in Hawkwind – loose, very loose. Huw did re-emerge a few years later, in a band called Widowmaker (not Dee Schneider's 1990s project, which we'll come to later).

So I was hoping for the guitar slot, but I wound up on bass instead. In fact, the day I joined Hawkwind was when I first started playing bass. It was in August, 1971. The band had an open-air gig at Powis Square in Notting Hill Gate, and the bassist, who was Dave Anderson at the time, didn't show up. But like an idiot, he left his bass in the van, which paves the way for a successor, doesn't it? You're almost inviting somebody to come along and take the job off you, which I did. Apparently, Dave didn't like doing free festivals, like the one Hawkwind was doing that night. He wanted to be paid all the time, and the band was into doing all these benefit shows. I remember us playing in defence of the Stoke Newington Eight, whoever they were. They'd been put in jail for some fucking thing and we thought it wasn't fair because we were freaks and everything wasn't fair because of the pigs – you know, all that crap that you talked to each other in those days. So we were doing all these gigs for these people, but the whole time we were getting conned. The organizers of those gigs had pockets everywhere. Quite a racket, that used to be. Still is, really. But once again, I digress.

Anyhow, here was Hawkwind at Powis Square with no bass player, and somebody was running around asking, 'Who plays bass?' Dikmik, seeing his opportunity to have a full-time partner in speed, pointed at me and said, 'He does.' 'Bastard!' I hissed at him, because I'd never played bass in my life! So Nik Turner, who played saxophone and sang, came over to me and said in very important tones, 'Make some noises in E. This is called "You Shouldn't Do That",' and walked off again. I mean, that's a lot of fucking information, isn't it? And then they opened up with another song anyway. It must have gone all right, 'cause I was with them for four years. They never officially told me I was in the band that whole time. Del Dettmar, the synthesizer player, sold me a Hopf bass, which he got at an auction at Heathrow airport for about £27. I still haven't paid him back for it.

As I said earlier, Hawkwind was a very loose outfit. Every few months, there was a change in the line-up; people would come and go. You were never quite sure who was in the band at any one time – at least, you were never sure who would show up. At one point, there were nine of us in the band and then just a few weeks later there were only five of us, and then there were six, and then seven and then five again. Every picture you see, it was different people in the fucking band. It was very strange. Dave Brock, who sang and played guitar, founded the band in July of 1969 and he's been its only constant member over the years. It's his band, really, the same as Motörhead is mine. Hawkwind would not exist without him. And even he would disappear occasionally. He would go through these, like, nature boy phases – that's what we used to call them – striding out into the fields with a staff, naked but for a loincloth, and you couldn't get to him. I mean, there was no point in saying, 'Dave, we've got a gig tonight,' 'cause he was gone, he was busy being nature boy, right?

In addition to being the main part of Hawkwind's power core, Dave also wrote most of the songs. But he would never write with anybody else in the band. At least with Motörhead, I give the others credit, but Dave was all self-sufficient. I learned a lot from him, really, about vision and tenacity – things I already knew about, but watching him bolstered my confidence. He just made me sure of it. He had his quirks, too, like his spanking fantasies. He used to pass schoolgirls on the road and lean out of his car, yelling, 'Spank! Spank! Spank! Hello, girls, spanky-spanky!' When he was tripping, he was always convinced that he'd bitten off his tongue. He never had, of course, but he used to keep a red bandana in his back pocket and he would wipe his mouth with it. Then when he saw the bandana was all red – aaargh! – and off he'd go! One time, in Grantchester, we pulled that trick on him and it took me forty-five minutes to talk him down (I was tripping at the time myself, so I probably wasn't doing a very good job!). Dave was always trying to beat the taxman out of money. One time he was explaining to us, 'I went and bought this new place. I've written it off against the old place and got this farm and they can't touch me.' And it transpired that as he was telling us that in London, the marshals were going through his house in Devon and taking all the furniture. Fucking miraculous, that.

Nik Turner was the other half of the power core in those days since he was the frontman, basically. He was in Hawkwind from the beginning, too, and he was one of those moral, self-righteous assholes, as only Virgos can be. Nik was the oldest one in Hawkwind – older even than Dave and I think that's where some of his behaviour came from. Like, on the one hand he could be very old-fashioned but he was also keen on showing off how outrageous he could be. I guess it was some sort of post-hippie, mid-life crisis. And he would do annoying things, like play his saxophone – through a wah-wah pedal – right on top of the fucking vocals. Whenever we got a new sound guy, Dave or I would tell him, 'Singing – sax out.'

I recall one time when Dave didn't show up for a gig in north London, and we rang up his house in Devon. His wife, who hardly ever spoke, told us, 'Oh, I don't know where he is. He took some mescaline and went for a walk. That was this morning and I haven't seen him since.' So Nik got this guy, Twink (who later founded the Pink Fairies), to play lead. The only guitar we had had two strings on it and he couldn't play either of them because he was a drummer. That was one of Nik's great decisions. He was also one of those who later got me fired from the band, so there you go.

But Nik was occasionally a source of high amusement. One time he walked up to the mic, holding his sax, which was plugged in, and he disappeared in this fusillade of blue sparks! We were all laughing, 'Yeah, great, Nik!' He finally shot back into the amps and they fell on him, which gave me immense personal satisfaction. Another time we had a gig on an open stage that had this moat running in front of it. So we were playing and it was pouring fucking rain – all these hippies were sitting under bits of plastic, just sopping wet and buying hamburgers for £15 – all that good festival shit. Part of the stage was under this bowl-shaped enclosure, but the front four feet were totally open and wet. Me and Dave were out there and Nik makes an entrance from the left, dressed as a frog – he had black cowboy boots, green tights, a green leotard and a full rubber frog head on. He was holding the saxophone and capering – he was a great caperer, Nikky. So he came capering along the stage and I said to Dave, 'It's about time somebody pushed that fucking frog into that pond –' and as I said it, he skated straight into the fucking water! I had to stop playing, I was laughing so hard. And then Stacia – our dancer – came up and tried to help him out and she fell in with him! I was on my knees, fucking helpless with laughter.

Another time we were in Philadelphia or somewhere like that and he was doing his trick with the joss sticks – he used to light these joss sticks and fill his mouth with lighter fluid. Then with all the lights out, he'd go POOM! and you'd get this big ball of fire. And this one night he overdid the lighter fluid. He went POOM! and set his hand on fire – there was this black silhouette hand in the dark surrounded by a halo of flames with a voice screaming, 'OW! OW! OW!' So we took him to hospital and he had blisters like sausages up his arm. But he still played that night, which showed fortitude, I will say that. He'd get drunk as a cunt on wine and once, in Switzerland, he walked out of the side of the stage and leaned on the PA and the whole thing collapsed on him. The only part of him sticking out of the rubble was his arm, holding the sax. Poor Nikky – he could be a bit accident prone.

Our drummer at the time was Terry Ollis – we called him Boris or Borealis. He used to wear nothing on stage. He'd come on wearing a pair of his old lady's knickers – that's all – but he'd take them off halfway through the first song anyway. He was a dynamite drummer, but his dick kept getting in the way – free fall, you know, and he'd wind up hitting it with his stick. Ow! – There'd be gaps in the fucking music. But he was still excellent, and an excellent character, too. He used to work at his dad's scrapyard on the outskirts of Far Westland, and he was always coming to rehearsals and gigs in weird clothing he found there. One day he'd show up in a German army outfit, and another day he'd show up in an old woman's shawl. Then he got into downers and that turned out to be his ruin. The last gig he ever did with us was at Glasgow University in January of '72. He fell out of the van on the way there. We stopped at a light and he thought we were there, so he opened the door and collapsed out onto the street. He was all over the road, his bags scattered and shit. We didn't know he'd gotten out, so we just drove on. Later, we found him and somehow we got him to the gig. I remember Nazareth was supporting us and when they finished, we put up our gear and he walked onstage and sat there with his drumsticks crossed on the snare all night. Never played a single hit. So it was obviously time for him to go. A shame, really. We replaced him with Simon King, whom I knew from Opal Butterfly. He was another one who wound up getting me fired from Hawkwind – and I was the one responsible for getting him in the band!

We also had this guy called Bob Calvert, from South Africa, who was the resident poet. Half the time he showed up for the gigs and the other half he didn't. When he was around, he'd read his poetry on stage, or that of sci-fi writer Michael Moorcock, which added to the band's mysterioso space warrior aura. But Bob had some very weird ideas. He wanted to go on stage with a typewriter around his neck on a guitar strap and type things and throw them to the audience. 'It's not gonna work, Bob,' I told him. 'It's never gonna work.' But he wouldn't believe me. Luckily, he never got a chance to try out that particular trick. Another time, when we were playing Wembley Stadium, he came on stage wearing a witch's hat and a long, black cape, carrying a sword and a trumpet. Then halfway through the second song, he attacked me with the sword! I was yelling, 'Fuck you!' and batting him about the head with my bass – 'Look, fuck off!' It was the biggest gig we ever played in our lives, and he was attacking me with a fucking sword – what's wrong with this picture, you know?

Bob was very bright, but he went nuts while he was working with us. He started taking a lot of Valium and hyperventilating and speaking much too fast and much too much. And he went down to this Buddhist retreat in fucking Devon or somewhere, and this guy who was in charge – Bob's new guru – was obviously a fucking charlatan. You know, hippies grouped around his feet, staring adoringly at this fount of wisdom. I just thought he was a cunt. And then Bob started getting really weird – 'You don't believe in this man, do you? You don't realize his greatness!' and all this shit. Eventually I had to pop him – he was playing with a piece of wire, and he hit me around the face with it, so I hit him back. He fell over and when he got up he was a much better guy. But he was falling apart mentally – he once got so bad, we put him in a cab with his girlfriend and sent him to check in at a mental hospital. Halfway there, he put a hammerlock on the driver, and the driver had to press a button under his dashboard so someone would come and fetch him. A real mess, Bob was. We had to keep sending him to asylums and they'd keep him locked up for like three or four days and then send him back out. It was a very difficult time for him; it was even more difficult for the rest of us! He's dead now, had a heart attack at much too young an age. He was quite talented, but he wasn't as brilliant as people make out now. Of course, when you die, you become more brilliant by about fifty-eight per cent. You sell more records and you become absolutely wonderful – 'Man, what a pity we didn't buy any of his records while he was alive, but still . . .' I'm sure that's where *I'm* going – 'How about Motörhead? What a brilliant band. If only we'd seen them . . .'

But I liked Bob. I played on his solo album, *Captain Lockheed and the Starfighters*, which he recorded in early 1974. He named it after that terrible plane, the F-104 Starfighter, which the Americans foisted on to Germany. There was a joke going round Germany at the time: 'Do you want to buy a Starfighter? Buy an acre of ground and wait,' 'cause they were crashing all over Europe. *Captain Lockheed* was a good album. Brian Eno produced and played on it, and some of the other guys who played on it were Dave and Nik, Simon King, Twink and Adrian Wagner. I must get a copy of it one of these days.

I had some wild times with Bob. When he got together with Viv Stanshall, the singer of the Bonzo Dog Doodah Band, it was like hell! Once I was with Bob and Nik, and we were on our way to eat. We picked up Stanshall, who was standing at the kerb. He was holding a briefcase and wearing this blue suit with big black checks on it, and his head was shaved because he was in the Sean Head Band at the time. And he had a Homburg hat on and he was chewing Valium. So we all went to this Greek restaurant and Viv and Calvert started smashing plates on the floor – off they went, screaming at each other across the table, having these convoluted intellectual discussions. Jesus – it went on for hours. Then we went back to Stanshall's place, which was quite near our house.

'Don't go through the door because of the turtles,' Viv told us.

He had all these tanks with terrapins in them, and these little walkways between, and of course, they fell off and went all over. So to get into the house, we had to go round the side of the porch and climb through a window into the hallway. So we got in that way, and Bob trod on a turtle and that started it between him and Viv all over again. Then we went upstairs and he had all these false limbs hanging off the ceiling and robots and these big piles of priceless 78s by people like Jelly Roll Morton, which Bob immediately fell into, knocking them over and breaking them. About three hours later, I decided to go home. Just as I was leaving one of them decided he *must* take a bath, and the other one got a chair and took it into the bathroom so they could go on screaming at each other! I thought I'd had enough – but I was wrong! At 7.30 AM, I was wakened from a dead sleep by Stanshall, standing outside my window screaming.

'You killed my terrapins!'

'You cunt!' I yelled back. 'It was Bob!' And I slammed the window shut.

Stanshall's dead now, too – he went in early '95.

In addition to the musicians and Bob, Hawkwind had several dancers. Stacia was the one who stayed with us the longest – she was there all through the time I was in the band and left to get married not long after I was out. She was six-foot-two in her stocking feet and had 52-inch tits. Quite an impressive sight. She was a bookbinder from Devon and when she first saw the band, she took all her clothes off, painted her body from head to toe and rolled around on the stage while they played. Then she wound up staying with them. She had a lot of male fans amongst our audience. We had a couple of other dancers, too – one called Renee was double jointed. She was small and blonde and looked very pretty until – presto! – she started her contortions and everything twisted all wrong. And then we had Tony, who was a professional dancer and could do pantomime.

Occasionally, Michael Moorcock would take part in some of our performances and recordings – he's on *Warrior on the Edge of Time*. More often, though, Bob would recite the stuff he wrote. Hawkwind was inspired by him – the name comes from Moorcock's *Hawkmoon* series of books. He was great. We used to go around his house for some free food now and again, and he would have these notices on his door: 'If I don't answer the first ring of the bell, don't ring it again or I'll come out and kill you. It means no, it means I'm not in, it means I don't want to see you.

Fuck off everybody. I'm writing. Leave me a-fucking-lone.' That was brilliant.

All our equipment was painted in psychedelic colours by this guy, Barney Bubbles – another one who's dead now. He used fluorescent, Day-Glo paint and we'd throw ultraviolet lights on them. He also did our covers for *Silver Machine* and *Doremi Fasol Latido*. He was really clever, and did a lot of trippy art for us.

The album covers in the early seventies were so much better than they are now – the designs were much more elaborate. If you can find an original copy of *Space Ritual*, you'll see what I mean. The whole thing folds out and it's loaded with art and photos and poetry. Now, that's well worth your money. When you talk about packaging and getting an idea across to the public, that's it right there. Nowadays with CDs, everything's smaller and the record companies are so fucking miserable and cheap and nasty. They won't spend five cents more to make it look better. And remember that long box thing when CDs first came out? What the fuck was that anyway? The CD was only half the size of the box, and you couldn't open the fucking thing up to get your CD out. You had to use a carving knife and you'd wind up cracking the jewel case and putting scratches all over it. And it took ages to persuade them to get rid of that long box. I remember them fighting over it when Motörhead was on Sony. People were leaving the company because of the loss of the long box! How's that for stupidity?

Anyhow, we made for one hell of a show. Hawkwind wasn't one of those hippie-drippy, peace-and-love outfits – we were a black nightmare! Although we had all these intense, coloured lights, the band was mostly in darkness. Above us we had a huge light show – eighteen screens showing things like melting oil, war and political scenes, odd mottoes, animation. The music would just come blaring out, with dancers writhing around onstage and Dikmik shaking up the audience with the audio generator. It was quite an experience, especially since most of our fans were tripped out on acid to begin with . . . not to mention everyone in the band. That included me and Dikmik, of course – just because we were Hawkwind's only speedfreaks, it certainly didn't keep us from indulging in anything else we could get our hands on! There's one legend about how I was so loaded that supposedly I had to be propped up against my amp on stage so I wouldn't fall over. Well, as loaded as I may have been, I remember that show and it's not true about my having to be propped up.

That gig was at the Roundhouse in 1972, when we recorded the songs 'Silver Machine' and 'You Shouldn't Do That'. That was a big venue. It was once an old engine shed, where they used to turn the trains around on a huge turntable. These rock 'n' roll people leased it and turned it into a venue by taking the turntable out and putting a stage at one end. There were still bits of loco-motive lying around inside and shit. It was a great place, but now it's used for theatre troupes – you know, Japanese acrobats and shit. Very interesting culturally, I guess, but . . . back to my story.

Dikmik and I had been up for about three days prior, whacking down Dexedrine. Then we got a bit paranoid and took some downers – Mandrax – but we thought it wasn't very interesting because it calmed us down too much, so we took some acid, and then we took some mescaline to make it more colourful. It started getting a bit freaky, so we took a couple more Mandrax . . . and then we took some more speed because we got too slowed down again. Then we went to the Roundhouse. Dikmik was driving and he was really interested in the side of the road, so he kept steering over to look at it. Finally we got up there and we walked in the dressing room and it was full of smoke – everyone was smoking dope. So we sat there for a while and somebody came in with some cocaine and we had some of that, and then some Black Bombers (or Black Beauties, as they're known in the States – uppers) arrived, so we each had eight of them. Oh yeah, and we took some more acid as well. By the time we had to go on stage, me and Dikmik were like boards!

'Fuckin' hell, 'Mik,' I said, 'I can't move. Can you?'

'No,' he replied. 'It's great, isn't it?'

'Yeah, but we've got to get onstage soon.'

'Oh, they'll help us,' he assured me.

So the roadies hooked our bootheels on to the back of the stage and pushed us up, and they strapped my bass on me.

'Right, okay,' I said. 'Which way is the audience, man?'

'That way.'

'How far?'

'Ten yards.'

So I stepped up – 'One, two, three, four, five, right. Hit it.'

And that was one of the best live gigs we ever taped. The jamming between me and Brock was great. But I never saw the audience! We got 'Silver Machine', our only hit – and a No. 2 at that! – from that gig! My vocals wound up on the recording, even though Bob sang it at the show. Bob wasn't on that night and he sounded horrible, so everybody tried overdubbing it later and I was the only one who sang it right. That was really my only time singing lead, except for 'The Watcher' on *Doremi Fasol Latido*, 'Lost Johnny' on *Hall of the Mountain Grill*, and 'Motorhead', which was a B-side for the single 'Kings of Speed' and later appeared on the re-release of *Warrior on the Edge of Time*. But I did sing a lot of back-ups.

It was magical, the time I spent with Hawkwind. We used to go to this huge, deserted estate and trip out. It had immense, over-grown gardens surrounding little pathways, ornamental lakes and tunnels all around this burned-out house. It was like madness in there. The whole band with about ten chicks and a couple more guys would all climb over the wall and we'd get high and wander around – you'd find the occasional person, tied in a knot under a tree, gibbering. That was a great time, the summer of '71 – I can't remember it, but I'll never forget it!

Maybe you're wondering, with the massive amounts of drugs I consumed in those days, why I never became a casualty. I did die once – well, the band thought I had, at least. But I hadn't. The whole thing started when we were going home from a gig in the van. This guy, John the Bog, was our driver – actually, *he* died, about two years after this incident, come to think of it. He was going down the road, dropping everyone off, and I was the last one. We were in the midst of dividing up about a hundred Blues (pills that had speed with downer mixed in them) between us. I had the bag on my lap and I'd just handed him fifty and I had fifty. Right then, a carload of cops pulled in front of us. Brilliant timing, that.

'Look, Lemmy,' John said, 'we're getting busted!'

Well, no shit! But I wasn't about to let that happen. So I said, 'Fuck this,' and ate all my blues – John did the same. So here we were, chewing fifty blues apiece. Let me tell you, that was fucking foul! And we couldn't exactly take a drink to wash them down, either, because the cops were standing right outside.

'Step out of the van.'

'All right, officer,' we mumbled through the mush in our mouths.

'What were you doing in the front of the van there?' one cop interrogated me. 'You were doing something with your hands when we pulled you over.'

'No I wasn't,' I insisted, drooling blue shit all the while.

But they missed that somehow and let us go. So John dropped me off in Finchley, where I was living in a house with the rest of the band. Apparently, I fell asleep and my metabolism hit an all-time low. It looked like I had stopped breathing, although I hadn't. But I was lying there with both eyes open, and it scared the shit out of Stacia. She freaked out.

'HE'S DEAD! HE'S DEAD!' she began screaming. Then she got Dave, and he was standing over me too, screaming, 'HE'S DEAD!'

Meanwhile, I was lying there thinking, 'What the fuck is the matter with these people? Can't they see I'm trying to get some sleep?' I wanted to tell them to shut up, but I was having kind of a hard time speaking. Eventually they figured out I wasn't dead and after a while, I was all right again.

Other than a couple of scares like that, I have to admit I had a lot of fun. So did everyone else. You have to realize, it was okay in those days to do shit like that. It really isn't now – everyone's into health and being politically correct, anti-drug and all that. But back in the Hawkwind days, drugs were our common denominator. It was the only way we freaks could tell if somebody was one of us. We were always showing up at our gigs completely spannered. And like I said before, sometimes those turned out to be some of our best gigs. There were also the legendary shows where we spiked the food and drink with acid. Actually we only did that a couple of times – one was at the Roundhouse, I recall. And since most of our fans showed up at the gigs already stoned, it didn't make much of a difference anyway. There was an innocence about those days, because we didn't know yet that some people would go nuts on acid, or that others would start putting needles in themselves and dying from an embolism. We started getting a few psychotics, but they were usually taken away after a short while. So we really didn't know about all that. It was all bread and circuses for us.

Because of our massive drug use, there was always the chance of running afoul of the cops. But as you can tell from my adventure with John the Bog, they were pretty thick. I'll give you another example of police stupidity. Often, cops would be lurking around outside the clubs. One time, I was leaving the Speakeasy with this guy, Graham, who was working for Jimmy Page and who later became Motörhead's tour manager. I had half a gram of speed on me and we were walking down the road to his truck, and these two cops, who were waiting in the doorway opposite the club, started following us.

'Let's do this quick,' I said, and quickly unwrapped the packet. Just as I had it opened in my hand, this arm came over my shoulder and closed over my fist – and contents!

'What have you got there, son?' the cop inquired.

'It's a . . . piece of paper.'

'Well, let's have a look, then.'

So I opened my hand and he took the piece of paper. All this white powder spilled all over his black cop outfit – he looked like he'd just been powdered like a baby! And he turns the paper over and said, 'Nothing on there.'

'That bitch!' I said. 'She didn't write her number down after all!'

'Oh, right,' he nodded. 'Let's have a look at your pockets.'

And there he was with the shit all over him – his mate didn't notice, either! So he searched the both of us, but we didn't have anything and they went away. How's that for dense?

But we did get busted all the time. Cops would be standing outside your house, just waiting for you. Finally, we got pretty good at stashing our contraband – Nik would hide stuff in his saxophone. And the undercover cops never did get that hippie look right. You know, the guy would be standing there, wearing a

Nehru jacket with a big green medallion, thinking he was really hip. Then you'd look down and see plastic sandals. It was fucking terrifying, really, at times, but it certainly never stopped us.

The first album I made with the band was *Doremi Fasol Latido*, their third. I played on three other full albums: the *Space Ritual* double live album, *Hall of the Mountain Grill* and *Warrior on the Edge of Time*. A lot of Hawkwind's best work came from the time I was with them. When it came to making the records, it didn't matter, really, who the producer was – Dave was always the one who was in charge. I didn't get any help, however, recording 'The Watcher', since it was my song, not Dave's. He was like that. Somewhere between *Space Ritual* and *Hall . . .* we did the *Greasy Truckers* album, which also featured several other artists. It was recorded in London at the Roundhouse on 13 February 1972. One side of the album is entitled 'Power Cut', and it's completely blank because the miners shut off all the power in England for about three hours that night – that's how they brought down the government. Everyone sat around in the dark, smoking dope, until it was switched back on again, and the gig continued.

Dikmik left the band around this time; he got sick of all the power politics and shit that was always going on within the band. So he went off and lived with this bird who was a great friend of mine who's living with Simon King now – London can be a very incestuous place. But while Dikmik was living with her, he became a pot dealer for ages until he got busted. He wound up spending six months or a year in jail and when he came out, he became a moocher, sleeping on the couches of his friends. He spent two years on my couch until I finally threw him out. It was a shame – Mik had a very incisive mind, but prison knocked him down and he never recovered from it. I think he was profoundly shocked by prison life. He changed when he came out – you become a victim instead of a predator and that's a terrible thing to see.

But the best thing about the band for me was that we got to play a lot outside of England, and I hadn't travelled for a long time. My first gig abroad with Hawkwind was the Olympia in Paris. A German band called Amon Duul II played with us – they had the industrial sound way back then, and they were very well known in Europe. We caused a riot at that show: it was just kids going nuts, really, but the CRS (riot police) came out like the fucking Gestapo. Another gig I recall doing was at the Lem Club in Italy – that really pissed Dave off!

I got to America for the first time in 1973, after *Space Ritual* was released. I took to it from the start – unlimited whoopee! It was fucking El Dorado for an Englishman. You've got to understand how drab and awful England was to grow up in back then – even more than now! Then you get to Texas – you can get England into Texas three and a half times! You can drive through Texas for two days and still be in Texas. And the clarity of the air in places like Arizona and Colorado is incredible. The first time I was in Boulder, I looked out the window and there was this range of mountains that looked like they were right on top of the hotel, but they were fifty miles away! We'd never seen anything like that, and it was the same for any European band.

Our first tour started off at the Tower Theater in Philadelphia, and then we went up to New York and played at the Hayden Planetarium – the comet Kohoutek was coming across, you see, and we were all very cosmically inclined. It came across all right, but it wasn't visible to the naked eye – bit of a swizz and that was about it. But we had a party at the Planetarium and saw this pro- gramme about Kohoutek and shit like that. It was a huge party, where I met Alice Cooper for the first time, and Stevie Wonder was there. In the middle of the lobby, there was this big lump of moonrock, and Stevie's minder brought him over, placed his hand on it – 'Moonrock, Stevie' – and led him away. Then during the show, I looked around, and there was Stevie Wonder again, with his minder telling him, 'It's going across now, Stevie, left to right.' Who's fucking nuts, me or them?

We took acid quite consistently all across America. In Cleveland, we were spiked three times with angel dust by three different sets of freaks before we went on, and none of us noticed. That's how much acid we were doing!

Then you come to Los Angeles and you think you've died and gone to fucking heaven. It's the palm trees. I remember our plane landing at LAX, circling around to descend, and I looked down – every yard had a blue pool and the palm trees were huge. And as we drove down Hollywood Boulevard, lined with all those palm trees, I thought, 'Wow, this is something else, this place.' And really, it was magical at that time, young men over from England. Of course, by the time I moved over years later, I knew it wasn't – intellectually at least. But you never quite lose that feeling of wonder.

As a matter of fact, it was in Los Angeles I wrote my last song for Hawkwind. It was 'Motorhead'. We were at the Hyatt on Sunset Boulevard – the hotel Led Zeppelin made famous with their tales of destruction. The Electric Light Orchestra were staying at the hotel the same time as us, and their guitarist, Roy Wood had an Ovation, which he lent me. So there I was on the balcony of the Hyatt, at 7.30 in the morning, howling away at the top of my voice. The cops seemed vaguely disturbed by my racket. They kept stopping their cars, getting out and looking up at me. But then they'd just shake their heads and take off. Maybe they thought they were hallucinating. Incidentally, on the original recording of 'Motorhead', the one for Hawkwind, there was a violin solo. If any of you out there think the violin is a sissy instrument, you've never heard Simon House. He played like a maniac and he ripped through that song. He did some great stuff, Simon. He ended up playing with David Bowie later on.

We toured America four times while I was in Hawkwind. Simon House, who played synthesizer and violin, came on just before the second tour. Eventually, he replaced Del Dettmar, but he and Del were both in the band at the tour's start. Del quit in the middle and went to live in Canada, where he built a log cabin with his own hands – literally. And he was a little fella, too! He built it for his wife, who was pregnant at home in England. About seven months later, when the cabin was finished, she and the kid came out by ship – and the kid was half Pakistani. Nasty shock, eh? Went straight to him, too. I don't think he immediately put her right back on the boat, but it was words to that effect. Very bad news.

Things with Hawkwind started to go downhill when the drum empire took over. That started in July, 1974, when Alan Powell joined. Simon King had injured himself playing American Football, and Alan filled in for him on our Norwegian tour. Then, when Simon came back a few weeks later, Alan wanted to stay because he was having so much fun, and he and Simon were mates and all that. So the two of them started playing together. That, as far as I'm concerned, was the end of Hawkwind because those two killed it between them.

I've seen a lot of pompous drummers in my lifetime, but when it came to this pair, it was ridiculous. Simon and Alan's two drum kits were set at the centre of the stage in this huge semi-circle of percussive effects, which we never used. There was an anvil and several bells, tubular and the hanging kind, and all sort of things that could be hit. It was quite amazing, really – jolly well made sure that you knew your place! But not me, of course. I gave those two fuckers no peace. I'd be standing by the side of them, urging, 'Hurry up you cunts! Slow – slow! Come on!' They may have hated it, but it sure kept the band going. But it wasn't just the goings-on with the drum empire that upset people. I was just too forward for the rest of the guys. During my years with Hawkwind, I really came out of any shell I may have been in, stagewise. I was always at the front of the stage and showing off, and since I wasn't the leader of the band, it was considered most presumptuous. And I'd started to write songs, which I think pissed everybody off as well. Not to mention the drug thing. See, I was the only speed freak left in the band. Dikmik had been gone for a couple of years, and I was a minority of one. I was the bad guy . . . as I still am today. So when I got busted going over the Canadian border for cocaine possession, they took that as an opportunity to fire me.

The really fucked up – but also lucky – thing about the whole situation was that I didn't even have any coke. It was May of 1975. We had just played Detroit, and we left early the next morning for Toronto. Some chick at the show had given me some pills and I had about a gramme of amphetamine sulphate. Apparently, when you're travelling from Detroit into Canada, you can go over the bridge or under the tunnel. The thing to do, if you don't want to be hassled, is go over the bridge, but we weren't paying attention. Under the tunnel we went and got a surprise awakening by the border police. 'Cause it was early and I wasn't thinking, I stuffed my contraband down my pants. Not a good idea – they searched us to the skin, and the cops got my stash. They took the amphetamine sulphate and put some of it in one of those vials that you shake up – if it turns a certain colour, then you're in trouble. But it doesn't differentiate between speed and cocaine. Well, it turned the right colour – for the cops, that is. 'This is cocaine, buddy, you're going to jail!' I said, 'I don't think so.' But the bastards kept me and the rest of the band went off to Toronto.

So there I was, stuck with the Canadian police. They didn't even bother charging me for the pills, but I was arraigned and sent down to jail on remand. This was, as you can well imagine, not a pleasant experience. I'd been locked up in cells overnight, but never in a serious jail like this one. I remember I was in the delousing room, ready for the spray when this wonderful voice behind me said, 'You're bailed.' Well, as I found out later, the only reason the band got me out was because my replacement wasn't going to get to Canada in time. Otherwise, they would have just let me rot. I wouldn't have rotted anyway – since what I had was amphetamine sulphate and not cocaine, the case was thrown out as a 'wrongful charge', and they couldn't charge you again for the same substance. So I was free and clear.

The band had got me a plane ticket and they flew me over to Toronto. I got there just after they'd finished the soundcheck. We did the gig to tremendous applause, then at four o'clock in the morning, I was fired. I was doing the wrong drugs, see. If I had been caught with acid, those guys would have all rallied around me. I think even if I'd been doing heroin, it would have been better for them. That whole hippie subculture was so fucking two-faced, when you get down to it. It was all 'Speed kills – wow, man, bad drugs', and stupid shit like that (and keep in mind, all the people I know who said that are now dead or messed up on heroin). Well, all I have to say is that at least speed keeps you functional. Why else did they give it to housewives for all those years?

Hawkwind had very bad timing, kicking me out of the band when they did. They were on the verge of really making it in America when I got fired, so they must have been fucking insane. But it wasn't because I was fired that they failed; it was because of who they got to replace me, in addition to firing me for all the wrong reasons. When I left Hawkwind, they got a guy called Paul

Rudolph to play bass. He used to be a great lead guitarist for the Pink Fairies, but he was a very, very mediocre bass player – the reverse of me, in fact. And he just saw the band straight into the Twilight Zone – it was a terrible fucking mess. They tried carrying on into Ohio, did about four more gigs and cancelled the rest of the tour. Dave, God help him, actually wanted to bring me back into the band, but the drum empire wouldn't let him. So the drummers and the bass player took over and the band went in a bad direction. They made a couple of – well, they weren't bad albums. Musically, they were excellent, but they were really naff. There was no nuts in 'em – when I left Hawkwind, the cojones came with me.

CHAPTER SIX

built for speed

I had my revenge on Hawkwind for firing me. By the time they got back to England, I'd stolen my equipment out of the band's storage space. I don't remember how we got in now, actually. We must have got somebody from the office to nick the key for me or something. In fact, I don't even remember who came along with me – it was Lucas Fox, probably, who wound up drumming in Motörhead for the first few months. He was the only one I knew who had a car. We had just got my stuff in the van when Alan Powell caught us. That was a nice coincidence, since I'd just seen his wife! He was shouting, 'Yeah, ya cunt! You thought you'd steal your stuff back!' We drove off, laughing, and I yelled back, 'Yeah, go and ask your wife!' But I don't think he did, because I saw her again the week after and she never mentioned it.

I was also busy doing other, more important things. Within

two weeks of getting back to London, I put together the band that was to become Motörhead. I wanted it to be sort of like the MC5, since that was the big hero band of most of the underground, and throw in elements of Little Richard and Hawkwind. And that's more or less how it turned out. We were a blues band, really. Although we played it at a thousand miles an hour, it was recognizable as blues – at least to us it was; probably it wasn't to anybody else.

It was pretty easy getting the band together, really – too easy, in fact. Within a very short period of time, I'd recruited guitarist Larry Wallis and Lucas Fox as the drummer. Larry I already knew – he'd been in UFO before they made a record, and he had been playing guitar for the Pink Fairies after the departure of Paul Rudolph, the guy who replaced me in Hawkwind. Pretty incestuous, eh? On top of that, the Pink Fairies and Hawkwind used to play on stage together billed as Pinkwind (Hawkfairies didn't work, really). Lucas was introduced to me by my roommate at the time, a girl name Irene Theodorou, who I called Motorcycle Irene, after the Moby Grape song. I'd begun living with her before I went on my last tour with Hawkwind. She wasn't a girlfriend of mine, just a friend, although we did have some wild times together. She was a very nice girl, and a good photographer. She did some shots of us in the early days. Lucas had been hanging around with Irene, hoping to fuck her. He never did, of course. He was a bit of a dork, but a very sound guy, really, and since he was always around, and a drummer, *and* had a car – he appeared very handy. I didn't want to sing; I wanted somebody else to do it. But the problem with that, of course, is you get stuck with a fucking singer! No matter – we never did find anybody else and I wound up doing the vocals.

At first I was going to call the band Bastard, a name which pretty much summed up the way I felt. But the guy who was managing us at the time, Doug Smith (he'd been managing Hawkwind – that's how I knew him), didn't think it was a good idea. 'It's very unlikely that we're gonna get on *Top of the Pops* with a name like Bastard,' he pointed out. I figured he was probably right, so I decided to call the band Motörhead. It made sense: 'Motorhead' was the last song I wrote for Hawkwind, and it was also the American slang for speedfreak, so all the pieces fitted. And it was a one-word name; I believe in one-word names for bands – they're easy to remember.

So I took my psychedelic-coloured amps, painted them flat black, and Motörhead got under way. The press was having a field day with us – my firing from Hawkwind had been in all the British music papers, and everyone wanted to know what I was up to. That was when I came up with the famous quote that first appeared in *Sounds*: 'It'll be the dirtiest rock 'n' roll band in the world. If we moved in next door your lawn would die!' Actually, I stole that line from Dr Hook, but it quickly became the first of Motörhead's many catchphrases.

Our first show was on 20 July 1975 at the Roundhouse. That was fast, considering I'd left Hawkwind in May. We opened for Greenslade, a kind of pomp-rock band formed by this guy, Dave Greenslade, who'd been somebody's keyboardist. All the bands in those days had intro tapes, and since I've always been a World War II fanatic, we used a recording from Germany of marching feet and people yelling '*Sieg Heil!*' It just sounded really powerful and incredibly cold, all those feet smashing on the German cobblestones, that *bromp, bromp!* tromping sound. That was our outro tape, too. I had a silver-painted human skull on stage, on the top of my stack. But in spite of these theatrical touches, I have to admit we weren't very good (bloody awful, let's face it!). Undaunted, we proceeded to go on a trek of England through most of August. After all, that's the only way you get better – you keep playing.

We were already attracting fans, though – punks, old Hawkwind fans and a horde of nasty characters were coming to see us. And some of them were really getting into it. One young kid showed up at our first show in white boots and a bullet belt, just like mine – and I'd only gotten the boots two weeks before, so he was really early. From the start, we were inspiring slavish fucking loyalty in people – that's the funny thing about Motörhead: our fans and our crews really latch on to us. The soundman we have now has been with us since around 1977. He made a bunch of money when he was working for Black Sabbath. The tour we asked him to do was only going to make him a third of the money, but there he was on the plane with Sabbath's crew, plotting all *our* sound and lights. Somebody told him, 'You should be doing Black Sabbath's stuff,' and he replied, 'Yeah, man, but these are my boys!' And he left that tour to come and do us. We've always had people like that. It's some sort of disease people catch from the ultimate underdog band.

And we were definitely underdogs at our next London gig, which was at the Hammersmith Odeon on 19 October 1975. We were supporting Blue Oyster Cult, but we certainly didn't get any help from them! In fact, they sabotaged us completely. They gave us no soundcheck, and the Odeon is notorious for its bad sound. I've noticed that a lot of American bands treat their openers poorly, like they want to destroy the competition before it even has a chance to compete! British bands don't do that – at least mostly they don't – nor does Motörhead.

That show earned us a new reputation and our own category in the *Sounds* poll for that year! We were voted 'Best Worst Band in the World'! Nevertheless, we had a record deal with United Artists – they were Hawkwind's label and they decided to hang on to me, at least for the time being. That was good . . . or so we thought at the time. So late in the year, we went down to Rockfield Studios, which is located on a farm in Monmouth, south Wales, to make a record. Dave Edmunds was going to produce it. Dave is one of my heroes. He became famous with Rockpile, and as a solo artist, but I knew him from Love Sculpture, which was his first band. They did an instrumental version of 'Sabre Dance', which was the fastest thing you've ever heard in your fucking life! It's some of the best guitar, too, because everybody was on pills then, and Dave was fast already.

Unfortunately, Edmunds only recorded four tracks with us:

'Lost Johnny', 'Motörhead' (two of the songs I wrote while in Hawkwind), 'Leaving Here' (an excellent Eddie Holland song – I used to see the Birds play in my Manchester days), and 'City Kids' (a Pink Fairies number that Larry wrote). Then Dave got signed to Led Zeppelin's label, Swan Song, and they took him away. That was too bad, because I really liked working with him – he was just like one of us. I recall one night, when we were listening back to a track, Dave stood up and said, 'Excuse me.' He went out of the door and threw up, then he simply came back, sat down and carried on. We used to find him slumped over the board with white noise howling out of the speakers. He also helped me fix a guitar. One of my strings kept jumping out of the nut – that thing that your strings go on at the top of the neck. So he told me, 'All you need on there is a bracket above it. Come with me.' And we broke through a window of this toolshed on the farm to get a drill. Then he smashed this old guitar, took the bracket off it, drilled holes on my guitar and put it on. It's still on there to this day. Good man, Edmunds, great spur-of-the-moment guy. And he's made some great records. He produced the Everly Brothers comeback album with Jeff Lynne, and the Stray Cats, among many others. After Dave, we wound up with Fritz Fryer as producer. He was in a sixties band called the Four Pennies who had a couple of No. 1s in England. A very good band, but they were a bit soppy. So Fritz finished up our record, which was a shame, really. He was all right, but he wasn't the man Edmunds was, which is not surprising, since he was the man Fryer was!

It was around the time Edmunds left that we changed drummers. We decided that Lucas had to go, because he was starting to get very weird. He was trying to keep up with my speed habit, and of course you can't! In fact, I don't especially recommend my lifestyle – it will slaughter the average person. This is no joke, and I'll tell you how I know: around 1980, I decided to have my blood changed – you know, the same process Keith Richards is rumoured to have gone through. It is a good idea, logically, because instantly you get untainted, fresh blood and your body doesn't have to go through all the stress of detoxing. So my manager and I went to the doctor, who took some blood tests and came back with the bad news.

'I've got to tell you this,' he said. 'Pure blood will kill you.'

'What?'

'You don't have human blood any more. And you can't give blood, either. Forget it, you'd kill the average person because you're so toxic.'

In other words, what's normal for me is deadly to another human – and what's normal for other humans is deadly to me, which is okay with me. I suppose that means I've made medical history of some sort. I'm gonna leave my body to medical science fiction! Me and Stephen Wright.

So keeping up with my habit was getting Lucas very tense. The veins on his head would stand out and he'd stare at you very intently for long periods of time without speaking. He'd be doing this, and the rest of us would look at each other, thinking, 'Well, he's obviously gone over the fucking top.' We were in the studio once listening to a playback and Lucas was leaning against the console. The top part was hinged a certain way so it could be cleaned, and somebody hadn't put the catches back right. And there was all this stuff on it, half-finished drinks and ashtrays and shit. So when Lucas leaned on it, the whole fucking console flipped open and everything fell in. Sparks flew – the whole fucking thing blew up! So he screamed and stepped back and knocked the phone off the wall, then he shot out the door. And Larry opened the door and called after him, 'Hey Lucas, don't walk past my fucking stacks – they'll burst into fucking flames!' So it was clear that Lucas was on his way out. I ran into him, funnily enough, a couple of years ago in Paris. He was dressed like a Frenchman, with a handkerchief hanging out of his pocket. Looking at him, I thought maybe he'd turned gay, but he said he was living with a girl over there. Lucas was a good enough geezer, really, and a good friend to me, but he just didn't have the bite.

Meanwhile, Phil Taylor had been hanging around. I met him about six months prior at this guy's flat – Paul, a guitar player. Paul's a great anti-heroin advertisement. He fell asleep, passed out on smack, with his arm leaning against an iron bedstand and his hand died. He'd cut all the tendons in his arm. I saved Paul's life – he was fucking dead, he was blue, and I beat him on the chest till his heart started again. He wasn't the first one I saved, and he certainly wasn't the last. But back to Phil.

He had a car, so he was able to give me a lift down to the studio, which was about two hundred miles from London. And he had mentioned to me that he was in the habit of banging on drums now and again, so we thought we'd give him a go. We played a couple of numbers down at the studio, and Larry in particular was taken with him.

'What a horrible little fucker!' he chortled. 'He's fucking perfect!'

Phil wound up overdubbing the drums on nearly the whole album. The only song he didn't do was 'Lost Johnny', because that track sounded okay as it was. Overdubbing drums is quite a feat, because the drums are what you usually base a song on – it's kind of like going ass-backwards. But Phil did it great, and for a very long time, he was an asset to Motörhead. One thing he couldn't do, though, was sing. On this album – which eventually was called *On Parole* – Larry sang on three of the songs: 'On Parole' and 'Fools', both of which he wrote, and 'Vibrator', which he wrote with his roadie, Dez Brown. (Dez also wrote the words for 'Iron Horse/Born to Lose'). Larry thought it would be good to have Phil sing on one track, so we tried him out on 'City Kids'. It didn't work – he sounded like two cats being stapled together. It was so funny that I was outside in the farmyard in the rain, on my knees, I was laughing so hard! So we had to scotch that idea.

We finished up the album, which also included 'The Watcher' (another song I wrote while in Hawkwind). Then the assholes at United Artists began hedging about the record's release. For months they fed us numerous lies, while still keeping us signed to the label. That, of course, kept us from being able to record with any other company. They wound up putting out *On Parole* four years later, long after we'd finally been released from our contract. They claimed that the UA staff had turned over and the new people had a new attitude towards the record. Strangely enough, their change of heart came just about the time we were starting to become really successful. Coincidence? I fucking think not! That was the beginning of our fucked-up dealings with record companies. Day one, Jack, and that was it!

It was around the time that UA was buggering us about that we also began our sordid history of various management changes. Doug Smith farmed us out to this guy from Belgium, whose name I cannot remember to save my fucking life. He was funny: he tried to talk British slang in a futile attempt to appear hip. In England, one might say, 'a bunch of cunts' to describe a group of guys. You never say 'cunt' about a woman in England (I discovered the difference in America quite early on, incidentally!). So the Belgian would come into a room and say, 'Where are my bunches of cunt?' Belgian translations of English are miraculous. But he was fucking hopeless, and faded out because he ran out of money.

Then for a while, we had this sweaty maniac, Frank Kennington, managing us. He was a friend of our guitarist, who by then was Eddie Clarke (I'll be getting to Eddie very shortly). Frank's father had a factory. I don't know what they were making – small things, I believe, small, indispensable shit . . . Lenses, that's it, lenses and prisms and things like that for industry. And Frank had taken the factory over from his father, so he had quite a bit of money. We rectified that situation, however, by bankrupting him completely! We owed the poor bastard some money till the day he died, in fact (although, incidentally, I finally paid him my share in 1996 – twenty years late! Still, better late than never). He eventually moved to America, where he was known (not surprisingly) as English Frank.

After we ruined Frank's financial affairs, we were managed for quite a while by this guy called Tony Secunda. I believe I met him through Chrissie Hynde, who I'd known for a number of years. Chrissie used to be a journalist for the *New Musical Express*, and I was always very impressed by the fact that though she had no tits to speak of, she could play very good guitar! She was very good indeed. She was squatting in Chelsea when I knew her, and I used to go round there and jam with her all night. Before she had the Pretenders, she was in a band called the Moors Murderers. That was in extremely bad taste. They all wore black, pointed hoods when they played – very bad taste, indeed. Luckily they never had a hit, or we probably would have never seen Chrissie's face – she would have been in a black hood for the rest of her professional career.

Anyhow, back to Tony Secunda. Tony used to manage the Move and Steeleye Span and he had a label, Wizard Records, in England. He was a very interesting man . . . from an anthropological point of view. A complete fucking lunatic. He went to Peru and came back with this Indian, who went everywhere with him. And he was doing cocaine like nothing on earth – teaspoons of the fucking shit. And he was paranoid about people eavesdropping. He used to mutter, 'Fucking earwigs! Listening to what I say, earwigs all over. Fucking bastards!' And this Indian would be standing behind him, arms folded across his chest. Really very weird.

But Secunda came up with some wild publicity schemes. He did this publicity stunt once where the Move took an atomic bomb to the middle of Piccadilly in Manchester for a photo shoot. And once, on being told that he had a very large tax bill coming up, he changed £20,000 into £1 notes. Then he dropped them through the ceiling at the end of one of Steeleye's gigs at the Hammersmith Odeon – he figured that since the government would have taken the money away anyhow, he might as well make it a deductible gift. Another Secunda stunt with the Move involved a pornographic postcard with British Prime Minister Harold Wilson, but that backfired on him. He had to apologize to the Prime Minister and pay all kinds of money and shit – libel, you know. While he was working with Motörhead, he had our logo painted on the side of this building on the main roundabout coming into London from the west. It only took us an hour to get it up – we put ten art students up on scaffolding and had them paint a square each – but it took the residents three months to get it taken off. So for those three months, we had top-drawer publicity. Free!

Originally, I had intended that Motörhead be a four-piece band, and we tried out a couple of different guitarists. One was Ariel Bender – known at the time as Luther Grosvenor – who was in Mott the Hoople and Spooky Tooth. We did a few rehearsals with him, but it didn't work out. He was a nice guy, but he just wasn't our type. He didn't have the same sense of humor as the rest of us, and I couldn't imagine being on a bus with him. So we carried on as a three-piece until we found Eddie Clarke . . . and wound up carrying on as a three-piece anyhow.

Phil met Eddie while they were both renovating a houseboat down in Chelsea. But it wasn't Phil who brought him to us, it was Aeroplane Gertie, who was a receptionist for this rehearsal studio in Chelsea. We were rehearsing there for free – if somebody quit early and there were a couple of hours left, we'd whip our gear in and use the leftover time. Gertie used to wear a hat with a plastic aeroplane stuck on it, hence the name Aeroplane Gertie. She was living with Eddie, and it was she who brought him round to the rehearsal studio. We decided to try him out, and it turned out to be a very weird situation. Larry didn't show up right away, so me, Eddie and Phil began jamming. It was going along pretty well by the time Larry showed up, hours later. Then Larry started playing along, but he was so loud that we couldn't hear anything else for half an hour. After that, he left and that was it, he'd quit the band. And Larry was the one who was always on to us about getting another guitar player, so go figure.

But Motörhead always worked really great as a trio anyway (and still does today). If there's two guitars, then you have to sort of toe the line a bit, because if the two guitarists ain't together – and the bass too, of course! – it's really messy. But with only one guitar player, you can do anything. I used to play all kinds of weird shit behind Eddie and it would work.

Right off the bat, I was trying to find nicknames for everyone. Nicknames are good, people like them. So Eddie became 'Fast

Eddie' Clarke, which was logical, really. I mean, he was a fast guitar player. Phil became Phil 'Dangerous' Taylor for a few months, but although the nickname was apt – he certainly was dangerous to himself! – it didn't last. It was Motorcycle Irene who christened him 'Philthy Animal' Taylor. By then, Phil and Irene were living together, so she knew whereof she spoke.

Eddie and Phil were great friends – at one point, Phil was living at Eddie's house. They were as close as brothers, which was occasionally problematical because they fought like brothers, too. Like one would turn around and the other would say something and the next thing you know, *bang*! They were beating the shit out of each other. The two of 'em used to fistfight all the fucking time. On the way to one gig we had in Brighton, Phil and Eddie were punching each other in the van the whole way down. By the time we got there, Phil had a black eye and Eddie's arm was bad. But when it was time to go on, I said, 'Okay, that's it. On stage.' And they both straightened up and went, 'Ahem! Okay!' and we did the show. Then when we were coming off the stage, Phil smacked Eddie in the back of the neck and sent him sprawling, and there they went all over again. As fighters, they were pretty well matched.

Eddie was always thought of amongst our fans as the quiet one, but he was more vicious than Phil. He really is a nasty piece of work when the fists start flying. I remember him and Phil both rescuing me out of a fight. This guy jumped me from behind in this boozer in Portobello Road, and Eddie and Phil got a hold of him and his two mates and they just wound them out the door and kicked them down the street! I never even got a chance to get a punch in. I couldn't get at them because Phil and Eddie had 'em busy. Incidentally, the week after that, the geezer from the pub broke a pool cue over my head! Those were the days, eh?

This new line-up of Motörhead had been working together for a few months when Tony Secunda got us a deal to make a single for Stiff Records. So some time during the summer of 1976, we did 'White Line Fever' – a song that the three of us had written together – and 'Leaving Here' for the label. Somehow, UA got wind of this and started giving us trouble because we weren't yet officially out of our contract with them. At that point, we hadn't talked to UA in months – I don't know why they gave a shit. But they kept the single from being released until 1977, which frustrated us.

All through the rest of '76 and early '77, we played gigs here and there, a lot of one-offs. I remember at one gig, in a disco place in Shrewsbury – Tiffany's, for God's sake! – Eddie and I both fell flat on our backs onstage. It was one of those slippery plastic floors with lights under it. But the crew only lifted me up – Eddie used to treat them like servants so they left him down there. There he was, lying on his back, waiting confidently to be picked up and it never happened. On the way to another gig, Phil was angry about something and kicked the side of the van, breaking his toe. By this point, the morale of the band was getting pretty low; all our efforts were getting us nowhere. We were starving, living in squats and nothing was happening. I was well prepared to keep going but Phil and Eddie wanted to give it up. It wasn't their band and they didn't have the commitment I did. So finally in April, after much debate, we decided to do a goodbye show at the Marquee in London and call it a day.

Around this time, I had hooked up with Ted Carroll from Chiswick Records. I asked Ted to bring a mobile studio down to the gig so we could document our farewell performance and our fans would have something to remember us by. Well, Ted apparently couldn't get the studio down to the Marquee, but he did show up backstage after we played, and he made us an offer.

'If you want to make a single, I'll schedule you two days at Escape Studio in Kent.'

So we went down to Escape with producer Speedy Keen, who had been in a band called Thunderclap Newman, which had a No. 1 hit in England with the song 'Something in the Air'. In two days, we recorded eleven backing tracks with no vocals. We all agreed there was no point in doing a single, because we wanted to at least leave an album as a memento. So we just barrelled our way through an album's worth of material in forty-eight hours with no sleep. Speedy Keen and the engineer, John Burns, were speeding out of their heads because they couldn't afford to go to sleep – they didn't have the time, and they wanted to make an album as much as we did. They mixed twenty-four versions of 'Motörhead' alone! Then they asked me which one I liked the best, as if I would remember. I mean, you can't tell after three. I just said, 'Fuck it! That one!'

At the end of the two days, Ted came down to hear two finished songs and we gave him eleven unfinished ones. But as he was listening, he was doing the boogie at the back of the studio, so we knew we'd got him! He gave us a few more days to finish vocals and such, and *Motörhead* was our first album to see the light of day. By then, we had wrestled our freedom away from UA, so we were back in business.

We recorded a total of thirteen songs for Chiswick and eight of them wound up on the album. Much of *Motörhead* was material from *On Parole*, which we re-recorded: 'Motörhead', 'Vibrator', 'Lost Johnny', 'Iron Horse', 'Born to Lose' and 'The Watcher'. We also did two new songs, 'White Line Fever' and 'Keep Us On the Road', and a Johnny Burnett song, 'Train Kept A-Rollin'' (you're probably familiar with Aerosmith's version of it – it was a hit for them). The other songs that didn't wind up on the album included 'City Kids', which was a B-side for the 'Motörhead' single; a ZZ Top song called 'Beer Drinkers and Hell Raisers'; 'I'm Your Witchdoctor' – a great song by John Mayall and Eric Clapton; 'On Parole', and an instrumental jam which was appropriately called 'Instro'. Those last four songs were released as *The Beer Drinkers EP* in 1980, long after we'd left Chiswick and not-so-coincidentally near the peak of our success. Once again, it was cash-in time – for the record labels, at least. I've never recorded more than we need since! But having said that, I don't begrudge Ted Carroll that – he saved my band, after all!

It was about this time that we were starting to have some differences with Secunda. For one thing, he wanted us to get our hair cut! Obviously we weren't gonna do that. Doug Smith started coming back into the picture when he put us on a tour through

England with Hawkwind, whom he was still managing. That was in June of 1977. But with our usual bit of luck, Phil broke his hand in a fight on the day before the tour. We were all at my house, painting our equipment, and this guy came over, a junkie who was a real drag. We told him to leave, but he wouldn't go, so Phil hustled him out the door and punched him. Unfortunately, this shoved Phil's knuckle back to about the centre of his hand. So we ended up gaffer-taping the drumstick to Phil's bandaged hand, and we did the whole tour that way. Other than that, it was a good tour, and things were fine between us and Hawkwind.

Phil injured himself again a couple of months later, with more disastrous results. We'd just started a headlining tour to promote the new album, which was due out in a few days, and we were supported by a band called the Count Bishops, who were very good. We called it the 'Beyond the Threshold of Pain Tour', which should have given us a hint. Round about the fifth show, Phil got into an argument with Bobs, one of our roadies, over Motorcycle Irene. This time he broke his wrist instead of his knuckle, so we had to cancel the whole tour. Tony Secunda fired Bobs that night, but it wasn't really Bobs' fault. It was unfortunate because Bobs had worked hard for us – he was actually going down to phone boxes with bags of two-pence pieces and getting us gigs. But in the end, I guess it didn't matter – we had to wait for Phil's hand to heal before we did any more shows, and we were offstage until November, when we did a show at the Marquee.

During the first few months of 1978, nothing much was

happening; the odd gig here and there, including one in Colwyn Bay, near where I grew up, but that was about it. Tony Secunda had had some sort of dispute with Chiswick and fired them. I believe it was also around this time that we parted ways with Tony. He bailed out, and eventually went to work for Shelter Records in San Francisco. In 1995, he died, rest in peace. This was a bleak period for us. It seemed like we couldn't even get arrested. Our lack of forward motion was getting to Eddie and Phil once again, so they went off and did some shows with Speedy Keen and a bassist, Billy Rath (who had played with Johnny Thunders and the Heartbreakers and Iggy Pop). They called themselves the Muggers. I think Speedy wanted to form a band with them permanently, and he might have been successful because we were about to break up. But finally Doug Smith took us back and got us a deal with Bronze Records, who had bands like Uriah Heep and the Bonzo Dog Doodah Band on its roster. It was just for a single – they wanted to see how it did before they invested any more money in us – but it turned out to be the beginning of our long-awaited upward ascent.

Not only did the Bronze deal give us a shot in the arm, we would have our biggest hits with the label. And, really, they treated us quite well there. Not that we appreciated it at the time. In fact, we found a lot to gripe about! We thought Bronze gave us a hard time, but considering the dealings I've had with record companies since, they were fucking great. Since then, I've often looked back on the Bronze days with nostalgia. The label head, Gerry Bron, and his wife, Lillian, were really enthusiastic about us and A&R exec Howard Thompson – who was the one responsible for signing us – was brilliant. They believed in us and made some good efforts on our behalf.

So that summer we went into Wessex Studios in London and recorded 'Louie Louie', with one of our own numbers, 'Tear Ya Down', as a B-side. Covering 'Louie Louie' was an idea Phil had come up with some months back, when we were still with Tony Secunda. We'd been sifting through some old songs, and I wanted to cover a Chuck Berry song, 'Bye Bye Johnny', or something like that, but 'Louie Louie' was the better choice, really. I think we did a very good version of it – people tell me that it's one of the few times it's been recorded where the lyrics can be understood! Actually, I only got the first two verses and then the last verse was largely improvised. We produced it jointly with this guy, Neil Richmond. We never did work with him again, but he was good . . . except for that weird clavioline thing he put in. I thought that was suspicious. We used to call him Neil Fishface. I don't recall why, 'cause he didn't really have a fishface – well, only from certain angles.

Anyhow, the single was released on 25 August 1978 (the photograph of us on the sleeve, incidentally, was shot by Motorcycle Irene). By the end of September, it had gone up to No. 68 in the charts, which was enough for Bronze to give us the go-ahead for a full album. As it was making its move up the charts, we started a tour around England, but before we took off, I had my brief excursion with the Damned.

In America, the Damned were never more than a good-sized

cult band, but in England they were much more famous. They were the true punk band, *not* the Sex Pistols. The Pistols were a great rock 'n' roll band, but really that's all they were. I actually gave Sid Vicious some bass lessons – he came up to me and said, 'Hey, Lemmy, teach me how to play bass,' and I said, 'All right, Sid.' But after three days I had to tell him, 'Sid, you can't play bass.' He said, 'Yeah, I know,' and he was all depressed and went off. Then a couple of months later I saw him down at the Speakeasy and he said, 'Hey, Lemmy, guess what! I'm in the Pistols!' 'What do you mean?' I said. 'I'm the bass player in the Pistols!' he said. 'It's great, innit?' 'You can't play bass, Sid.' 'Yeah, yeah, I know, but I'm in the fucking Pistols!' Steve Jones just taught him the basic bum-bum-bum-bum. That's all he had to do, really. Anything more complex than that on the album, it's either Steve or Glen Matlock. Sid – he wanted to be in a punk band so bad. He'd been in a band called Flowers of Romance for about three weeks, and in Siouxsie and the Banshees for about three days – he just talked everybody into it. But he was very good for the image. He was perfect – fuckin' hell, he out-Pistolled the Pistols as far as image was concerned!

Even though he couldn't play bass worth a damn, Sid was a nice enough geezer. I got quite friendly with him. But he used to get into all sorts of fights. One night at the Marquee, he mixed it with Bruce Foxton, the bass player out of the Jam and Bruce stuck a broken glass in his face. I was walking down Wardour Street towards the Speakeasy, and the lights were still on at the Marquee so I put my head in there – you might find some birds, you know – and there was Bruce, going, 'Fuck me,' and all this. I said, 'What's up?' and he said, 'I just fucking glassed Sid. I think I cut him.' I said, 'Well, I'm sure you cut him, else he'd still be here jumping on you.' He was worried that he'd hurt him bad, so I went to the Speak – there used to be all these cinema seats in the front of the stage for a while and Sid was sitting right in the middle of them, all on his own. So I went over to him and said, 'What's up, Sid?' 'Cunt done me,' he said, and he had this three-cornered fucking wound going right through his cheek. 'You wait till I get better,' he promised, but he never did try and do Bruce again.

One time he was trying to take a bird into the toilet for something or another and this huge Maltese bouncer who was really a hard man said, 'You can't go in there!' And Sid just went for him! I'd never seen anything like it – the geezer was down on the deck, rowing backwards on his elbows up the stairs, horrified 'cause this fucking bundle of pipe cleaners in a pair of tennis shoes was kicking the shit out of him. The guy didn't know what to make of it – Sid frightened him to fucking death! Anyway, that was the punk era for you.

So I like the Pistols, though as I said, I thought they were really a rock 'n' roll band. And I never liked the Clash, for that matter. Joe Strummer was better in the 101'ers, the band he had before the Clash. When it came to punk, the Damned were the real thing. They never quite got it together, but they were great fun. Dave Vanian couldn't sing, none of the guitar players could play, and the drummer, Rat Scabies, just sort of went along with it all. But they were fucking crazy – I mean, seriously in need of professional help. One time we supported them at the Roundhouse with the Adverts. And at the start of their show, Captain Sensible – there's a true maniac for you – came out wearing a pink ballet tutu, fishnet stockings, a pair of hobnailed boots, these big wing-tipped shades, and orange hair. And the punks all spat on them, and by the end of the gig, the band was skating around in this green goop all over the stage. They were soaked in it. And then the Captain took all his clothes off . . . of course, he used to do that at most of the gigs. When they played at another London club, the Rainbow, he took a piss on the front row. The audience was throwing seats at him, and he was throwing them back – while pissing down his leg, I hasten to add. Just your typical mid-seventies punk show – and then some.

Anyhow, I'd got to know them over the years. I met Rat at Dingwalls. I was at the bar and this over-scruffy urchin came up behind me and said, 'Hey, you're fucking Lemmy, are ya?'

So I replied, 'Yeah, I fucking am.'

'Yeah? You fucking think you're a rock star or something?' the little bastard inquired.

'No,' I said, 'but you do. That's why you're talking to me.'

'Fair enough,' he shrugged. 'I'll buy you a drink.'

The Damned went out of business for a while, after Brian James left the band. Then when they reformed, the Captain wanted to play guitar. It was probably his idea to ask me to fill in on bass for a gig at London's Electric Ballroom. They were calling themselves the Doomed for that show, but they returned to being the Damned shortly thereafter. We had about five hours of rehearsal. I learned eleven of their songs, and they learned one of mine, which they wound up fucking up on stage. I shouldn't have even bothered having them do one of my songs, really. But it was fun, playing with those boys.

So much fun, in fact, that Eddie, Phil and I wound up doing a recording session with them, too. We recorded a couple of songs – a version of the Sweet's 'Ballroom Blitz' and a Motörhead tune, 'Over the Top'. That was a joke. The Captain was watching cricket on TV and wouldn't come out of the TV room, for starters. And Eddie and Phil were fighting, as usual. Dave Vanian showed up late, and by then we were all drunk as shit. He took one look at us all, spun on his heel and walked straight back out. In the end, only me and the Damned bassist Algy Ward were still alive, so to speak, so we just went in and fucked around. I did a bass solo on 'Ballroom Blitz' and he did the vocals. That song wound up as a B-side to the Damned single, 'I Just Can't Be Happy Today', but we had a rough mix that was much better than the one that appeared on the record. We never did get around to putting vocals on 'Over the Top'. Oh yeah, and we broke the toilet bowl at the studio, too. I think the Captain kicked it in. But back to Motör-business.

We toured through September and October, and on 24 October, we filmed our first *Top of the Pops* appearance. *Top of the Pops* is a terrible programme, really. They had bands on the show who were either in the Top 30, like Slade and the Nolan Sisters (I did a record with those 'innocent little virgins' once – more on that later), or who the programme thought were headed for the Top 30. There was no regard to anything like talent – it was just reflecting the charts. We weren't anywhere near reaching the Top 30 at the time ('Louie Louie' had peaked at 68), but this friend of ours who worked at Bronze, Roger Bolton, used to work for the BBC, so he had a lot of handy influence. Roger wound up getting us on the show about five times before we really had a hit! In fact, Roger's efforts on our behalf helped us quite a bit on our way up the charts, for which I will buy him a drink any time.

So we went down to the labyrinthine BBC studios to tape our appearance. It's like a rat's nest in there – hundreds of studios and corridors – and you need a guide to take you to the studio. It's lunacy. Some day, all the guides are gonna be ill and everybody's gonna be fucked. We were supposed to re-record the song, but no one ever did. We just used to remix the original track slightly, put the vocals up a little bit higher or something. Then we'd put our amps up, lean the guitars on them and turn everything on. Then the inspector from the BBC would come round to the studio to make sure you'd done the work. He knew what was going on, of course, and we knew that he knew. It was all a game – tacit agreement, we'd call it. At least we really played on our records, instead of having studio musicians, like a lot of pop stars did.

The *Top of the Pops* people treated us all right, but only because they had to. I don't think they liked us much, really – especially because I won £100 on the one-armed bandit that was in their canteen. That pissed off everybody from the BBC, because they'd been waiting for it to pay off!

By this time we had already worked up several songs for the upcoming album, playing them on stage, and we were looking for a producer. We wound up getting Jimmy Miller, who had produced *Exile on Main Street* and *Goats Head Soup* for the Rolling Stones. So things were really starting to look up for us. Our years of struggling were paying off, and by now Phil and Eddie had stopped complaining about lack of momentum (that doesn't mean they stopped complaining, however!). The kicker was in November, when we headlined the Hammersmith Odeon, the same place where Blue Oyster Cult had so soundly fucked us over three years earlier. It was fully packed with 3,000 fans cheering us on. You could feel the energy – our rise up the rock star food chain had begun.

CHAPTER SEVEN

beer drinkers and hell raisers

We only had a fortnight to record *Overkill*, our second album and first for Bronze. Considering our chequered recording history, however, it was a world of time for us, and besides, being quick in the studio has always been natural for us. The whole experience was pure joy. We recorded at the Roundhouse Studios, which were next to the club of the same name in north London. Jimmy Miller was excellent, as were Trevor Hallesy and Ashley Howe, the engineers. *Overkill* was supposed to be something of a comeback album for Jimmy Miller, which is exactly what it turned out to be for him. He had gotten very heavily into heroin (which likely began when he was working with the Stones) and he had lost it for a couple of years. Since *Overkill* charted right away – it eventually peaked at 24 – he got a lot of work from it, but months later, when we were working with him on *Bomber*, it was sadly clear that he was back on smack. Come to think of it, he must have been doing it during *Overkill* too because he'd already started showing up late now and again to the studio and coming up with completely preposterous excuses. One incident will give you a good example of his modus operandi.

This particular day, he arrived five hours late for a session, and we were all sitting in the studio, twiddling our fucking thumbs at a thousand bucks an hour, muttering, 'That bastard! He cometh not.' Finally, he showed up and before he was even through the fucking door, he'd launched into his tale – that way, of course, we didn't have room to start in with, 'You bastard! Where have you been?' and all that.

'Guys! Guys! You wouldn't *believe* what happened!' he said. 'I called this taxi and it didn't come, so I had to call another one, and then that arrived in the *snow*, you know what I mean? And then he ran out of gas, so we had to push it to a filling station! And then the thing on the solenoid was gone, so I had to call another cab from the filling station and he didn't arrive for ages. And anyway, he broke down on the way after that too, and I've been walking through the snow for three hours! Look at my clothes!'

We knew he'd been rolling in the snow outside for three minutes to get his drawers wet – I looked out the window and saw him doing it as a matter of fact! But at least he was jovial, and he got the job done. And he took the trouble to be original, God rest his soul.

As is usual with Motörhead, there were quite a few new songs that we'd already been performing live. 'Damage Case', 'No Class', 'I Won't Pay Your Price' and 'Tear Ya Down' were among those. Others we wrote in the studio. 'Capricorn' (which happens to be my astrological sign) was written in one night. Eddie's solo for that one, I recall, happened while he was tuning up. The tape was running while he was fooling around with his guitar, and Jimmy added some echo. When Eddie finished tuning, he came in and said, 'I'll do it now,' and Jimmy told him, 'Oh, we got it.' That saved us some money!

'Metropolis' was another fast one. I went to see *Metropolis*, the movie, at the Electric Cinema in Portobello Road one night, then I came home and wrote the song in five minutes. The words don't make any sense, though. They're complete gibberish:

> *Metropolis, the worlds collide*
> *Ain't nobody could be on your side*
> *I don't care.*
> *Metropolis is something new*
> *Ain't nobody got their eyes on you*
> *I don't care*

See what I mean?

But some of my lyrics have more meat on 'em. I always wanted Tina Turner to record 'I'll Be Your Sister', for instance – I like writing songs for women. In fact, I've written songs *with* women. I've been called sexist by some factions of radical, frigid feminists (the kind who want to change the word 'manhole' to 'personhole', that kind of crap), but they don't know what they're talking about. When I find good women rockers, I'll lend them a hand. I'll never get any kind of credit for helping to advance women in rock 'n' roll, but I have. Girlschool is an example. They were never that well known in the States, but in England they were quite popular for a while. In March, 1979, when we began our *Overkill* tour – our first big outing, really – they were our opening act. A lot of their early success came from their association with us, and they wound up being quite an asset for us, too.

It was one of the guys in our office, Dave 'Giggles' Gilligan, who found Girlschool originally. The band was from Tooting, south London. I listened to a single called 'Take It All Away' that they'd put out on some little label and thought they were fucking excellent. Plus I liked the idea of girls being in a band – I wanted to stick it up these pompous bastard guitarists' asses, because Girlschool's guitarist, Kelly Johnson, was as good as any guitarist I've ever seen in my life. The nights when she was really on, she was as good as Jeff Beck. So I went down to see them at a rehearsal they were having. I thought they were great, and I went back and told the others, 'They're coming on tour.' The boys were a bit weird about it at first, but after the first night they played with us, they shut up.

Not only were Girlschool an excellent band, they were really feisty and they didn't give a fuck. One night, a couple of days after the tour started, they walked out and some guy in the audience shouted, 'Go on! Get 'em off!', and Kelly walked up to the mic and said, 'You get 'em off. We could all do with a good laugh.' I thought that was really good – I like chicks who stick up for themselves. Then they kicked into their set and proceeded to knock the crowd on their ass.

During the first week of the tour, we were in Edinburgh, and a few of us were sitting in the lobby of the Crest Hotel – it was me and Eddie, and Kelly and Girlschool's singer, Kim McAuliffe, with her boyfriend Tim (he later wound up being the boyfriend of their drummer, Denise Dufort. See? There's not much difference between male and female rockers). I don't recall where Phil or the rest of Girlschool were. And I fed Kelly Johnson the worst fucking line I ever fed a woman in my life:

'How'd you like to go up to my room and watch *The Old Grey Whistle Test*?'

Fuck me, that's lame, isn't it – 'Would you like to go to my room and watch TV?' But she said, 'Yeah,' which only goes to show! So off we went. And I heard that later, Kim leaned across to Eddie and said, 'Let's go to your room and watch *The Old Grey Whistle Test*,' too. Eddie was a bit embarrassed, but she got up and led him to the elevator, with Tim still sitting there in the lobby! And Tim walked out of the hotel, got in the van and drove home to London, stranding all the chicks at the hotel. So we had to take them on our bus with us for the tour, which suited me fine. They were great people, and really funny.

A couple of them were real handfuls – Kelly could behave almost like Keith Moon: she used to get drunk so she couldn't even see and then try to take baths and fall over in the tub, shit like that. Eventually Kelly left the band because she fell in love with Vicki Blue of the Runaways and she moved to the States. Vicki got her a green card, so maybe they got married? When I was having the overnight relationship with Kelly, she hadn't yet realized she was gay, or bisexual. But I knew, when I was with her, that something was wrong, like she was trying too hard and it wasn't working. But then, some time after she and Vicki broke up, she got married to some guy, so I think it was maybe she just didn't fancy me! But whatever. She's an excellent guitarist and a really nice person and whatever she fucks doesn't matter. She's an old friend of mine – all of Girlschool are. I'd go to bat for them anytime.

As always, I digress, and frankly, this is where my mind starts to wander anyway because much of the next several years are a blur. That's what happens when you start to be successful and you're in a rock band. You're either on the road for months, or in the studio, or people are leading you around somewhere – to a TV show or a radio station or whatever – and most of the time, you're not even sure about where you are. It all starts to blend together and everything looks the same.

Some incidents stand out, though, and Finland's Punkahaarju Festival, which we played in June 1979, is certainly one of them. And not because it was a great gig, either. In fact, it was fucking horrendous. It took place at the side of a lake, in a forest of pine and birch, like fucking *Peer Gynt*, you know. And the crowd was really fucking dour, we played badly, the sound sucked, and it was too bloody anticlimatic for words. When we came offstage, we thought, 'Ohhh, what a fucking awful gig,' and I said, 'Well, let's run out through the equipment.' So I went round behind my stacks and ran out through them and they all fell over, *BA-DOOM*! And Eddie was trying to knock his amps down – God, he was terrible at that! Ed could never knock a stack over. Then Phil – Clumso the Wonderdog – walked through his drums, but I think he did as much damage to himself as he did to the gear. Our roadie, Graham, got so excited that he pushed the PA over on the crowd. And there's more.

We were given this terrible caravan as a dressing room. There was no cooling in it, and Finland in the summer is fucking hot with loads of little mosquitoes flying around, not the frozen place it becomes in the dead of winter. *And* there was no booze in there, either – horrors! So we were sweltering in this thing and Chris Needs, a writer for *Zig Zag* magazine, was walking about with this tree, for some reason. It was a small tree, but nevertheless he put it through one of the caravan's windows while he was trying to talk to us. I guess he forgot he was carrying it. So we felt, well, we fucked up the caravan now, so we had better disguise the fact by sailing it into the lake and setting it on fire – give it a Viking funeral. And it went out very well, floated off in a very Arthurian manner, flames and smoke pouring out of it, and it sunk in quite a dramatic display. That wasn't the end of it.

Back at the hotel, Phil and Eddie took all the furniture and everything out of their room and put it up in the garden outside. It was a complete replica of the room's layout only out of doors – like I said, Finland summers are warm. Then we had a food fight on the bus on the way to the airport. Well, we had to do that because the driver told us in a very firm Finnish accent, 'Anything is happened to my bus, make dirty, then is coming trouble!' So immediately all the packed lunches came out and started flying. The bus looked totally destroyed, with fruit and eggs all over it, but it wasn't actually damaged. Then when we got to the airport customs area, the trouble really started.

'I think you have done something very terrible in Punkahaarju,' the customs guy told me.

'Not me, guvnor!'

'Come this way, please.'

So they stuck me in this room and took my passport away. And one by one, everyone else came in, too. We all got thrown in jail, the band and the crew, except for Rish, our roadie who also did the front of house sound. He'd signed in at the hotel as Rish, which wasn't what his name was on the passport, so he wound up going straight through, getting on the plane and flying home, wondering why there were all these empty seats around him. The rest of us were stuck in this Finnish jail for three or four days. All we had between us to read that whole time was one copy of the *Melody Maker*, and I read that thing, literally, from cover to cover. I read the date, page numbers, the adverts, every fucking word. And the food was crap, too.

Finally, we got deported. They put us on a plane to Copenhagen, then we had to change over for the flight to London. The first flight went okay, except that Eddie immediately poured his vodka and orange down the neck of the woman in front of him – we were celebrating because we were free. Then we got on the second plane and before we took off, the captain came storming down the aisle.

'I have heard about you and your being deported from Finland,' he glowered. 'If you try anything on this plane, I will have you arrested in London.'

So we didn't do anything the whole way back to London, but when we landed, there were all these cops on the tarmac. 'Oh fuck!' we thought. And then they arrested the captain! It turned out he was flying the plane drunk, which only goes to show.

A couple of weeks after our Finnish excursion, we went back in the studio and began working on our next record, *Bomber*, with Jimmy Miller. By then, he was completely out of it, and that got to be a little much. He would say he was going to the toilet for a moment, then he'd be in there for an hour and when he came out, he'd be nodding. Once he went to the men's room and he never came back at all, so we went in and he was gone! Apparently, he'd left to find his dealer, and we found him in his car, asleep at the wheel. Even when he was around, he was *in absentia*. When we had the rough mix down, we transferred it to quarter-inch tape and we started playing it back. Jimmy was nodding out in his chair the whole time we were setting it up, and when the music came on, he woke with a start, he looked at us, and started moving the faders up and down like he was working! And the tape wasn't even going through the desk – that was a bit of a giveaway. Poor bugger – he died a couple of years back. It's a shame; he was truly a good guy.

Ironically (or perhaps not so ironically), *Bomber* has one of my first anti-heroin songs on it, 'Dead Men Tell No Tales' (which, when we play it live, is often called 'Dead Men Smell Toe Nails'). It was about someone else, though, not Jimmy. *Bomber* is also the one album where Eddie sings a track, 'Step Down'. He'd been bitching that I was getting all the limelight, but he wouldn't do anything about it. I got sick of him complaining, so I said, 'Right, you're gonna fucking sing one on this album.'

'Oh no, man,' he protested. 'I can't sing, man. I don't fucking got no voice . . .'

'You're a perfectly good singer, man, get on the fucking microphone.'

So he did it with much grumbling. And it was like pulling teeth to get him to do it live. He hated it, but really, he was a good singer, Eddie. I don't see why he didn't do more of it. Later on, when Wurzel was in the band, he wouldn't sing either, and he was good too. And he used to sing in all his other bands. Whatever – I came to the conclusion long ago that there's something wrong with you if you're a guitar player. They whine about how artistic they are, and they *never* get any recognition, and they think they're the main force of the band – which, when it comes to my band, is really dangerous.

Overall *Bomber* was a good record, but there are a couple of really naff tracks on it, like 'Talking Head'. 'Bomber', 'Stone Dead Forever', 'All the Aces' – those were great. 'Lawman' was a weird pace for us – that was quite nice. *Bomber* was basically the transition record between *Overkill* and our next album, *Ace of*

Spades, and that was its function, really. And it peaked at No. 11 on the charts, so it got us up another notch successwise.

In the middle of making *Bomber*, we played the Reading Festival. We were on the same night as the Police and the Eurythmics. That was the great thing about the Reading Festival in those days – there were a lot of different kinds of bands on the bill. Rock 'n' roll hadn't yet become the categorized mess it is today. We were selling Motörhead flags that year, and they were flying in abundance during that show, much to the consternation of some of the more pretentious critics in the audience.

After Reading, we finished up mixing *Bomber* and Bronze threw us a record release party at London's Bandwagon Heavy Metal Soundhouse. That was awful – I've always hated those things. You're supposed to be all things to all people all night, which is impossible and fucking unpleasant besides. Phony bullshit is what it is. We were far more excited about getting back on the road: we had a few dates in Germany, our first, and then it was back up and down England again. Plus, we had a new toy on stage: our infamous 'Bomber' lighting rig.

The rig was a replica of a German WWII bomber, made out of heavy aluminium tubing, forty foot by forty foot. It flew four ways, backwards and forwards, and side to side – the first lighting rig that ever did that, by the way. It was heavy as hell, and if it had ever fallen it would have smashed us flat. But it was an impressive prop, and we used it for several tours. We never got the chance to take it to the States, though, because it was too massive for the venues we played there. So America, unfortunately, has never received the full Motörhead attack.

By this time, the band was generating quite a bit of money – for somebody, not for us. After *Bomber* charted at 11, it was clear that we would continue to get even bigger. But none of us in the band ever really saw a return. All we made immediately went into more elaborate stage productions. We were all right, though. Around the time *Overkill* came out, we were put on wages, and we finally found decent places to live. Before that, we were always living on somebody else's couch. Eddie was sharing with five other people, so his flat was halfway decent. Phil had been sharing a place with a couple of guys in Battersea. But for ages, I was crashing at people's flats and walking around London with this little World War II tank map case that contained a tape recorder, five tapes and a pair of socks. It didn't have a map in it, though. I needed one too, wandering around London. I quite liked drifting about like that, really – you go and live with chicks for a week and disappear. That was quite fine. But that all changed when our records began selling – our living conditions showed much improvement, even if they weren't exactly castles.

Of course, having a home isn't all that important when you're spending most of your time on the road. We did something like fifty-three gigs with two days off before having a break. On our dates through England, we had Saxon supporting us. They were nice guys, but kind of weird because they didn't drink or smoke. They had a tea urn in their room. We found that a bit odd. Interestingly, their drummer, Pete Gill, wound up joining

Motörhead a few years later. He'd started drinking heavily by the time he joined us, however. He drank even heavier after he joined! The tour with Saxon was also where I discovered acupuncture. Biff, Saxon's singer, and I both lost our voices (apparently living healthily didn't get him any farther than my lifestyle got me). Phil knew this amateur acupuncturist, and she put pins all over me and hooked them up to a 12-volt tractor battery. My voice was back in twenty minutes. Biff didn't try it out so he suffered.

In the midst of our travels, Bronze put out an EP of four tracks ('Leaving Here', 'Stone Dead Forever', 'Dead Men Tell No Tales', and 'Too Late Too Late'), recorded live while we were gigging. As a joke I told the label to call it *The Golden Years* – turned out they *were* our golden years (I think I sort of knew, really). The songs were pretty badly recorded, but the record got in the charts.

In July we played Stafford Bingley Hall and we were presented with silver discs for *Bomber* – it had sold over 250,000 records. And they had this Queen Elizabeth impersonator give them to us. The three of us got down on bended knee to receive them, like we were being knighted. Actually, that woman impersonates the Queen to this day, but she looks a bit rough now. The real Queen isn't looking all that great these days either, for that matter. In fact, *I* was feeling a bit rough at this particular show – I collapsed backstage after we'd finished and had to be revived for the encore. I don't recall why – I'd probably been up for three days. So I blacked out, but Phil and Eddie, those two miserable bastards, thought I was goldbricking! I was sitting there with damp towels on my head and those two cunts were standing there going, 'Fucking hell, man, you fucking stayed up for three days! How dare you! You motherfucker!' They were worried about the slant on their careers it would cause and shit like that. Jesus! Talk about the pot calling the kettle black! Whenever Eddie got really drunk and obnoxious, he would always go on at me for drinking – in the press! He'd say, 'Lemmy drinks too much,' and he was always drunk when he was doing the interview! But nobody ever mentioned that.

After that gig, I told the papers that I'd collapsed because I'd had three blow jobs that afternoon. The part about getting the blow jobs was true, actually. There were chicks all over the place, and there was this really cute little Indian bird – she was two of them. There was this room in the hall that was full of cushions and shawls hanging down. It was like some Maltese fucking dream. So I locked myself in there with her and wouldn't come out – well, wouldn't you do the same? See? Wonder where *she* is now?

Not long after Stafford Bingley Hall, we went into rehearsals to prepare for our next record. *Ace of Spades* was one of our longer albums, in terms of the recording process. It went easier than our previous albums, because we were on a roll, and we couldn't be stopped then. Well, we can't be stopped now, but we couldn't be stopped nationally then because the band's popularity had been building – *Bomber* did better than *Overkill*, and *Ace of Spades* promised to do even more. We were on our way up, and we knew this one was going to be a hit. We felt good. I didn't realize then how doomed we were. It was the end of something, really, instead of the beginning. *Ace of Spades* was the ultimate record for that particular line-up of Motörhead. I only started thinking about that when we were recording *Iron Fist* – out of the frying pan into the bear trap!

We were at Jackson's Studios in Rickmansworth for about six weeks, from the beginning of August 1980, until mid-September. Our producer was Vic Maile. I knew him from the Hawkwind days, when Vic was with Pye Records. He used to own a mobile studio – Hawkwind hired it out to do *Space Ritual* and he came along with it. Vic was a great man and a great producer, really brilliant. He had diabetes, of which he later died. It's just an on-going thing – the nice guys always go. That's why I'm still around.

The songs on *Ace of Spades* are considered classics by Motörhead fans, and I must say, they are an excellent bunch. We really enjoyed doing 'em. Those were good times; we were winning, and we were younger, and we believed it. The older you get, the less you can believe. It's not your fault, you know. It just comes to you that everything isn't corn flakes and skittles and beer. It's a jungle out there. But I never cared about it when I was young. I wasn't starving, you see, and I was having a good time. It certainly beats high-paid plumbing!

Like always, there were a lot of funny little segments in the songs. We had a tap-dancing part in 'Ace of Spades' – you know, *ding-dang-dangady*. We always imagined ourselves tap-dancing at that point. I used gambling metaphors, mostly cards and dice – when it comes to that sort of thing, I'm more into the slot machines actually, but you can't really sing about spinning fruit, and the wheels coming down. Most of the song's just poker, really: 'I know you've got to see me read 'em and weep', 'Dead man's hand again, aces and eights' – that was Wild Bill Hickock's hand when he got shot. To be honest, although 'Ace of Spades' is a good song, I'm sick to death of it now. Two decades on, whenever people think of Motörhead, they think 'Ace of Spades'. We didn't become fossilized after that record, you know. We've had quite a few good releases since then. But the fans want to hear it so we still play it every night. For myself, I've had enough of that song.

My chief memory of '(We Are) The Road Crew' is Eddie lying on his back in the studio, helpless with laughter, his guitar feeding back all over the place, halfway through what was supposed to be his solo. And we left it on because it was so fucking funny. That song was my first ten-minute lyric. That's how long it took me to get the words down in the studio. I remember going off somewhere because Vic had to go eat something – it had to do with his diabetes. He hadn't finished buttering his first cracker when I was back in there, telling him, 'I've done it.'

'Fuck off,' he said, 'I haven't even eaten yet.'

When he realized I really had finished the lyric, he was astonished. I was quite surprised myself. Ten minutes of real work ain't bad. I've dashed through a few more songs that way since then.

One of our road crew *cried* when we first played that song for them. I'm not going to say who it was. We took the lot of them up to the studio one day and played them the track. And this one guy cracked and broke down right then and there. He was weeping, 'Oh, that's a great one. That's great.' It was really nice that it affected somebody that deeply. Bands as a rule don't treat their crews too well. I try to.

I've caught hell from feminists for several songs I've written, but for some reason, they never said anything about 'Jailbait'. They never mentioned anything about that, and it was fucking blatant! But basically, my lyrics on *Ace of Spades* came from what I know personally. Like 'The Chase Is Better Than the Catch' – well, it is, isn't it? I mean, whenever you move in with somebody, it's fucking gone, you know. They leave their knickers in the bathroom and they have horrible habits that you didn't know about, which you become aware of almost immediately. It's fatal, you know – to have a relationship is fatal to the relationship.

We did the photo session for the album cover on a crisp, cold autumn day. Everybody thinks we did it in the desert, but it was in South Mimms, north of London. The Western motif was Eddie's idea; he had an aching desire to be Clint Eastwood. Keep in mind that at this point, I was the only one who had been to America. We all looked pretty good, dressed up as gunslingers, though. We had a slight problem with the wardrobe – the spade-shaped studs on my pants were too far apart. I took them off one leg and put 'em all on the other, so it turned out I could only be photographed from one side. But other than that, it went quite well.

After we finished the album, it was back to all those TV shows and interviews, which seem to blend together in a haze. But there were some highlights. One was in November, when we went on an ITV show called *TisWas*. It was a kids' Saturday morning show that featured a rock band every week. Chris Tarrant, who hosted the show, was a real strange person, but he knew what kids want to see: kids want to see grown-ups fuck themselves over, you know; they love that shit. There were buckets of water everywhere on this programme. It wasn't warm water, either – it was fucking cold and they were slinging it all over. And there was the Phantom Phlan Phlinger: he'd come up to somebody during the show and go *bhuuf* with this huge fruit pie. It was great fun, completely slapstick. We were on that show a couple of times.

Once, we were on with Girlschool and we were having a game of musical pies. The pie stopped in my hand and I had to smash it in the face of Denise, Girlschool's drummer. The poor girl was cowering a bit, but it was like, 'Sorry. I've got to let you have it, babe.' Everybody who went on got it, bad. At one point on this November show, Eddie Clarke was decimated by about six buckets of water. It was funny as shit. And they had this cage there, and they'd put people in it. Viewers wrote in for weeks ahead of time, volunteering to get in. There was a waiting list to be stuck in this cage, where everything in the world was dumped on them. They had this big trough full of green gunge – viscous, garbagey slop – and they'd tip that all over 'em at the end of the show. Phil had volunteered to be in the cage, but our manager, Doug Smith, went in – then they wouldn't let him out again. Ha-ha! So we had some revenge on the son of a bitch. Great show.

Our 'Ace Up Your Sleeve' tour that fall was fucking mammoth.

We barrelled through all of Great Britain with the 'Bomber' rig, the 'Overkill' backdrop with its flashing eyes, and on a couple of the earlier shows, we also had these lighting tubes forming a gigantic Ace of Spades playing card. The latter didn't last very long – it was a bit on the fragile side and I believe it met an untimely demise. It was around the time of this tour that our old label, Chiswick, released the *Beer Drinkers* EP, the leftovers from the *Motörhead England* album sessions. The record charted, peaking at 43, and although we didn't see any big monetary returns, it was good for us. Anything's good that gets the name around, you know.

We finished up the 'Ace Up Your Sleeve' tour with four nights at the Hammersmith Odeon, and then an aftershow Christmas party was thrown for us at the Clarendon Hotel. There were some fire-eating strippers there – all good, wholesome English fun. I don't know where they came from – it was some publicity-type scheme. If it had been somebody else's party, I probably would have enjoyed it, but as I said earlier, I hate those things if I have to be involved. It's terrible because you've just come off stage and you're knackered. The last thing you want to do is to go to some fucking room upstairs at a boozer and be *sociable*! I mean, who needs it?

After a gig, I prefer to get laid immediately, if possible (as you may have gathered). I like to get one on one with a chick and just go someplace with her. I don't really mind where. A club or the back of the bus or whatever, you know. One time, I vanished with this chick out the side door of Hammersmith Odeon right after our gig. Her name was Debbie and she used to be a Page Three girl in the *Sun*. Saw quite a bit of her for a while. (Debbie, sadly, is no longer with us – rest in peace.) I walked off stage and gave the guitar to the roadie. Debbie was standing there, so I grabbed her and we immediately nipped out the door, joining the crowd that was walking away from my own gig. There I was in the middle of all these people walking down the road. A couple of them looked – 'That's Lemmy.' 'No, it's not! Can't be. Forget it. It can't be him.' They couldn't believe I was out that quick, so nobody asked me for an autograph, nothing. It was really funny. I'd fooled them, stonewalled them!

In late December, we popped on over to Ireland to do a few more dates. That's where Philthy broke his neck. It was in Belfast after a gig, and he was on a staircase, playing 'Who can lift each other up the highest' with a large Irishman. The Irishman lifted Phil up the highest, and at the same time, took a step back to admire his work – into thin air. They went backwards down the staircase, with Phil flying, and he landed on the back of his neck. We went over to them – the other guy got up, but Phil didn't.

I said to him, 'Come on, man.'

With stark terror in his eyes, he looked up at me – 'I can't fuckin' move.'

We took him to hospital in Falls Road. Keep in mind that this was Belfast on a Saturday night, and Falls Road is a Catholic area. Jesus Christ, you know! There were fuckin' *bullets* going by! We went into this hospital, past the gunshot wounds and the bomb-blast wounds, and they took him in. They had him braced on a table with his head propped up so he couldn't move it – well, he couldn't move it anyway.

'I'm dying for a piss,' he moaned as he was lying there. When he said that, our tour manager, Mickey, grabbed me and pulled me out the door.

'What's the matter?' I wanted to know.

As we were just through the threshold, we heard a nurse saying, 'I'll just put this catheter in here, Mr Taylor.' Then as the doors closed . . .

'AAAAAARGH! YOU BASTARD!'

'I just wanted to get out of there before the screaming started,' said Mickey.

I suppose Phil had assumed they were going to somehow walk him into the toilet, let him have the piss there and bring him back. He was lucky – he could have been paralyzed forever.

Finally, Philthy emerged, wearing this huge brace on his neck. I cut a bow-tie out of black gaffer tape and stuck it on the front so he looked like a Spanish waiter with a goiter. Phil's done lots of other stuff besides that. We were going to do a book called *Hospitals I Have Known Across Europe*, by Phil Taylor – a guide to European emergency rooms, you know. He's not real graceful, you see. On the bus during one tour, he was almost completely prone at all times because he couldn't get his bus legs together. The guy couldn't walk down the aisle. He would affect this very strange, stiff-legged gait, which he thought would help him stand up, but in fact laid him flat nearly always. He spent that whole tour on one knee on the bus, mobile proposing across Europe!

With Philthy out of action, we had to postpone the European tour we had planned at the beginning of '81. Meanwhile, Girlschool were at Rickmansworth, making a record with Vic Maile. It was Vic's idea to have Motörhead and Girlschool record a single together. The song we did was 'Please Don't Touch', which was originally recorded by one of my favourite groups of days past, Johnny Kidd and the Pirates. The band had some attention around 1977, after John died, as the Pirates. This cover wound up being part of a record called *The St Valentine's Day Massacre EP*, which was released on 14 February. The flipside had us doing the Girlschool tune, 'Emergency' (Eddie's second vocal), and also the girls covering 'Bomber'. Denise Dufort played drums on all those tracks, since Phil couldn't. That single turned out to be the biggest hit either Motörhead or Girlschool ever had in the British singles chart. It went to No. 5, and we went on *Top of the Pops*, billed as 'Headgirl'. Although Denise played the drums on the show, Philthy made an appearance, dancing around and adding a back-up vocal or two.

About a week before that *Top of the Pops* appearance, both Motörhead and Girlschool were filmed in concert for a Nottingham TV show called *Rockstage*. It was held at the Theatre Royale. I've still got a video of that performance. At the end of 'Motörhead', I leapt on to the Bomber lighting rig, pointing my bass at the audience like a machine gun, as one does – and got stuck halfway up. The guy who was in charge of lifting the rig left me up there for what felt like fucking years, but it was only a couple of minutes. I had this curly lead and it was stretched out tight. It was fuckin' pulling me out of the plane and I was thinking, 'You bastard! If I ever get down alive, I'll fucking kill you!' You can't tell that from watching the show, however – the effect looked great. The guy responsible for that SNAFU miraculously and wisely disappeared after the show.

In late February, *Sounds* magazine ran its 1980 readers' poll results and we came out on top in everything. I think we even nabbed 'Top Girl Singer'! Oh, except for one category – I came second for 'Male Sex Object', below David Coverdale. I didn't mind – he had more hair!

By March, Philthy had healed enough so that we could resume touring. We went all through Europe with Girlschool, and then came back and did four dates in England. We recorded all the English gigs for our live record, *No Sleep 'Til Hammersmith*. Originally, we were going to make it a double album but we didn't quite have enough material. It would have been three sides, which would have been a bit of a con. Incidentally, none of the recorded shows were at Hammersmith – they were at West Runton, Leeds and two dates in Newcastle. The last three dates turned out the best, and we chose the songs from those shows. It was also Leeds and Newcastle where we were presented with silver and gold albums for *Ace of Spades*, a silver disc for *Overkill* and a silver for 'Please Don't Touch'. This time they gave 'em to us backstage, however.

We didn't stick around for the release of *No Sleep 'Til Hammersmith*. By mid April we were off in the States for our first tour there. We were opening up for Ozzy Osbourne on his

'Blizzard of Oz' tour. While we were doing that, the record came out and immediately charted at No. 1. I heard about it in New York – I was still in bed when somebody phoned me.

'You went straight in at number one,' I was told.

'Uhhh – call me back, will you?' I mumbled and hung up. Then about ten minutes later it hit me and I was up like a shot. That was the height of our popularity in England. Of course, when you've peaked, there's nowhere to go but down. But at the time, we didn't know we'd peaked. We didn't know anything.

CHAPTER EIGHT

keep us on the road

So here we were in America, blissfully unaware that Motörhead had already reached its peak in Britain. And we did have a great time – Eddie and Phil had never been to the US before; I, of course, already knew my way around. But it's always refreshing seeing a place through new eyes. Phil – Clumso – managed to go all the way across the US without suffering any major injuries, although the salad nearly killed him in Florida. He and Eddie, see, they were used to English salads where you get a leaf and a couple of boiled eggs. So at this restaurant in Florida they both ordered double salads – and I didn't discourage them. I just watched as the waiters rolled up with two carts – an acreage of fucking greenery! Phil and Eddie practically had to fight their way out through this treacherous

Mugwambi swamp. Myself, I won't go near vegetables – too healthy for the likes of me.

I'd never met Ozzy, nor anyone in his band before but I got to know them during this tour. Rudy Sarzo and Tommy Aldridge were nice enough guys, but they were quiet, like. They were just, you know, the bassist and drummer. Rhythm sections never get much attention, really, unless the band belongs to one of them. Randy Rhodes was Ozzy's guitarist back then, and he was a much bigger deal. I believe he'd been writing songs with Ozzy. My big memory of him, however, was that he was terrible at Asteroids, so I wound up beating him at Asteroids all the way across America. I was quite friendly with Randy so I found it a terrible shame when he died in a plane crash a year later. Nevertheless, I have to say he wasn't the guitar player he became after his death. As with Bob Calvert, a guy who was more or less ignored during his lifetime suddenly becomes a huge genius. Randy was a good guitar player, to be sure, but he wasn't the great innovator he was later made out to be. God knows what people will say about me after I'm gone!

Ozzy was a nice guy – still is. Very twisted, but nice. Of course, you're going to be a bit warped when people are throwing half a dozen doves with broken legs and wings on stage every time you play a gig. Other things landed at his feet too – frogs, live rattlesnakes, a deer's head, a bull's head, all because of that story about him biting the head off a dove during a meeting with his record label. I don't know how he went on working after that tour. He must have been constantly freaked, never knowing what was going to come flying up at him. Makes you kinda feel for the guy, doesn't it?

Ozzy really was having a rough time on the tour we did with him. He nearly died on this trek: he was at the height of his nervousness and the depths of his despair, and he was just overdoing everything. We kept finding him flat on his face, passed out on the floor everywhere at the beginning of the tour. Finally his girlfriend (and later, wife) Sharon took over and pulled him out of it, and that was great. I've had some ups and downs doing business with Sharon since then, but I've got to give her that. You wouldn't have any more Ozzy Osbourne records if it wasn't for Sharon, and I think Ozzy would be the first to acknowledge that.

The Americans didn't quite know what to make of Motörhead at first. We had quite a few jaws dropping to the floor during the Ozzy tour. Some places understood what we were about – we got a rousing response on the coasts, New York and LA. They also liked us in Detroit and Chicago, which are still a couple of our main areas today. Ohio was good, too, and we've won over Texas since then. But apart from that, we might as well not have bothered that first time around – they were baffled by us completely. I think a good portion of the Midwest was rather frightened by us; most of the audiences didn't know who we were. An American label, Mercury, had picked up *Ace of Spades*, but nobody seemed to know about that. The label did absolutely nothing to promote the record (and what else is new?). So we were this strange, unknown entity every time we hit the stage.

We did have our few fans, though. One of them was Lars

Ulrich. He wasn't Metallica's drummer then – he was just this little teenaged kid living in LA. He loved us. As a matter of fact, he was in charge of the American Motörhead fan club, which, I assume, consisted of guys like him, who owned tons of import records. Those kids were big supporters of the New Wave of British Heavy Metal movement, which took off around this time. The NWOBHM was great for some bands – it sent Iron Maiden over the top. It didn't do us much good, though. We came along a bit too early for it . . . and then our popularity resurged just a bit too late for the big metal and hard rock boom of the late eighties.

So our first American tour was a mixed bag, but the ironic thing is that when we got back to England, we headlined a huge show at Port Vale Football Club in front of 40,000 people, *over* Ozzy Osbourne; so that gives you an idea of how massive we were at the time in Britain. That was probably our loudest show ever, and by then we'd already earned a reputation for the sheer volume of our gigs. (Admittedly, we did like it loud – we couldn't hear it otherwise because we were deaf!) At Port Vale, we built the entire stage out of PA – I mean everything: it was all speakers, everywhere, to the tune of 117,000 watts. At soundcheck, a guy rang up from four miles away to complain that he couldn't hear his TV . . . and that was just Eddie's guitar! Plus, there was the requisite spectacular publicity stunt that night. During our show, this plane flew low over the field and dropped these guys with Motörhead parachutes. Six of them landed smack in the middle of the field, but unfortunately one of them missed and went into the allotments next door. This one old geezer witnessed the whole thing – he'd been standing there with a shovel, guarding his allotment from the hippies, you know. And he said, 'Ay, that last lad came down like a sack of shit – *phoom*! On the ground. They took him away in a Dormobile.' I assume that wayward paratrooper recovered from his injuries, because we didn't hear any more about it.

We were also quite popular with the cops back home – they were always trying to bust us in those days. It was very different from what it is now: we couldn't go out of the house – the cops were just waiting outside the front door or failing that, they'd bust you on the street. Around this time – August of '81 – they caught Phil with about £5 worth of pot, and he ended up in court being fined £40. Stupid, petty shit, isn't it? But it wound up making news because we were these famous, bad-ass rock stars. Motorcycle Irene was with Phil when he got busted and they found pot on her too. But she only got fined £20 – maybe because she had bigger tits than him!

Minor hassles aside, we had a lot of fun with our fleeting time at the top. One very satisfying moment was when we played the Summernight Festival in Nuremberg, Germany and we were billed over Blue Oyster Cult, who had so soundly screwed us over at our first Hammersmith Odeon gig. We didn't do anything particularly nasty to them, though – after all, they were old news. We just didn't lend them the PA, that's all.

It was also around that time that I made a record with the Nolan Sisters. It was just a one-day gig – I got a phone call and did it for a giggle. It was a song called 'Don't Do That', and the band included me on bass, Cozy Powell on drums and ex-Whitesnake guitarist Micky Moody. Colleen and Linda Nolan sang, and Status Quo's road manager Bob Young also added some vocals and harp. We called ourselves the Young and Moody Band, and made a video for the tune, too. The Nolan Sisters were great fun – we used to run across them quite a bit because they were on the charts at the same time Motörhead was. Everybody thought they were soppy little popster virgins but they weren't. They'd been around – they'd played with Sinatra at the Sands in Vegas. They were tough chicks, managed by their father, but they were really great. And funny as shit. Once our manager, Douglas, was talking to Linda Nolan in the *Top of the Pops* bar, and he dropped some money on the floor. When he bent down to pick it up, Linda smirked and said, 'While you're down there . . .' That was the last thing he expected out of a Nolan Sister! Maybe wishful thinking and he dreamt it up, but it shocked the shit out of him.

I don't understand why people want to think that women don't like sex, or that the ones that do are terrible and depraved. Everybody likes to fuck. We should have grown up to that extent by now, where we recognize sex for what it is – fun and recreation. I've said many a time that sex is the most fun you can have without laughing. Like I mentioned at the beginning of this book, part of the reason I got into rock 'n' roll was for the chicks, and everyone in Motörhead has always had as many as they could get their hands on . . . or who could get their hands on us. One time at Bolton Casino, I was sitting at this table and this girl came up and blew me right there. Eddie swung by to say, 'We're ready to leave, lad.'

'Could you hang on a minute?' I asked, very strained-like.

Then he saw the high heels protruding from underneath the tablecloth and got the idea. So he left us alone and I drifted back into the ecstasy.

Pleasant interludes like that happened all the time. When it came to chicks, we weren't really worried about quality in my band. And, actually, quality is certainly in the eye of the beholder. What people call quality is usually better dressed, which doesn't cut any ass with me. I've met chicks who look like bad ladies who have more brains, better conversation and are just all-around sexier than the best dressed models in the world. It's true. Those model types are like fuckin' thoroughbred horses – they look good but they're dumb as shit. I've had a lot of what people would call slutty chicks around, and I like them because they're honest and up front. They're like me – they say, 'I like fucking! Let's go!' And, really, that's the way it should be.

Obviously, rock stardom has its ups (and you can take that several different ways!), but there was the occasional downside. At the beginning of Motörhead's career, we used to hang out in the bar with the fans before the gig, but eventually it got to be too much. You start getting fans who think they're in the band – they dress up as me and after a while when they look in the mirror, they see me instead of themselves. That can get very weird. There were guys all over the place called Lemmy, and loads of kids called Lemmy, too, poor little fuckers – one is a girl! Another guy gave his son Kilmister as a first name. And there's cats and rats and dogs and fucking parakeets, all named after me. We were inundated with adoring fans, not to mention the occasional nut, so eventually we had to stop being as accessible as we once were. That was a shame; I always missed that, because when you hang out with the kids you get an idea of what's really going on out on the street.

A lot of bands divorce themselves from that as soon as possible and I think that's a big mistake. Some bands never even meet their fans, don't even know who they are or what they look like. They just see the spotlights shining in their eyes, then they go off-stage into their own little world. Musicians who do that are missing out on a lot. I still like talking to fans today . . . except for the occasional drunk fucker who insists on singing 'Ace of Spades' in my ear nonstop! We have made a few albums since the *Ace of Spades* days, after all – if he's drunk and starts singing something from one of our last couple of records, I might not mind so much!

Another problem with being very popular is that some people claim that you've sold out. But really, that's more their problem, not mine. Commercial is whatever people are buying, that's all. That doesn't mean the music changes. For example, our first album didn't sell very well, so we were still street credible. Then *Overkill* was a minor hit, and some of our fans left us because they thought we were 'going commercial'. That was really stupid – couldn't they tell the music was basically the same, just a little better because we were a tighter unit after playing together for a few years? By the time *No Sleep 'Til Hammersmith* came around, there was a small backlash going on with the requisite cries of 'Sell out!' Since that was a live album of songs from when we weren't 'commercial', it looked like they needed a damn good thrashing for being elitist, overfed snobs! We knew we were doing just what we wanted to musically, so that was easy to ignore.

It was Motörhead's best year ever, 1981, but it ended on a very bad note. We spent the last part of the year touring Europe, and my flatmate, Andy Elsmore, got murdered. He was a little gay guy who used to run a porno cinema. Somebody came into my house while I was away and stabbed him fifty-two times in his face, neck and chest, then put a knife through his asshole and pulled it through to the front. And they cut his dick off, and shoved it up his ass. Then they set the place on fire in an attempt to disguise the murder. Still, poor Andy managed to crawl all the way down the corridor to the TV room before he died. That's where they found him. It was a terrible fucking thing.

The media, of course, didn't get it right – the headlines said things like, 'Motörhead involved in drug slaying', or some fucking bullshit. It had nothing to do with us, and I'd been gone a month so I didn't know who Andy was mixing with. It was obviously some gay hate killing, otherwise they wouldn't have bothered sticking his dick up his ass. That's definitely an anti-gay thing. A tragedy.

But back to the band. At this point in our career, unfortunately but perhaps inevitably, we started getting complacent. Everything we'd done up to that point had turned to gold. We thought it was just going to carry on magically. But *Iron Fist* was not the record to follow up an album that went straight in at No. 1. To be honest, we were screwed anyway. *No Sleep 'Til Hammersmith* was live, and you can't follow up a live album that sold the way *No Sleep* did. We wound up getting a lot of mixed reviews, which didn't surprise me in the least. It did surprise Eddie, who produced it with Will Reid Dick, and I think it broke his heart in a way. But the record didn't do too badly sales-wise. It peaked at No. 4 – not as good as our previous couple of releases, but still quite respectable.

The disillusionment hadn't really set in yet, however, and we began our UK tour with high hopes – the dates were very good. Our manager, Douglas, had come up with the idea of the Bomber lighting rig, and since that worked out so well he now fancied himself as A Man Who Knows About Stage Shows. So he had to outdo himself for our *Iron Fist* tour. We didn't even know what kind of marvel he'd cooked up until something like three days before we hit the road – 'We made it and you can't change it now.' It was quite dramatic, really. The curtains would open up and the stage would be absolutely empty – nothing, not even the red lights on the amps. We were up on the ceiling, see. We had a stage that was on four gantries, with all the equipment on it – the drums, the amplifiers, the lights, the whole stage, was in the roof. Then the music would start and we'd come down, out of clouds of smoke and coloured lights, and as we were making our descent, this huge fist would open up and there were searchlights at the tips of its fingers.

Naturally enough, the fist didn't work properly the first night, and we got stuck going back up as well. The stage rose about halfway and stopped moving and the curtains caught on the stage. People could see us milling about, going, 'What the fuck are we gonna do now?' and 'How do we get down off of here?' Philthy, of course, nearly stepped from his kit into oblivion – Eddie caught him just in time. But after the first couple of days, it worked great. We never used the fist again, though. That went straight back to the shop and it stayed there.

Tank, a band Eddie had produced, opened for us on those dates. That was our friend, Algy Ward's band. He had been in the Damned but got fired, and then he formed Tank. He was bass player and leader of his band, as was I, and he felt very good about that. They'd done very well on tour with us in Europe, but in England, they had wife trouble. The wives wanted to come on the road and, of course, they were only new boys so they let them, and that's death for any band. I'm not coming off chauvinistic by saying this but wives separate the band, plain and simple. Let's say you have three guys in a band – maybe they go to three hotel rooms after the gig, but they're the only ones in their rooms. But if your old lady's along, you get off stage and you have to hang out with her. You don't discuss the gig with the rest of the group and you don't go back to the hotel bar for a drink because you're with your old lady, right? She's standing there and there are a lot of things you won't say in front of her because you think she'll be bored or you've got to pay attention to her. So that completely fucks up the communication within the band. And also, a lot of wives are in their husband's ears – 'The other guys would be nothing without you. You don't get enough credit,' and the rest. It causes a lot of grumbling and dissension and can destroy a band. I've seen it happen many times – it's happened within my band! So as a result, Tank wound up doing very badly with us in the UK.

Since we were still big rock stars, we were pulling all sort of *Spinal Tap* shit. (Incidentally, *Spinal Tap* was a very accurate film. Whoever wrote it must have spent some time on the road with rock bands.) We were bad boys in those days . . . but then, we still are today, only everyone's used to it now! People get horrified by Motörhead – 'The fuckin' cheese isn't here! Where's the cheese!' 'Sorry, man, we couldn't get it.' 'OH YEAH? CAN'T GET ANY FUCKING CHEESE IN A BIG TOWN ON A WEDNESDAY AT FUCKING SIX O'CLOCK?! GET OUT AND GET THE FUCKING CHEESE!' 'Cause it's not the cheese that matters, is it? It's the principle that they didn't bother, that's what pisses me off. I'd send the promoters and their minions on all kind of errands – 'Get out there and get me this shit!' If it's on the rider it had better damn well be there. If the drum roadie wanted Twiglets (and ours did), he got them. Our present guitarist, Phil Campbell, sent out for Chinese food at one show, and he told the guy to get a portion of Ben-Wa balls, too – and the guy came back with them! But here's one thing that has always puzzled me, and it happens in every country in the world. Your rider says you get so many towels, right? And they give you these tiny, foot-square pieces of cloth. What the fuck is that?

We took no shit from anybody. At one point we were scheduled to play at this radio station, Radio Clyde, in Glasgow. We were supposed to be doing a soundcheck, but the guy was a real dick and he kept us waiting for ages. Radio people are notoriously unsympathetic to anything you're doing, because they're so self-important. So after sitting there for a while, I said to Eddie, 'Fuck this. Let's do 'em.' So we unwound the firehose from the wall, stuck it through the door of the studio, jammed the door shut and turned it on. And we left. They didn't ask us back – rather unsporting of them, really.

The cops really got on our ass around this time. They went through everybody's house, the roadies' hotel, even our manager's house. I was in a hotel in Swiss Cottage, so they missed me. They had this serious operation going: dogs, door smashers and all, and out of everybody – twenty-five crew, three bandmembers, the manager and his wife and their staff – the cops came up with all of a half gramme of cocaine, I believe, a little bit of dope and one Mandrax. We went down to the nick and I asked, 'What reason did you have for mounting this massive operation?' 'It was an anonymous tip off,' the magistrate said. 'We heard you were selling acid to the audience from the stage.' Jesus, what idiocy! I'm singing and playing bass – when am I going to have time to go down front and say, 'Anybody want any acid?' Not to mention handing out change – I would have needed a change belt instead of a bullet belt! Fucking assholes – as if the cops don't have real drug pushers to chase. Or why aren't they out catching the Yorkshire Ripper, people like that, instead of fucking around with a band who's just playing gigs and taking a few drugs on their own? Of course, telling them this never goes down well with the cops.

I imagine that my comments on wives still have you radical feminists out there fuming (but then, if you get pissed off that easily, what are you doing reading this book?). But fair's fair – as I've mentioned before, I'm more than happy to work with female performers. Before Motörhead began its American tour, I popped in at a studio in London to visit this all-girl band from France, Speed Queen, who were making an album. The singer, Stevie, was great – she sounded kind of like a singer that's around now (and, incidentally, getting far less attention than she deserves), Nina C. Alice from a band called Skew Siskin. They both have real rough voices – like Edith Piaf, only with guitars. I even added some backing vocals to one of their songs. The album was in French, though, so it never got heard anywhere but France. A few days after that, Motörhead flew to Toronto so that we could record an EP with Wendy O. Williams. That session resulted in the demise of what many Motörhead fans call our 'classic line-up' (although those who think that way probably haven't heard the band in the last few years).

Wendy O. and her band, the Plasmatics, have been pretty much forgotten nowadays, but she was a completely outrageous punk rock agitator. She sawed guitars in half with a chainsaw and blew up police cars on stage. Once she drove a car into a pile of explosives on a New York harbour and jumped out at the last minute. After she did that, she went straight to Florida to wrestle alligators. I thought, 'This chick's fucking excellent!' Plus, I'd seen pictures of her, and she did take a good picture. After our EP with Girlschool hit, people were always on us to collaborate on records, especially with girls. And I really enjoy making records with birds. Eight geezers in the studio can really be a drag – recording with girls usually produces better results, because it causes an interesting kind of friction, and also the scenery is a bit better! Abrasiveness and scenery – I'm all for both, and it was clear I'd get that from Wendy O. It was touted as this extraordinary combination of punk and heavy metal – two warring factions at the time. The songs we were going to do were a Motörhead tune, 'No Class', 'Masterplan', which was a Plasmatics number, and as the single, 'Stand By Your Man' – yes, the country song.

Eddie was supposed to produce the tracks for us, and unfortunately he had Will Reid Dick – whom I generally refer to as Evil Red Dick – in tow again. The session was problematic to say the least. Wendy took a long time to get in tune, and it wound Eddie up. She tried her parts a few times and she sounded terrible, I will say that. You'd think she was never going to get it, but I knew she would if I just worked with her. In addition to this, Eddie wasn't playing guitar – he was only working as producer. We were using Wendy's guitarist from the Plasmatics, with me and Phil on bass and drums. Eddie just wasn't acting terribly thrilled with the whole scenario and finally he said he was going out to eat, but we found him in the other room, sulking with Evil Red. It was bullshit. We could have worked through our problems if Will Reid Dick hadn't been there, because Eddie would have had nobody to go off with, away from the band. He would have had to stay in and lump it, then it would have been done and forgotten. But we ended up exchanging a few words and Eddie left the studio. Later, Phil and I went back to the hotel. Phil went ahead of me, and he came up and told me, 'Eddie's left the band.'

Actually, Eddie used to leave the band about every two months, but this time it just so happened that we didn't ask him back. We didn't try to persuade him, which is why he stayed away – that surprised him a bit, I think. But we were just tired of him because he was always freaking out and he was drinking a lot back then. He's become very much better now since he stopped. So Eddie did our first two American dates, Toronto (there's a video of that gig, but Eddie was terrible and so was I – I got cramp halfway through the show and couldn't play), and New York. We had to get another guitar player fast so we could continue the tour, and we chose Brian Robertson, who had been in Thin Lizzy. Technically, he was a better guitarist than Eddie, but ultimately he wasn't right for Motörhead. With Robbo our slide downwards began to pick up speed, which was unfair really, because the record we made with him, *Another Perfect Day*, was very good.

Looking back – and I must say, hindsight is 20/20 – it was good for us that we fell when we did. We wouldn't have been going now if we had carried on getting more and more famous. We would have wound up a bunch of twats with houses in the country and gotten divorced from each other. So it was just as well, I think, for Motörhead's moral overall. It's important for a band to be hungry because that is the motivation that makes all bands work. And if anyone knows about being hungry for long periods of time, it's me.

But back to Robbo. I'd known him for years – we met under a table at Dingwalls. There was a fight going on and all us cowards were hiding. Yellow streak aside, he was one of Phil's heroes, because Phil is a complete Thin Lizzy freak. And Brian was great on stage with them. He used to wear a white cord suit – quite striking with his curly, longish hair. He was available so we flew him out immediately, and he arrived in Toronto with reddish-dyed short hair. I was fucking horror-stricken, but I thought to myself, 'Well, he's enough of a trouper.' It turned out he wasn't, though. He wound up being just a pain in the ass. He was the only person in any of my bands that I threatened with physical violence – he was threatening me back, to be fair. We both had a chair in our hands and we were going to hit each other with them. But that happened months later: when he first got in Motörhead, the only hint of impending doom was the fucking red hair.

Gradually, we got more clues. When Brian first came into the band, I said to him, 'Remember when you were in Thin Lizzy, you had that thing with Scott Gorham, where he'd wear the black cord outfit and you'd wear the white one and you each used to flash over to the sides of the stage? That'd be great. I wear black. Why don't you get that white outfit back out?' 'Oh no, I couldn't do that, Lemmy,' he said. And there was other shit, like he wanted a contract with us for only one album at a time. Basically, he wanted an out beforehand in case Motörhead didn't happen for him. All this was easy to ignore in the beginning because for a while he was dead on. After he hooked up with us in Toronto, he only had a few hours of rehearsal before our first gig with him at Harpo's in Detroit, but he played like a demon. We finished the American tour in June and then went off to Japan – our first trip there – and he was great the whole time.

Japan loved Motörhead from the start. Brian had already been there with his band after Thin Lizzy, Wild Horses, and he told me with all confidence (and with his broad Scottish accent), 'Don't think you're gonna get all this acclaim like you're used to here in Japan. You won't because they don't do nothing. They just sit there and clap their wee hands.'

'Oh, don't be too sure about that, Brian,' I said. 'You're in Motörhead now,' which probably irked him like shit.

So we got there and sure enough, the first time the curtains opened across the stage, it was all, 'AHHHH! REMMY!' Blian got a bit upset by that. 'Blian Lobertson' – that's rather unfortunate, isn't it?

I loved Japan as much as they loved us. It's a complete culture shock because nothing there is like it is in the West. The girls go out in bunches over there, but they don't mind a bit of adventure. A big group of them will come into your hotel room and all take their clothes off – it's very much a bonding thing with them. It's because they don't have this guilt we do, courtesy of our stiff Christian upbringing. In Japan, they have Buddha, which is much more civilized. Most Japanese girls are very, very pretty, and everyone's polite, which I like. Good manners cost nothing, and most people in America, England and in many parts of Europe are mainly arrogant, brutal, stupid assholes who don't give a fuck about anybody. They push you to one side and elbow you out of the way. They don't do that in Japan. But make no mistake, they're very horny as well.

There are places we wound up visiting every time we went back – Pip's bar was one of them (unfortunately, it closed down a while back; now it's a karaoke bar!). They were very friendly there, and they didn't care if you fell on the floor. Plus they had a couple of pin tables, which was great drunken entertainment for me. But that's nothing compared to the amusement arcades. The amusement arcades are unbelievable – it's like being in the Starship Enterprise. The weirdest thing I've ever seen in Japan, however, was about twenty Japanese rockabilly fans walking down the street. They had it down – the quiffs, the leather jackets, the walk. Japanese teddy boys, that took some getting used to.

It was back in England that Brian started getting very strange. He did fine on our first show there, which was at Wrexham Football Club. We were headlining, and down near the bottom of the bill was a new band from America called Twisted Sister. It wasn't long after this gig that Twisted Sister became huge MTV sensations – keep in mind, MTV was just starting up in 1982 – but this was the band's first time in England, ever, and they were *terrified*, the poor bastards. I ran into them backstage – here was this group of big geezers, all dressed like women, and they were so nervous they were spitting teeth. I could see that they were going to just fall to bits, so I said, 'Listen, I'll go out and introduce you if you want.' And they were all, 'Oh yeah, please!' So I went out there and said, 'These are some friends of mine, so give them a fucking break – Twisted Sister.' That made sure they wouldn't get bottled off, at least. And they went on and blew the place down. I introduced them again when they played the Marquee – I mean, I would expect them to do the same thing for us, and the band's singer, Dee Schneider, did so a couple of times. He also got us on MTV, when he had his own show. We had some good times with Twisted Sister. Later on in the year, they were on *The Tube*, a TV programme that recorded in Newcastle, and we went up and jammed on 'It's Only Rock 'n' Roll' at the end of the broadcast. I ran around one side and as I was putting on my bass, Brian suddenly appeared on the other side and – *BANG!* – he fell straight on his face. It was funny as shit. You could always rely on Brian for some unintentional entertainment.

He was less than entertaining at our show after Wrexham, however. It was a stadium gig at Hackney Speedway in London that the Hell's Angels put on. Everybody who worked on that show – the crew, everyone – were Hell's Angels. They lost a fucking fortune putting it on, and they never promoted another show after that. I remember one of the guys, Goat, was telling me, 'I know where I can steal a generator. Up the motorway, they've got loads of them. Nobody'll miss it.' 'I think they'll miss it,' I said, 'and I think they'll catch you doing it.' Somehow they got a generator, though. So here we were, surrounded by these massive, tough bikers, and Brian comes out on stage with his red hair, wearing these green satin shorts. A lot of muttering was going on: 'Who's that cunt with the fucking shorts on?' 'That's Motörhead's new guitar player.' 'Ah. Let's kill him.' You could feel the terrible undercurrent. Brian doesn't know how close he came – I stopped them, but they really were going to kill him. After all, he was reflecting badly on them. The Angels are aggressively masculine, and they don't like shit like that! There he was, poking it right in their eye. Whereas that's laudable in a sociological sense, he really could have picked a better place to make a statement.

Brian's fashion sense continued to shock and horrify fans throughout our tour of Europe at the end of the year. Let's face it, ballet shoes and Motörhead do not mix! He stood out like a sore thumb, and I guess that's what he wanted. He was trying so hard to proclaim to everybody that he wasn't actually in Motörhead, and he was just a guest artist. Our record label didn't like him, either. I think Bronze would have preferred us to break up at this point, really. The *Stand By Your Man* EP didn't get much promotion. But we did go into the studio in March of '83 to make an album.

Another Perfect Day shows a lot of Brian's influence, which musically, wasn't a bad thing. Even the producer, Tony Platt, was Brian's boy, but he did a very good job so I have no complaints about that. Brian, of course, was his usual pain-in-the-ass self, but we dealt with it. The only thing I didn't like about the record was there was a bit too much guitar – some of those solos didn't have to be that long, God knows! But other than that, I thought it was excellent. Our fans hated it, though. They thought we were 'going commercial' – there's that word again! It got up to about No. 20, and that was it, so it wasn't as 'commercial' as people claimed it was. But *Another Perfect Day* has stood the test of time – a lot of fans have recanted now and come to like it. But that didn't help us back then.

I think *Another Perfect Day* was a good change for us, and maybe it was a mistake that we didn't experiment more earlier. Maybe we should have carried on in that direction . . . but not with Brian! After the album came out, we toured with him through England and America (*that* was a loony tour – they didn't know what to do with us so they kept billing us with bands like the Outlaws!), and the audiences just hated him. For one thing, he refused to play any of the old songs we were known for – 'Ace of Spades', 'Overkill', 'Bomber' and 'Motörhead'. He didn't want to be associated with the past. Actually, Phil was in agreement with him on that, and I could see their point, but let's face it, the kids want to hear the old stuff. I mean, if I go to see Little Richard, I want to hear 'Long Tall Sally', and if I don't I'm gonna be thoroughly pissed off. Even though I'm sick to death of it, Motörhead *should* do 'Ace of Spades' – people want to hear 'Ace of Spades' and you can't fight that. To refuse to play it – or those other tunes – is very bad news. And then there was Brian's clothing thing, too. On our last tour with him, he was wearing what looked like sweat pants, only they were made out of gabardine, and he had them tied up at the bottom with two strips of old, white towel.

Plus the blazing red hair. He was just being awkward for the sake of it.

But I didn't fire Brian for any of those reasons. I would have kept him in the band forever if he was playing all right. It was just when he started fucking up that he became unbearable. We were part way through a European tour, in the fall of '83, when it just got ridiculous. We were playing at the Rotation Club in Hanover, Germany, and we had just done 'Another Perfect Day' and he started playing it again. So I stalked over to him and said, 'You cunt! We just played that!'

'Oh, sorry,' he said, and he started it again a *third* time.

At that point it was, 'Good night from him, good night from me and thank you very much' time. We cancelled the rest of the tour because we knew we couldn't go on like that. Brian was a mess. Once in Spain, I found him in a hotel lobby in front of a display of those knick-knacks hotels have – crystal teddy bears and shit like that. He was leaning with his head against the glass like he was looking into it, but I went over to him and he was asleep, with his bag over one shoulder and a bottle of Cointreau in his hand. We got him into the car and took him to the airport, and propped him up in one of the chairs in the waiting room. He laid there unconscious with his head thrown back and his mouth open and little kids were putting cigarettes out in his mouth, 'cause they don't care in Spain. He wasn't much livelier on stage, so he had to go.

After we got back from the aborted European tour, Phil and I went down to Brian's house in Richmond and fired him. It was fairly amicable, really – he was expecting it.

So Motörhead was down one guitar player once again. I finished up the year by singing and playing bass on 'Night of the Hawks', for Hawkwind's EP *Earth Ritual Preview*. By then, the only person from my time who was still in Hawkwind was Dave Brock – but of course, it's his band. As Motörhead is mine. I knew my band was going to carry on, regardless. I just didn't know who was going to be in it next.

CHAPTER NINE

back at the funny farm

Finding a new guitar player wasn't a difficult process, really. I just did an interview in *Melody Maker* in which I mentioned that we were going to get somebody unknown this time around, and the applications flocked in. It was so simple, in fact, that we wound up choosing two guitarists.

After trying out about seven or eight guys, Phil and I narrowed it down to two contenders. Some of the others were good, but they just weren't right for Motörhead. In the end, Phil Campbell and Mick 'Wurzel' Burston were the only ones I would have gone near. I had never heard of Phil Campbell's prior band, Persian Risk, but apparently they had recorded a couple of singles. He was in London, playing with his band when we were trying out people, and on their way out of town in the van he said, 'Let me off here, lads. I've just got to go and see somebody about a dog,' or some such lie – you can't really tell them you're going for an audition, can you? After all, you might not get it. Phil was quite nervous, but he was so sure of his ability that he practically walked in as if he was just showing up for a rehearsal. He laid a couple of lines out and went zapping back out, rushing around, speeding out of his head. If this gives you the impression that he was something of a maniac, you're right. I only found out just how much of one later on. He's definitely added to the Motörhead legend over the years.

Wurzel, on the other hand, was nearly a basketcase when he came in. But I was already favourably inclined towards him from the letter he sent me. He'd enclosed a silly looking photo of himself and a note that read, 'I hear you're looking for an unknown guitarist. Well, there's nobody more unknown than me.' That warmed my heart immediately. When he came in to audition, however, he was shaking from fear. On top of that, he had walked all the way from the station carrying his guitar and his bag of pedals. No doubt his arms were killing him.

'I've got a list of songs – ' he said, and the paper was rattling in his hand.

'Give me that, for fuck's sake!' I said, snatching it away from him. 'Don't worry. Sit down, have a couple of vodkas, man. You'll be all right.'

So he had a couple of drinks, after which he played for us and he *was* all right. Usually at auditions, they fly you in for ten minutes and send you flying back out again, but I don't see any sense in that. If you want a good guitar player, let him play his best. Wurzel later said in the press that that was the fairest audition he ever did. And it worked, obviously, because he wound up getting the gig.

We liked both Phil and Wurzel immensely (incidentally, both of them lied about their ages – Wurzel said he was younger and Phil said he was older. I'm the only one who never seems to lie about his age). We couldn't decide between the two of them, so we had them both come back. The plan was to hold a battle of the guitarists to see which of 'em came out on top. Then, the morning of the final audition, Philthy left the band.

Our manager, Douglas, called me up early, at nine that morning and said, 'I'm coming to pick you up in five minutes.'

'What for?' I asked.

'We've got to see Phil Taylor,' he told me, and I knew right then what was up.

I hadn't been seeing much of Phil but I had been getting the impression that he wasn't really keen any more. Although we didn't discuss his reasons for leaving the band, I think part of it was because he wanted to become a serious musician, or whatever it is that people think heavy metal isn't which, if you ask me, is total bullshit. To this day, metal is one of the bestselling types of rock – in fact, it *is* true rock 'n' roll. And it takes as much talent and determination to get anywhere as just about any other form of music. And it's fun – so what more could you ask for? Anyhow, I believe that was one of his reasons. And our troubles with Brian Robertson aside, Philthy was one of the biggest Thin Lizzy fans in existence. Although he fired Brian from Motörhead along with me, he still believed that Brian was a loftier pinnacle to reach for than Motörhead was – he must have thought that because he wound up doing a band with Brian for a while. Or who knows – maybe he just wanted to get away from me!

Anyway, Douglas and I went round to his house and he told us, 'I'm leaving.'

'Man, your timing is great!' I said. There we were with auditions to do that day with two guitarists who had travelled from Cheltenham and Wales. Now I didn't have a drummer. But I have to admit, Phil was a gentleman about the whole thing. The band was committed to appear on a *Young Ones* show not long after he left, and he came back and did that with us. He did leave decently, unlike some of Motörhead's former members.

That was small comfort, however, when I had to face Wurzel and Phil Campbell that afternoon. For a timeframe of a few hours, I was the only member of Motörhead. I really didn't know what to do, so when I got to the rehearsal room, I said to them, 'Look, Phil's a bit late. You guys talk amongst yourselves a minute, have a drink. I've just got to go across the road.' Then I went out and played one-armed bandit in the boozer for a quarter of an hour. When I came back, I caught a bit of their discussion.

'If I played this, then you could play that part –' I could hear.

They were already talking over how to persuade me to take them both. But they didn't have to try because I'd been thinking along the same lines. A four-piece is a lot more capable of playing different stuff – with two guitar players you're bound to get that.

Obviously I had to take a reduction in money, but it proved worth it for the next decade.

Once that was decided, I broke the news about Philthy's leaving. Things were a bit downcast, but only momentarily. Phil Campbell suggested Pete Gill as a replacement, and that seemed like a good choice to me. I remembered him as being a real attacker from the tour he did with us in 1979, when he was with Saxon. Later I heard that Brian Downey, Thin Lizzy's old drummer, was interested in the gig – I wish I'd have known about that (and wouldn't it have burned Philthy!). But Pete did all right for us for a few years. We asked him down to a rehearsal and he was all for it. He came and we played about two songs and then we all stood there with stupid smiles on our faces because it sounded so great.

Pete was something of an odd character. He was drinking when he first joined us and he's one of the funniest cunts in the world when he's been drinking. But then he stopped drinking and became this born-again jogger, and he was kind of difficult after that. He wasn't really jogging anyway. He only used to go down to the caff and have breakfast, then jog back, as if he'd been jogging the whole time. I know this because we followed him one day! He started to do some really strange things, Pete. He used to take his clothes off at odd moments. The first gig we ever played with him, there was a power-cut in the middle of the show, and he jumped up and dropped his trousers, which I thought was a very unusual reaction. Sometimes he'd just pull his dick out. Like, we'd be on an airplane and as the stewardess walked by, he'd pull it out and wave it behind her back. Then if she turned around, he'd put his paper over it. It really got to be a drag. Motörhead is nothing if not democratic, but I don't think it's fair to be waving your dick around when people are minding their own business and might not want to see it. Then there were the items he had sitting in the back window of his car – a riding crop, a hard hat and this colourful umbrella. I don't pretend to know what was going on in Pete's head, but later on I heard he came out of the closet and admitted he was gay. That made some small sense out of a few of his actions. One thing that never made *any* sense was the black notebook he kept with him at all times. Phil Campbell found it after Pete had been with us for two years. He peeked in it, and it was some sort of diary or ledger or something. Ten days after he had joined the band, Pete had written down, 'Phil Campbell owes me fifty pence.' Jesus, talk about wasting your time! But of course, all this was in the future.

At the time, having a completely new bunch of geezers to play with was brilliant. It took ten years off me, easy, 'cause they were so excited. First off, we did six dates in Finland to warm up, and we had an hysterical good time. All the way through Finland, we were dissolved in fits of laughter. We were playing really well and we were out of it with joy. In fact, it was probably the best time we ever had with Wurzel. One night, he was so drunk, he was lying in bed and the roadies were pouring beer over him. And I nicked his bird, which was only fair play because he already had mine! Man, those Finnish gigs were like Fellini's *Satyricon* backstage. It was so horrifying, it was great! I got some wonderful chicks on that tour. One place, I remember, we had to drive through four miles of quarry to get to this hut where the gig was, and it was *packed*. I don't know where the fuck those people came from! But I pulled this incredible chick that night – sixteen years old, just beautiful. She took her clothes off and I fell to my knees in tears and thanked God.

At another show, the Finnish lighting guy wound up in a wardrobe with this chick – he couldn't go anyplace else because we were in the crew room and we wouldn't let him in the band room, of course. So he took this bird into the wardrobe so she could suck him off, but we turned it round so the doors were facing the wall. They were in pitch darkness and the chick started gurgling and threw up in his jeans. There he was, stuck with this sick bird moaning around the floor, surrounded by this terrible stench! Finally he broke through the back of the wardrobe. Those shows were great fun.

Back in London, we did a gig at Hammersmith Odeon straight away – it was 7 May 1984. At that show, Pete Gill and Rat Scabies ran upstairs and smashed a sink off the wall of the men's room. We got fined for that by Hammersmith Odeon, but no matter. We murdered the audience that night – it was a complete triumph. We'd just had a new Bomber rig made – half of the old one had been stolen by gypsies. They'd broken into the compound and absconded with various bits of it for scrap metal. That second Bomber rig was nearly lethal. After one show we did with it, we found a split in the metal in the back of the wing, so the rig was liable to collapse at any second. And had it fallen, believe me, we would have been thoroughly crushed. As it was, I got hit on the head by the thing regularly. Still, it was a great prop.

Obviously, Motörhead was ready to take the world by storm once again. Our fans were ready for it, and we certainly were ready for it. Our record company, however, had lost it, as far as we were concerned. We had bitched a lot about Bronze during the time we were working with them, but looking back on it now – especially considering the subsequent labels we went through – the people there were really great. But by 1984, Gerry Bron had stopped being interested in us personally, and that rankled us a bit because Motörhead was his star turn. Bronze signed a lot of people off of our reputation – Girlschool, Tank. They even got Hawkwind.

Our trouble with Bronze really began after Eddie Clarke left the band. They didn't like Brian Robertson, and they didn't seem to have much faith in the new line-up, either. For our next album, they wanted to do a compilation of our old songs – that was an indication. When people start putting together compilations of a band's prior shit, you know they're readying the death knell. Bronze seemed to think we were finished, and anything more that we did would fail miserably (boy, did we have news for them!). No doubt they would have preferred for us to break up. There was no way that was going to happen, though, and I insisted that if they wanted a compilation, they were damn well going to add some new songs by Motörhead's new line-up. I also took charge of selecting the old tracks that appeared on the record, and wrote a commentary about each song. So that wound up being *No Remorse*.

During the latter part of May, we recorded six songs. Four of them – 'Killed by Death', 'Steal Your Face', 'Snaggletooth' and 'Locomotive' – ended up on *No Remorse*. The other two tracks we did went on the flipside of the 'Killed by Death' single and were both called 'Under the Knife' – they were two completely different songs, however. Maybe that sounds confusing, and it was meant to be. That's what's missing from record companies – that kind of lunacy for its own sake. That's the great British legacy to the world, humour like *The Goon Show*, *The Young Ones* and Monty Python. Some people don't get it, which is too bad for them. You're supposed to laugh in life. Laughing exercises all the facial muscles and keeps you from getting old. Looking stern gives you terrible wrinkles. I also advise drinking heavily – it helps the sense of humour! Smoking pot helps the sense of humour no end, but after a while you lose it altogether and all you can do is talk about the cosmos and shit, which is really boring.

But like I was saying earlier, our problems with Bronze were no laughing matter. They did promote *No Remorse* and the single very well – I will give them that. But it had the aura of a last hurrah. They advertised the record on television; it wasn't all that great, really – just a live shot of us making a racket and touting us as 'the loudest band in the world', and all the usual schmear. Nothing to write home about there. We did a photo shoot for the single that was funny as fuck, though. Each of us in the band were supposed to illustrate the different ways to be killed by death – they put me in an electric chair, Wurzel was shown being crucified, Phil was being burnt at the stake and Pete faced a firing squad. For that last shot we were dressed up as Mexican revolutionaries with rifles and all, and we took a break to buy Cornish pasties at the supermarket next door. It made the shoppers rather nervous. They backed themselves up against the wall, in fact, but we told them, 'It's all right. Robbers don't look like this. Too obvious.'

We also went to Arizona to film a video for 'Killed by Death' – I don't remember who paid for that, I don't think Bronze did; no doubt we probably did. MTV banned it for a really stupid reason. I was riding a motorcycle in it with this girl and I put my hand on her leg and slid it up behind me. You didn't see me grabbing the offending public hair, but nevertheless they didn't like that. It was bullshit – that was when they were playing the hell out of Michael Jackson's 'Thriller' video, which had people coming out of the ground with shit pouring out of their nose, but they didn't seem to have a problem with that!

Anyhow, photo shoots and TV commercials aside, things just weren't the same with Bronze, and we decided we wanted off the label. What ensued was nearly two years of legal shit which kept us from recording an album that whole time. We also had other annoyances to deal with, too. Phil Campbell was still tied up with Persian Risk's old label, and Pete Gill was in litigation over some money Saxon apparently owed him. So while the whole band wrote the music for the new songs we recorded, only Wurzel and

I were able to take credit. Things were just ten times more complicated than they should have been all around.

Since we couldn't put any records out for the time being, we just did what came naturally – we spent all our time on the road. Our first gig after the *No Remorse* sessions was for the annual TT motorcycle race on the Isle of Man. We drank lots of free Pernod that day and later I woke up in bed thinking it was really fucking warm in the hotel room. Then I noticed my feet were on fire! I'd fallen asleep holding a lit cigarette and the bed was in flames. I had to scoop up all the sheets and chuck them in the bath. Shit like that used to happen to us all the time – once, at the place where I used to live, I woke up and the whole mattress, except where I was lying, was *red*. The cigarette had burned through the bedclothes into the mattress, and it was about to blow up. I hurled myself off the bed, fast, and just as I did, it exploded – fire up to the fucking ceiling! That scared the shit out of me.

After the Isle of Man, we headlined the Heavy Sound Festival in Belgium. That was a classic line-up for the era – on the bill with us were Twisted Sister, Metallica (by then I'd gotten to know them fairly well and to this day, they're amongst our biggest fans), Mercyful Fate and Lita Ford (who I knew from her time in the Runaways), plus a few smaller, long-lost bands. A little over a month later, we toured Australia and New Zealand for the first time.

Travelling from England to New Zealand is a real pain in the ass, by the way. It took us a nightmare flight of thirty-two hours to get there – three-hour layover in Sydney and propeller plane to the island included. Then we got to the hotel and discovered that, yes, the tap water *does* go round the sink in a different direction! I turned on the TV to find a two-year-old episode of *Coronation Street*. It was a bit of a culture shock – things are very weird down there. We died a death in Dunedin, our first gig. Then a few days later, in Palmerston North, they had a riot. The audience was freaking out and running around – some guy got stabbed in the buttocks and the theatre was fucking destroyed. It got better, though – Wellington and Auckland were good. Then we went to Australia and that was very good indeed. Australia is great, because it's like the old American frontier. When you get away from the big cities and drive to the small towns, it's all verandahs and old sidewalks. You go into the bar and the fan's going round and there are flies everywhere and the town drunk is slumped over the counter, just like you see in old saloons in the movies.

They really loved us in Australia and especially Melbourne, where our main fan-base is. They gave us new guitars at one gig. Wurzel got a blue one, and before we went on stage, we could hear the audience singing, 'Who's the man with the blue guitar? Wurzel, Wurzel!' One guy followed us all over the continent – he pawned his VCR to do it. He beat us to town on the trek from Adelaide to Melbourne, which is a long fucking way. His car was dead, 'cause that's not a hospitable climate! But apparently it was worth it to him, and he wrote about the experience later.

We stopped home in September just long enough to work up a couple of new tunes that later wound up on *Orgasmatron*, and then we did a few dates in Hungary – this was before the

Communist thing went down. It was a very weird experience. No customs at all to deal with – we went straight through into the VIP lounge with all these Russians looking bemusedly at us. Obviously, if you're going to be a promoter in Communist Hungary, you're going to know the border guards, right? No doubt about that! There was a car on the tarmac and we were whisked straight through with top-notch treatment, went right to the venue in Budapest, soundchecked and were taken back to the hotel. The next day we went to the gig to find a whole army lined up around the site, and these Hungarian freaks just ran right through them. They were excited because I think we were the first band to play there for a long time. What a sight – thousands of people storming the Hungarian army! We performed in front of an audience of 27,000. Great show. The killer was it was in Hungary so nobody heard about it. I always find that when you play in these depressed, so-called Third World countries, the people are much more trusting and kind. They're more enthusiastic about everything. Considering that, what has civilization done for us? Blunted our sensibilities and made us less open and tolerant. Civilization is apparently a curse – God bless the open market!

Back in England, before starting off on our tour to promote *No Remorse* (it had come out in the UK the month before), we made an appearance on ITV's *Saturday Starship* (a kids' Saturday morning show – the successor to *TisWas*). Apparently some people complained because we were rehearsing early in the morning for the show in the station's parking lot. I don't know what the problem was – 8:30 AM was the time they gave us to rehearse and they put the stage up in the parking lot for us. Then we did the 'Wooaarrggh Weekender' festival in Norfolk, which was put on by the magazine *Kerrang*! That was a terrible show, and as is typical in the world of Motörhead, it was broadcast.

Halfway through our British tour, Wurzel had to go to hospital because he had kidney stones, so we finished up the dates as a three-piece. Our last gig at Hammersmith Odeon, he was allowed to play on a few songs. They put him in a wheelchair and two porno-'nurses' rolled him out on to the stage. The whole place was cheering for him – keep in mind that at this point he'd been in the band for less than a year! Plus, we got a silver disc that night for *No Remorse*. For a band that was supposed to be finished, I'd say that was a rather impressive showing.

We spent the last part of '84 touring America. It was the first time for Phil and Wurzel (Pete had already been there with Saxon) and I played tour guide for them. I really enjoyed myself on that trip because the last couple of years with Phil Taylor and Eddie hadn't been that much fun, and with Brian, it was no fun at all – that was a year and a half of fucking torture, in fact. But like I said, when young guys join the band, it really takes years off you. We finished out the year by filming a video clip for MTV – they opened the door to find us all singing a hideously off-key rendition of 'Silent Night'. Then we ended December by doing a few dates in Germany.

Those were actually our last shows for a few months. We spent the first part of '85 doing TV appearances – most of them for Britain, a couple for Sweden. We were on the debut show of

left: My grandmother showing off the hurdle she made in woodwork!

below: Father showing his RAF–ness.

below: Wedding of adored parents. *left* to *right*: unknown; my Uncle Colin; Vic; my Mum; my Gran; unknown; my Auntie Joyce. An optimistic group!!

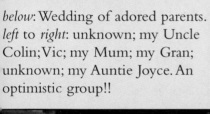

above: Even then! Me and cousin Caroline whose only appearance in the book this is!

right: My mother explaining to me that I am a month premature and be glad I wasn't an Aquarius.

Above: I saw ya! Note withered right arm!

Right: Age 4 ½. Who needs teeth anyway? Ok, Gummy!

below: Me and Hicka
– Hicka is the one
in the bridle

left: 'Monarch of the Glen' – this is me on Goldie when I worked at Hewitt's Riding School at Benlech on Anglesey, where we pulled the Girl Guides! Goldie had his own plans for the evening.

below: Me and my mate Krystof with our horses.

below: Simon House, Dave Brock, self, Nik Turner and Simon King: **Hawkwind**. We were probably trying to levitate or something.

below: Rehearsal for unlimited Whoopee – 1971. This is the picture they put on the front of the *NME* to advertise the Space Ritual Tour – without any of the others. I'd been in the band ten months! Ho Ho!

left: Paul, my son, aged 5 – he could already play better than me!
right: Paul and his wife Uma. Attractive couple, eh?

top: Motorcycle Irene, Philthy Animal and me. I cannot for the life of me remember the name of the other girl – she will now hunt me down and kill me.

bottom: We don't need no 'steenkeeng batches'!

below: What an unfortunate pose!

above: Phil Campbell, falling backwards, is
saved by his gallant bass-playing comrade.

below: Just like that!

above: Jesus, were any of us ever *that* skinny?

above: I *love* this picture. Macho in extremis!

left: Say what?

below: The best picture any of us will probably ever get of ourselves. The reason is a *secret*.

above: 10th Anniversary. *left* to *right*: Wurzel, Lucas Fox, Pete Gill, Brian Robertson, Phil Campbell, Phil Taylor – back row me and Barry Wallis – I think Phil just elbowed me in the balls!

right: Lemmy with starfish caught while scuba diving.

above: And on the seventh day – FIRE! FIRE!

ITV's *Extra Celestial Transmission*, or *ECT*, or 'Eric Clapton's Tits', as I fondly called it. It was this heavy metal show, and they asked the audience to 'dress outrageously'. In the spirit of the occasion, I had the make-up department do an incredibly realistic double scar down my face, and I dressed all gangster-ish, in a white double-breasted jacket – a favourite of mine – black shirt, white tie and wraparound shades. A couple of Hell's Angels friends of mine saw our appearance and offered to kill the guy who gave me the scar!

I also made a few appearances on my own here and there. I flew over to Germany to perform on a TV show with Kirsty MacColl (rest in peace: she was a really great bird). I was on guitar, dressed in shades and a teddy-boy outfit, and I sank to my knees doing a solo – actually I had no idea what I was playing! Frankie Goes to Hollywood was on the same show, and I came up on stage with them, too. They were all very pleased, for some reason, and later, when they had a gig at Hammersmith Odeon, they asked me up for 'Relax'. I was supposed to play guitar during it, but I didn't know the chords. Nobody knew who I was anyway – Frankie's crowd wasn't exactly Motörhead's – and they were well bemused.

They had a party at the Holiday Inn in Chelsea that night, which we went to. Gary Glitter was there with a drink *and* a cigarette in each hand – he didn't know whether he was on his ass or his elbow. And there were two girls in basques hanging around who desperately wanted to fuck Frankie's bass player (only Holly Johnson and the other singer were gay). That's all they wanted, and he was the only guy they didn't fuck. They had everybody else, including Motörhead! You'd get a blow job and as you were leaving, they'd say, 'If you see the bass player . . .' But he'd left with his wife over two hours before. The last time I saw Holly Johnson was at a Frankie show at Wembley, and he had this huge gay geezer as his boyfriend, who was very obstructionist. One of those types that protects people from everyone, even their friends. Holly was leaving the band, and I told him not to. I said, 'You're making a terrible mistake,' and it *was* a mistake because no one's heard of him since, or any of the others. And they were *huge* for a while.

I also met Samantha Fox that year. We were both judging this spaghetti-eating contest (there were some fucking animals at that thing!). I'd been a fan of hers since she was a Page Three girl, and we were thinking of doing 'Love Hurts' as a single together. I did a tape and gave it to her to listen to, but our schedules got in the way and unfortunately it never happened. She's another one that's practically disappeared. She was very cute, but I think she was kind of misdirected. Her father was her manager, which is always a mistake, and he managed her right into oblivion. But she seems to have reappeared once again – Motörhead recently did our first-ever shows in Russia, and we went to a club owned by the promoter and there was Sam Fox! We had a great reunion there!

Even though Motörhead couldn't make any records for the time being, it didn't stop us from doing other things, such as benefit records. Gerry Marsden of Gerry and the Pacemakers got a bunch of geezers together to sing 'You'll Never Walk Alone', with the proceeds going to the Bradford City Football Stadium Fire Disaster Fund. Wurzel and I were on it, along with Phil Lynott and Gary Holdon, among others. That song went to No. 1 and earned a gold disc. I also produced a Ramones song along with Guy Bidmead – 'Go Home Ann' from their *Bonzo Goes to Bitburg* EP. I wish it had been one of their faster numbers like 'Beat on the Brat' or 'I Wanna Be Sedated'.

At the end of June, Motörhead was coming up on our ten-year anniversary, and we did a couple of shows at Hammersmith to celebrate. Those were fun gigs. The first night, everybody who'd ever been in Motörhead showed up on stage, which was amazing. Wendy O. Williams and Girlschool were there, too. The second night, everybody showed up again, except for Larry Wallis. Even Lucas Fox was there, and he'd only been in the band a few months. Since we couldn't get three drum kits on stage, we hung a guitar around Lucas, but he wasn't supposed to be plugged in. Of course, he *was* plugged in, while Brian Robertson wasn't. Typical. And Phil Lynott came on stage because he just couldn't resist it. We were doing 'Motörhead', but he had no idea what he was playing (Eddie Clarke was over there, going 'E!' – he didn't remember, either)! Phil was a good friend of mine, but he'd never heard our signature tune. We were recording those shows, and Vic Maile did a special mix of it with Phil's bass up front and gave it to him, just to embarrass him. He had his revenge posthumously, though, when I went on stage with Duff McKagen's band a couple of years back at the Hollywood Palladium. They started playing 'The Boys Are Back in Town' and I didn't know it! I was supposed to do a different song with them, but they switched on me.

Anyhow, the second gig ended with a huge birthday cake being rolled out, and this little bird jumped out of it with these big balloons under her T-shirt. I took her home that night – actually I was going out with her at the time. Katie, her name was . . . what a little beauty! We released a video of that gig, called *The Birthday Party*. Our manager also wanted to release it as an album, but we said no. I thought it would damage video sales, and I also thought it was a con, another cash-in thing. We didn't think it was good enough as an album, either – after all, we hadn't played for five months before those two shows. It became an issue between us and Doug Smith. That went on for years, fighting and bitching. He finally won. It's hard to think now why we were so adamant, but at the time it seemed real important.

After the Hammersmith Odeon gigs, we toured Scandinavia for a month. We played just about everywhere there was to play – above the Arctic Circle, every shit-ass town. They have fairs in the summer in Sweden, so we did all of them, all of Norway and a couple of dates in Finland (our last gig was in Gothenburg, Sweden – our present drummer, Mikkey Dee, was living there and we never knew!). We called it the 'It Never Gets Dark Tour' because it *doesn't* get dark there in the summer. The sun just gets low on the horizon, then comes up again. In Norway, we had the promoter from hell. He kept telling us the wrong distances from gig to gig so we kept missing the ferries – Norway's all fiords, and you have to keep catching ferries and we missed about half of them and had to take speedboats. It was really annoying, not to mention expensive, and we were constantly late for gigs. Once when we got to the show really late, we walked into the dressing room to find a bowl of cold water with, like, one fucking beer in it, three yoghurts, a few biscuits and fruit and nuts – you know, bear food. So I said to the promoter, 'Hey! Come here a minute!' and I hit him with the three yoghurts before he got out the door. A bit later on the door opened a crack and a bottle of vodka was rolled across the floor to us. Finally in Trondheim we got totally fed up with him and covered him with squirty cheese. It was the fifth time we'd had to take a speedboat and we were two hours late for the show and we were really pissed off. Kids always think it's the band's fault when the gig starts late. So there we were on stage at last, and this cunt of a promoter was leaning against the PA like he was some Big Deal because it was in his hometown. And our roadies came up behind him and grabbed him, handcuffed him, dragged him out on stage and pulled his trousers down. Then they squirted him with the squeezy cheese and mayonnaise and anything else they could get their hands on. Our tour manager at the time, Graham Mitchell, walked up to the mic and said to the audience, 'See this asshole? That's why we're late tonight!' And, *per-doom*!, we pushed him off the stage. The guy wound up going to the police station – like that! Covered in slop, and in a taxi! After the gig, in the dressing room, we got the inevitable loud *thump-thump-thump* on the door, and it was this giant fucking cop – the Norwegians are real tall – who looked like the super-Gestapo.

'I sink you haff done somezing very awful to this person,' he informed us.

'Yeah? Well, he told us all the wrong fucking directions,' and all: we told him the story.

'Yes, yes, yes!' he said. 'But zis is no reason to cover a man viz cheese!'

It was the cheese that seemed to bother him, not the assault. It was a cheese thing. Strange.

When we got back to London, we did a few things around town before heading back to the States. Hawkwind was doing an anti-heroin gig at Crystal Palace, and I got up and did a couple of numbers with them. At this juncture I would like to mention that I think these anti-drug gigs are a joke. They're generally set up by people who are smashed out of their minds, which already defeats the object. And what do you do with the money you get from an anti-heroin gig, anyway? Not buy drugs with it?! They just set up clean-up centres or rehabs that really don't work. No drug taker worth his fucking name is ever going to listen to the people who are in charge at those places because they run them like youth clubs, which is the very reason you started taking the stuff in the first place, as a mark against your parents' generation. You don't want to be herded somewhere and told you're a bad boy. That isn't the way to do it: you lock 'em in a fuckin' room until they're clean and then let 'em out and see if they stay clean. That's all you can do. And actually, it's not even much use doing that, because a smack addict has to want to be clean. They've got to come to you. You don't do things like offer them rehab instead of jail, either – obviously, who's going to choose jail, for fuck's sake? They go to rehab to get the heat off 'em and maybe get rid of the annoying girlfriend. Then they get clean and it's cheaper for them for a couple of months afterwards 'cause they only have to take a fraction of what they were doing before. From my vantage point, the whole 'Drug War' is a fucking mess.

Anyway, enough of that. Wendy O. Williams and the Plasmatics were playing at Camden Palace, so me and Wurzel got up and did a couple of our own songs with them – 'Jailbait' and 'No Class'. They released a video of that show, if you can find it now. The next month, November, we were in the US, and I finished up the tour by appearing on MTV with Dee Schneider. By then we'd had very good news: our litigation problems with Bronze were over and we could begin 1986 by making a new record.

CHAPTER TEN

(don't let 'em) grind ya down

O f course, Motörhead didn't wind up on just any record label. Our manager, Douglas Smith, had convinced us that it would be best if we went with his company, GWR (an acronym for Great Western Road, where his offices were located). So our manager and record label were under the same roof. Plus Doug and his wife were handling our merchandising, too. Anyone could probably have told us this was a very unhealthy situation, giving our management this much power, but no one did. So, ignorant of business affairs as always, we forged ahead with the recording of *Orgasmatron*.

Orgasmatron was our first full studio album in three years and the line-up, except for me, was completely different from *Another*

Perfect Day, but that didn't faze us any. Between the recording sessions for *No Remorse* and all the touring we did, the four of us were rather used to each other by then! We made the record in eleven days, which as you might have figured by now, was no big deal for Motörhead. It was very easy, in fact, because the guys were so glad to be there. We gave our producer, Bill Laswell, a bit of a fright the first day, however. Me and Paul Hadwen, the fan club secretary at the time, had been drinking in this boozer when we saw an advert in the paper for Fat-O-Grams. We immediately thought, 'This is just the thing for Phil Campbell!' so we booked one. Then we went in the studio with Bill Laswell and his engineer, Jason Corsaro. They'd just come over from the States and they didn't know us at all – I'd met Bill for half an hour before this and, of course, nothing had been mentioned about Fat-O-Grams and such. So Bill and Jason were being all gung-ho American – 'Let's get it on, boys. It's gonna be great!' etcetera. But there was this large lady standing around the lobby (Phil later said he thought she was somebody's mother), and she came into the studio after us, asking, 'Which one's Phil?' And Phil said, 'I am.' WHAM! She tore off her dress and there she was, this huge woman in a little, skimpy outfit with the tits cut out, singing 'Happy birthday to you – !' (I suppose it may not have been his birthday – but we told *her* it was!) And she grabbed Phil and stuck his head between her tits – all we could see was just this little tuft of hair sticking out between 'em! Then she started slapping him with them! Nearly knocked him out. It was fucking great, and Laswell and Cosaro were edging behind the desk, going, 'What the fuck is *this*?' That was their introduction into the world of Motörhead.

As it turned out, Bill was good for getting sounds, but he fucked everything up in the mix. It was a much better album when he took it to New York than when he brought it back. A bunch of us – our people, Laswell's people – got together for the grand, first-time playing and our publicist brought a case of champagne to ring in the occasion properly. It was dreadful. *Orgasmatron* was mud. There was supposed to be a four-part harmony on 'Ain't My Crime', but he wiped three of them out! I won't bore you with the rest of the 'highlights'. Suffice it to say that our publicist was edging the crate of champagne back under the desk with her foot, while Laswell's manager was standing by the door, bopping determinedly. It was hopeless. I tried to remix some of the record, but Bill and Jason weren't being particularly helpful because 'it was our mix and *we* liked it and that's the way it was and this difficult musician was coming over trying to teach us our own job' – well, I suppose I *am* difficult, if you consider wanting to get the job done right 'difficult'!

I didn't come up with the title *Orgasmatron* right off the bat. The album's working title was *Riding with the Driver* (each Motörhead studio album, except *Bastards*, which we made in 1993, is named after one of its songs), but that track didn't turn out as good as we'd hoped. I didn't even know at the time that an 'Orgasmatron' was a contraption in some Woody Allen film – I never saw the movie – but I've been told about it quite often since! However, I made up the word on my own. A lot of our fans consider this album one of our 'classics', and there are some great songs on it – the title track and 'Deaf Forever', for example. I'll always have problems with the way it was mixed, though. As far as I'm concerned it was only half the album it should have been. I do want to note, however, that there's a great picture of Lars Ulrich on the original album sleeve. He had come up to see us at the Beverly Sunset a couple of years before while we were in Los Angeles, and he got a bit ill. He was still a youngster in those days, but it's a fallacy to say I taught him how to drink – I actually taught him to throw up, and that's what he did, all over himself – that's what he got for trying to keep up with older people's habits! A photo of that classic moment in rock history appears on *Orgasmatron*.

With a new album to promote, we were on the road again, and Douglas had to outdo himself once more with the stage set-up – hence the *Orgasmatron* train, to go with the record's cover art. The drums went on the front of the train, and it came out on rails in the middle of the stage – basically Pete was riding out to the front on the train. But it never fucking worked. You couldn't get the rails on the stage properly and things like that. Douglas did have some great ideas – the Bomber rig was brilliant – but this one was a very botched job. That and the infernal Iron Fist. But the train came with us through most of Europe.

Orgasmatron really should have brought us back up to speed – our new record with the new line-up and all – but nobody bought it. Or I should say nobody was able to buy it. GWR farmed the album out to various distributors around the world, most of whom did a shoddy job of getting it in the stores. But we played all the usual places – Europe, the Castle Donnington festival, England and the States. We started off the US tour with Megadeth opening up for us, but they were a very new band then and they blew it. The first night, in Oakland, they had their stage banner stretched out on the floor across our dressing-room doorway, and since we're no respecters of tradition, we walked straight across it. The band's manager dashed in, freaking out – 'You walked on our banner!' And I said to him, 'Look, there was no way of getting into our dressing room without walking on your banner. Why didn't you put it some fucking place else!' We were running late at soundcheck that night – it was the Kaiser Auditorium, I recall. The first show is always fraught; we had new guys in the crew and people were still setting shit up and learning. And that manager stormed up to our soundman's desk just he was finishing up the drums and said, 'You guys have to get off stage now. It says in my contract that my band has a soundcheck now.' Dave, our sound guy, turned around and stared at him.

'I'm sorry?' he said.

'Tell your guys to get off the stage,' this idiot commanded.

So Dave pulled out the copper's truncheon that he keeps behind the sound desk.

'If you don't go away, I'm going to hit you very hard between the eyes with this.'

So the guy went away, ranting and screaming backstage. Meanwhile, Megadeth's frontman, Dave Mustaine, came in to apologize and he crashed out in our room! Poor Dave was a bit out of it at the time – he's since cleaned up. And there was the fucking manager, stalking around outside, unaware that his star was possibly dying on our couch! But to be fair to the band, although we threw them off the tour the next day because of all the shit with the manager, it wasn't really their fault. It was the manager – we should have just thrown *him* off the tour, really. Years later, at the NAAM show, Dave Mustaine came up and apologized to me for it. That was really big of him, because he didn't have to. We could have just gone on leading parallel lives and it would have been all right. More power to him. He's a smart man, Mustaine; he's got freckles, but he's a smart man.

Overall, that wasn't our most stellar tour through the US. In New Orleans the audience was spitting at me (punks, you know!) and I warned them that I would leave if they didn't stop. And they didn't stop, so I left, and there was a riot with firehoses and all kinds of shit. Then in Aurora, Illinois, Graham, my roadie for years, smashed my favourite bass – it sounded great and I played nothing else from the time I got it till he broke it. He didn't do it on purpose, but he came to me with the two ends of it hanging around his neck, laughing. It was still repairable after he broke it, but he took it into the parking lot and smashed it to smithereens in a fit of pique, so I fired him.

During the short breaks in between all these various tours, I made all sorts of cameo appearances. I played an outlaw (typecasting, don't you think?) in a video for this song, 'I Wanna Be a Cowboy' by the band Boys Don't Cry. I got up at Hawkwind's gig at the Reading Festival and sang 'Silver Machine'. Then there was Boss Goodman's testimonial at Dingwalls. Boss was a roadie, then a manager for the Pink Fairies and then he ran Dingwalls. He became one of those mover-and-shaker types. A nice guy, and he was having this testimonial because he was retiring, which in fact turned out to be true – I haven't seen him since. Anyhow, Wurzel and I played some numbers with Rat Scabies of the Damned and Mick Green from the Pirates. Larry Wallis was supposed to play with us as well, but he was also playing in two other bands that night (including his own Love Pirates of Doom) and he refused to come and rehearse with us. He was such a drag that Mick Green finally told him, 'Look Larry, we'll be all right, you know what I mean? Thanks anyway.' We didn't need Larry anyhow – Mick's a great guitar player, and we did a good show. Also in the midst of all this Motörhead did the inevitable BBC 'Peel Sessions' recording, and I appeared briefly in a Doctor and the Medics video. *Orgasmatron* sales may have been disappointing, but our visibility factor was certainly high in 1986!

Early in '87, I had a featured role in the film *Eat the Rich*, and Motörhead did the soundtrack – mostly songs from *Orgasmatron*, plus the title track. The movie was made by the Comic Strip people, who were also responsible for *The Young Ones* TV show, and a few other projects. One of their earlier shows, called *Bad News*, had been about a mythical heavy metal rock band – a bit like *Spinal Tap*, but better, actually (and I'm one to know!). Bad News, the band from the show, had opened for us at Donnington, and we were all chatting at the gig and eventually

Peter Richardson, who was the film's director, rang me up and asked me if I wanted to be in a movie. I got the part as simply as that.

To be honest, I don't like making movies – I've been in several of them now. It's dead boring. They tell you to show up on the set at four o'clock in the morning and then at three that afternoon they say they don't need you. So it's just waiting around all day, basically, with a bunch of fucking actors. *Eat the Rich* wasn't so bad, though. I spent a lot of time drinking with Nosher Powell, who had the lead role as the Home Secretary. He has a club now in south London, frequented by villains and gangsters of all shapes and sizes. My character was called Spider, and I was supposed to be working for this Soviet double agent, Captain Fortune, played by Ronald Allen, who was in *A Night to Remember*, the Titanic movie from the fifties. I won't get into the plot of *Eat the Rich* here too much – it's a black comedy involving cannibalism in a smart restaurant, with lots of political overtones. Quite a few people did cameos – Paul and Linda McCartney, Bill Wyman, Koo Stark, Angela Bowie (not that she's any big deal – her claim to fame is that she was married to David Bowie). It's a very English film, really. A lot of Americans don't get it, but I think it's quite good.

My part didn't require any major sort of acting; I just played myself – I even used my own clothes. The director's instructions for me pretty much consisted of 'Walk over here and say this'. If you happen to rent the video, look closely at the scene where I'm riding a motorcycle – it's not really me. They shot that when I was off touring America with Motörhead, and I had to leave a set of my clothes behind. They ended up having a girl double for me . . . a big girl. Good, eh, trivia fans!

The director ended up having all of Motörhead in the film: we replaced the band in the ballroom scene. It was a secondary idea he had halfway through shooting. If you watch very closely during that scene, you'll notice that the band changes all the way through it. First there's none of our mob in it, then there's just me playing and the rest of the band are straight guys, and then Phil appears and then Wurzel and Phil Taylor appear (I had just fired Pete Gill that morning and Philthy shot down real quick in his car to do the scene). So much for continuity!

The sacking of Pete Gill was a long time coming. Peter was his own worst enemy, he was another one who wouldn't just be content to be in the band. He went up against me on a couple of decisions, and he was making Phil and Wurzel upset too. I got tired of him moaning, so when he kept us waiting while he hung around in the lobby of his hotel for twenty minutes while he read the paper or something, that was the proverbial last straw. I know it sounds trivial, but most flare-ups in families are, aren't they? And a band *is* a family. I let him stay for a couple more months, but it wasn't the same. I mean, enough's enough. I already knew Phil Taylor wanted to come back. He'd been playing with Frankie Miller, along with Brian Robertson, and it wasn't working out very well. One time Motörhead was flying home from a tour of the States, and Frankie Miller, Philthy and Robbo were on the same plane. That was very weird to begin with, and then the three of them started fighting amongst themselves in mid-flight. Some time after that Phil came round and asked for his job back, but we told him, 'Well, we've got to keep Pete at the moment,' not yet knowing all the conniving that was to ensue. I'm too honourable for my own fucking good – Brian Downey from Thin Lizzy asked for the gig around the same time and I turned him down!!

So the situation with Pete came to a head the day of the shoot. He took so long to do everything, and we were always having to wait for him. It was just getting up my nose, because after all, I'm a speedfreak and I don't like waiting. That morning, we got in the car and went down to the hotel to pick him and Phil Campbell up. Phil came bopping out of the hotel immediately, but Pete was still in his room, not dressed and we sat there for half an hour while he fucked around. Then he was saying goodbye to people in the lobby, and we were supposed to be at this shoot! Film people were sitting with their cameras on idle. So finally he came out, but I was fed up. I rolled down the car window and said, 'Fuck you! You're fired!' and we drove off. And that was it. Last I heard about Pete, I believe he was touring with some alternative version of Saxon. It's got three original members of the band who had all been fired, so they were calling themselves Son of a Bitch, which was Saxon's original name.

Anyhow, with Pete gone, we gave Phil Taylor his job back. It was a mistake in retrospect, but then everything is easy in retrospect, isn't it? The situation worked all right for a while, but things weren't the same, and I should have known they wouldn't be. But by June, we were back in the studio, recording a new album, which would be *Rock and Roll*.

Rock and Roll is a fair album, but it isn't one of our best. There were problems in the studio – nothing truly disastrous, just a series of little annoyances. Our biggest mistake was choosing Guy Bidmead to produce it. He was an engineer, really, so we were pretty much producing ourselves. Guy had looked like a good idea, though. He had worked a bit with Vic Maile, who helped on our two most successful albums and he had engineered the tracks we recorded for *No Remorse*. But the chemistry wasn't quite right. It wasn't Guy's fault, really – it was us, too. We were calling all the shots and whoever was nearest the desk would generally be the loudest! There was quite a bit of confusion when we were making that album. And Wurzel was having a bad time personally. His old lady kept coming up to the studio and chasing him around, causing all manner of family arguments while we were supposed to be working. That certainly didn't help. A lot of times the way a record turns out depends on what the band members are going through while they're in the studio. If a guy's getting harassed at home or he's got some money problems or whatever, it affects his performance 'cause his mind won't be on the job one hundred per cent. In addition to all of this, we didn't have enough time to do the songs properly and when that happens you're pretty much wasting your time.

That said, we did have some amusing moments. One of the studios we used to make *Rock and Roll* was Redwood, which was co-owned by Michael Palin, and it turned out that the engineer had worked on all of the Monty Python records. He played us some great outtakes that Python never put out. We also asked Michael Palin to come down and do a recitation to put on the album. He showed up, dressed in this perfect 1940s-cricketer outfit – the striped blazer, the duck trousers, the fucking white pumps, a V-necked sweater, with his hair all brushed over to one side. A complete vision. And he walked in saying, 'Hello, what sort of thing are we going to do now, then?' I said, 'Well, you know in *The Meaning of Life*, there was this speech that began "Oh Lord –"'

'Ah!' he said. 'Give me some cathedral.' And he went in and he did it. It was great.

Even though we've done better records, both before and since, *Rock and Roll* did have some great songs, like 'Dogs' and 'Boogieman'. We played 'Traitor' for years. And Michael Palin's 'Oh Lord, look down upon these people from Motörhead' speech at the end is classic. But overall it just didn't seemed to work. Still, it's not a *bad* album – I don't think we've made a bad one.

Anyway, with a new record done, there was the usual promotional stuff. MTV Europe had an 'International Lemmy Day', which frankly, I remember nothing about. And of course we spent the rest of the year touring through England and then Europe. We were supposed to begin 1988 by touring through the US with Alice Cooper, but we missed a month of it because the fucking American immigration department took so long to give us our work permits. It was just a lot of bureaucratic bullshit. I mean, we bring foreign money to America and they don't give a fuck about that. They'd rather give amnesty to all illegal immigrants. Actually, I missed out on that by one year – I had been living in America for six months when the amnesty was granted in 1991. If I'd known it was coming I could have stayed out beyond my work permit and then got amnesty and a green card. I can't get a green card because I got busted there for two sleeping pills in 1971, so obviously they have to watch out – dangerous drug fiend, right? Brilliant thinking, that.

Anyhow, the Alice Cooper tour, once we finally got on it, was a pain in the ass. It wasn't Alice's fault – he had no idea what we were being put through by his tour manager. That guy was a complete cunt. He made everything really difficult for us – since he was working for the top star, somebody else had to suffer and be made to look bad. We couldn't do this and we couldn't do that: fucking arrogant sons of bitches – how important do they think they are? It's only a band, not the Houses of Parliament – not that *that's* that important either. Finally, this idiot took away our 'all-access' passes and replace them with passes where we could only go backstage up to when we played; so after we finished our set, we couldn't get in. Naturally, I wouldn't stand for that kind of shit, so I went around the crew and said, 'Give me them fucking passes!' and gathered 'em all up. Then I walked straight into the production office, threw them down and said, 'There, look! We're out of here.' And as I was leaving, Toby, Alice's accountant – who had a brain – came and spoke to us and gave us our passes back. Toby still works for Alice; the other guy doesn't. Need I say more? I talked to Alice years later, and he never knew any of this happened, that his people were doing things in his name that made him look like an asshole – something he definitely isn't. One thing, though – I've never understood his fixation with golf. I mean, what is the deal with that? You hit a ball with a stick and then you walk after it and you hit it again! I say if you hit it and then you find it, you got fucking lucky, pal! Put it in your pocket and go home. (Thanks, George.)

We had our own kinds of recreation. Phil Campbell pulled one of Alice's dancers. I never forgave him for that, because she was so beautiful. Gail was a great girl and we still see her when we go through Chicago. And an Alice Cooper show is always an impressive thing to watch. I'm a big Alice fan. On a less pleasant note, it took some effort to get to some of those venues. I remember going up to a gig in St John's, Newfoundland. We had to load all our stuff on a ferry and it was fucking freezing, so cold that it bit straight through you, and there were icebergs in the water. In the middle of the night, we came out of the cabin to get something out of the bus and I slid all the way across the deck to the railing and nearly went over into the fucking sea. The story of the *Titanic* has fascinated me for years (well before the film and all the fuss) and the whole time I was thinking, 'This is what it was like when the *Titanic* went down!' 'cause we were at the same latitude. In fact, our next date was in Halifax, Nova Scotia, which is where they brought all the bodies. Imagine jumping into that water voluntarily! The shock when you hit it must have just fucked you up. So on the metal wall, next to the rail where I'd landed, I wrote, 'Remember, and be thankful it wasn't you on the *Titanic*, 1912, 14th of April.'

We spent a good portion of 1988 on the road. It had been our natural habitat for a long time and it's still that way today. It's funny – the metabolism you need to tour is unlike anything any doctor has come across. Ever. Forget the Elephant Man – at least he was all in one piece and working in the same direction, deformed as he was. *We* are deformed. Not *that* much, just slightly deformed . . . correct that – we're very deformed! The physical requirements for touring are unique (we're no good for anything else). You've got to get up on stage every night and suddenly be energetic within minutes or everybody in the world is gonna *die*! They're going to go home and shoot themselves because you didn't go on stage that night. We've gone on stage in all kinds of conditions. Once, in April of 1988 in Paris, Phil Campbell broke his ankle – he was fighting with Phil Taylor and they fell under a table and only one of them got up. He did the gigs we had scheduled after that in a cast. And I've already enlightened you on the various states of Philthy's health (both physical and mental). We have missed a gig here and there because of injuries or illness, but those have been very, very rare occasions. I can't understand any other way of being alive than playing in a rock band all over the world. For two years we were home for one month in each year. It was great fun, though. Kind of blurred, but fun!

Occasionally during the brief periods of time we spent at home, we'd attend some really stellar event. That spring we saw the Rolling Stones play a surprise show at the 100 Club, an old jazz club on Oxford Street that turned to rock and blues. That was an extremely good evening. Everyone – Jeff Beck, Eric Clapton and the like – showed up with their guitars and jammed, so it obviously wasn't that much of a surprise. The real surprise was Wurzel. I think he was even a surprise to himself!

We got to attend the after party at Keith's suite at the Savoy because a friend of ours, Simon Sesler, had an uncle who worked for Keith. But Wurzel had already begun his evening of terror at the 100 Club by knocking Bill Wyman flat on his back! He was flying down the stairs and Wyman just happened to be in his path. We managed to arrive at the party without any further mishaps, but there were more to come. For a while, we were sitting and talking with Simon when Kirsty MacColl came by with her new husband, producer Steve Lillywhite. Kirsty was a great old friend of mine – I was in a video of hers once – so I gave her a big hug, and Wurzel turned to Steve Lillywhite and said, 'Who's that old boiler that Lemmy's got a hold of?' Steve gave him this look and replied, 'That's my wife, actually.' 'Ah!' said Wurzel. 'Could I have some more coffee, please?' Then about a half hour later, he was standing by the bar next to Ronnie Wood. Jo Howard, Ron's stunning wife, walked past, and everything was moving, you know what I mean? And Wurzel leered, 'Eh, I'd like to fuck her, wouldn't you?' And Ron said, 'I do, actually. She's my wife.' Talk about putting your foot in your mouth – Wurzel had both feet in up to the knees! Luckily, it wasn't catching, because I was standing around when I heard this voice behind me say, 'Hello, Lemmy. I've always wanted to meet you.' I turned around and it was Eric Clapton. This was big news for me because I remembered him well from the Bluesbreakers and the Yardbirds. So I managed to say hello without grovelling – I mean, Eric!

I also wrote some songs that year for people other than Motörhead. We were rehearsing in the same area as Girlschool and we all went to a pub, and I wrote 'Head Over Heels' there for them. I scribbled it down on the back of a beer mat or something and Kim took it away with her. I also wrote a song, 'Can't Catch Me', for Lita Ford's record, *Lita*, which turned out to be her most successful album. We were in LA at that time and she came down to our hotel, the Park Sunset, and told me she needed songs. Once again, I wrote it right there and gave it to her – I wrote it as a twelve-bar, but she didn't record it that way. I'd known Lita since 1975, when she was in the Runaways – at their first gig in London, Joan Jett wore my bullet belt. I thought Lita was the best thing in the band: she had great tits and played mean guitar, but Joan *looked* meaner – probably because she was! Lita made a great solo record but then I think she let the people around her have too much of a say in her career – for a start, she was too dressed up, and it looked like she was being pushed way too hard to try to be the 'next big thing'. It just didn't work for her. She was a real rock 'n' roller, not the glossy chick they made her out to be. Then her mother died, and she was really devastated by that. Last time I saw her was a few years ago at a music convention in LA. We were on a panel together, but she was quite short – just 'Hi, Lem' and a quick squeeze and she was gone. She didn't hang around at all, which I thought was very strange. So, Miss Ford, give me a call – we'll talk!

A lot of performers from the eighties haven't fared very well – that's obvious from watching *The Decline of Western Civilization, Part II: The Metal Years*. Where are all those people now? That film probably helped kill their careers – it made everyone who liked heavy metal look like morons. I was filmed for a segment of that, but I came off okay – no thanks to the director, Penelope Spheeris. She took me up to Mulholland Boulevard, in the Hollywood Hills and the camera crew was about twenty yards away from me. Penelope had to shout her questions at me.

I said, 'Can you ask me questions from a bit closer?'

'I don't want to be in the shot,' she said.

'You don't have to be in the shot!'

'Nah, I'm going to read them from here.'

Fucking idiots – they could have come closer, used a different lens or something, but no! It was a stupid movie, anyhow. Everybody always says I'm the best thing in it and I tell them, 'The only reason I was good is because all the rest of them are so terrible!'

I've had to do a lot of strange appearances. I was interviewed on the radio by some TV psychiatrist – that guy used to reduce a lot of people to tears on his show (*Room 13*, I think it was called) but not me, as you might imagine. I was also on a programme with The Joan Collins Fan Club, which was just one guy, Julian Clary, who's famous now under his own name. He's gay, so I guess as far as Joan Collins was concerned he was both the Bitch and the Stud. He was all right – very bitchy and camply sarcastic, and I love that kind of humour. I think Julian's going to end up as a modern-day Noël Coward. But him and me together on a TV show certainly made an odd combination. A couple of years ago I – along with a lot of other heavy rock performers – did a video for Pat Boone because of the album he made covering metal tunes. This is not as weird as you might think. I thought he was an excellent performer in his day.

Anyhow, back to *my* day (or with this particular period of time, you might call it 'dog days'). In 1988 we also did another live record, *No Sleep At All*. We figured we might as well, since we had this relatively new line-up and all. It was recorded at the Giants of Rock Festival in Hameenlinna, Finland in July. But it was a mistake and failed miserably sales-wise. The record itself is all right. It could have been better no doubt, but we had Guy Bidmead mix it because we wanted to give him another try, mainly because he had been Vic Maile's boy and Vic was a great live mixer. After that, I think we finally figured out that Guy just wasn't Vic Maile. Don't get me wrong, though – after all I've said about Guy, it was only 'cause he was taking orders from us. He was too nice! Vic knew when to tell us to shut the fuck up!

Of course, we went on the road and toured behind *No Sleep* – nothing new there! When we went through the States we opened for Slayer. Tom Araya is a really nice guy (plus he plays bass and sings, as I do!), but I'm not so sure about the band's philosophy of terror and gore. They don't realize what they're doing. Like, in the middle of their show, Tom would say something to the effect of, 'Do you want to see blood?' One day I told him, 'You don't want to be saying that, Tommy. Someday that's gonna backfire on you.'

And he insisted, 'Oh, these are my people, man. I understand them and they understand me.' Then the very next night, in Austin, Texas, there he was – 'Do you want to see blood?' – and half a chair went past his head, missing him by about an inch. He lost it altogether! He got on the mic and gave the audience a fucking sermon, waving his finger about and stomping up and down. He was beside himself with fury, and when he came off the stage, I was standing there, going, 'Uh-huh, your people, eh?' I enjoyed that tour quite a bit, actually. On the last night during Slayer's set I went behind guitarist Jeff Hanneman and just stood there – dressed up as Adolf Hitler.

We took a short break at the beginning of 1989, during which Phil Campbell went off to Germany to do some tracks for some Swiss band called Drifter. Then, after we went through the UK, we headed to South America for the first time. We'd never seen anything like Brazil. On one hand, you've got Copacabana beach, with bronze billionaires and their molls, then 200 yards away there are people living in cardboard boxes amongst sewers running through the sand. You've got shopping malls with everything in them that you could possibly want and next door, literally at the edge of the parking lot, is a shanty town with one wire running from the telegraph pole with a light bulb in each cardboard box. We saw a guy sleeping under a bridge with a table, a chair, a sofa and a picture on the wall – five feet from the traffic. That's where he lived! Unfortunately I see the US heading in the same direction. Great Britain already seems like a Third-World nation, and judging from all the homeless people around, it looks like America isn't far behind. Can somebody tell me why the richest country in the world has bums living on the streets?

Anyhow, we played four dates in Brazil – two in São Paulo and one each in Porto Alegre and Rio. The venue in Rio was underground – an incredibly hot concrete bunker. They weren't these massive stadiums that one had heard about, although we did play those when we came back. It wasn't that great a tour the first time we went, but it was amazing all the same. We went home with mountains of practically worthless currency – it was like Weimar Germany. Interesting place, but rather frightening, really.

Another country we toured that year was Yugoslavia. That was where Phil Campbell made one of several attempts to quit Motörhead – for a while it seemed like he was quitting every other day. I'm not sure what was really going on with him at the time – it seemed like he was having a nervous breakdown or something. Anyway, we were driving across Croatia, in the mountains. It was in the middle of fuckin' nowhere – all they've got up there is sheep, goats, crags and the odd shepherd – and it was the middle of the night, and Phil was having a row with somebody. I forget what the problem was, but he was storming up and down the bus, packing his bags and yelling, 'Stop this bus!' The Yugoslav bus driver didn't care: he stopped the bus and – *froom*! – opened the door. So Phil stepped out of the bus with two suitcases into three feet of snow. There was a blizzard howling horizontally as he looked around. On one side of him was a snow drift and down the valley, miles away, there was one light. It went out as he was looking at it. Fucking great, that was – a treasured moment in Motörhead history.

Needless to say, Phil didn't quit the band that night. He did keep trying, though. We were on our way to Berlin and he was doing it again – 'I'm leaving the band!' He came up behind the bus driver and said, 'Take me to the airport.'

'This bus is going to the gig,' I said.

Phil wasn't about to let that stop him. 'Well, I'm hiring the bus as well as you are and I want to go to the airport!'

'This is paid for by the *band*,' I replied, 'and you are now a civilian. The band is going to the gig on the band's bus. So if you want to go to the airport, you get out and get a fuckin' taxi, right? And you can ring one from the gig because you can't use the band's mobile phone any more. Okay? You're a civilian now, Phil!' This bit of news was met by a lot of muttering under the breath and again he gave up the idea of leaving.

He tried once more at the beginning of another German tour. He left the band the first night we got to Frankfurt, before we'd even gotten started. Nothing would do but he had to go to the airport – no matter that it was half-past eleven and all the planes were gone. He went there anyway and slept in a chair: when he woke up, somebody had stolen all his bags. After that, I think he learned his lesson and stopped trying to quit the band. Phil is still with us today and other than me, he's the longest-running member of Motörhead. He's also a constant source of amusement. Many's the time he's walked out of a gig into the back of the gear truck, thinking it was the bus. He got into a bass bin once – thought it was his bunk. No end of fun, Phil. He's sort of like our Keith Moon. Incidentally, he's also an excellent guitar player. And a Taurus.

But back to the Yugoslav dates: we had two in Ljubljana. During the first one, Wurzel fell off the stage – one minute he was next to me and the next he was gone, straight down. That wasn't the sturdiest stage that was ever built, either. I remember walking into a hole near the back. On the second night, something happened that was potentially far more disastrous. During the first song before the solo, some asshole threw a razorblade at the stage – the guy had even taped it between two coins to give it more thrust – and it cut my hand wide open. I didn't really feel it, so I didn't know what had happened until I began seeing all this red on the floor of the stage. Then I looked at my hand and realized it was gushing blood like a motherfucker. But I wrapped a rag around it and we finished the show. It was a terrible wound, though. When we came offstage, I took the rag off and blood spurted all over the walls, amidst cries of disgust from the rest of the band. So I went to this Yugoslav peasants' hospital and got stitches, but over the next four days, my arm slowly began to turn black – blood poisoning. We stopped in Nuremberg on the way home, and I saw a doctor there, thinking German doctors were good, but this guy *really* fucked it up. I'd been asking our manager, Douglas, to fly me home so I could get this mess taken care of, but he didn't want to pay for the plane fare. If it had been up to him, I would have had to take the bus all the way back to England. And when I say my arm was black, I don't mean blue –

it was *black*, with a bit of red. I almost lost my thumb and a finger! It was so bad that our tour manager finally said, 'Fuck this,' and put me on a plane. I was in hospital in England for two weeks with my arm hanging in a sling – all because of some little fucker who thought it was smart to throw a razorblade at a band.

In fact, I'll tell you exactly how smart that guy was – after he did it, he stood there pointing at himself, saying, 'It was me!' Naturally our crew headed his way, rubbing their hands together – 'Oh really? A live one!' They kicked the piss out of him, and when they were done, the Yugoslav police kicked the piss out of him as well, and *they* are professionals. And believe it or not, he was still there at the load-out, yelling, 'Come on, man!' and all that. A real diehard idiot. I'll never understand that – I could see him hating me for some odd reason. I could see him premeditating the thing and doing it. But I can't see him going, 'It was me!' to *my* people! I wonder where that guy is now – probably having a great time, running around killing women and children. Probably a cop.

Anyhow, the police loved me that night because I carried on playing. If I'd stopped in front of those 6,000 people, there would have been a riot. There were a lot of riots going on back then . . . but anyhow, I was their hero for keeping the show going – that year, at least. I don't suppose I am now after the double whammy we got hit with when we came back to play again: Phil Campbell and Phil Taylor both wound up in hospital and we had to cancel that show. I remember going up to Wurzel's hotel room.

'Gig's off, Wurz,' I said.

'Why?'

'Drummer, guitarist can't do it. They're in hospital.'

'Have they been run over?' Wurzel asked.

'In a way, yeah.'

The both of them were flattened by some 'brown speed' – well, it wasn't speed at all. *Brown* speed? – I said to Phil Campbell, 'Didn't you think?' and he said, 'No.' Phil Taylor, too – they both should have known better; speed ain't brown! But no – they wound up being carried past each other in the hospital corridor. What were they thinking? That was almost as stupid as that guy yelling, 'It was me!'

In June, our fan club had its ten-year anniversary and threw a party at the Hippodrome. I met Wendy there – Naughty Wendy from Redcar. I was walking around a corner at the theatre and there was this bird with these fantastic eyes. She was just tremendous. I don't remember anything about the party after that – I was with Wendy. She was a great girl, very supportive of me in all sorts of ways. I saw her not too long ago when I was in England and it was nice to see her again. I hadn't seen her for eight or nine years – luckily she hadn't changed into a drooling hag. Some of them do, you know!

The Hippodrome was a big venue in London – as indeed it still is! It was famous for dancing bears in the nineteenth century, but by 1985 all they could get was us! I used to go up there on 'heavy metal night' and try to hit on all the girls who came to see the good-looking bands! Well, you never know! I got more than I bargained for one night when I went up there and ended up on stage with Jon Bon Jovi, Richie Sambora, and Dave 'Snake' Sabo, Rachel Bolan and Sebastian Bach from Skid Row. We did Creedence Clearwater's 'Travelin' Band' and 'Rock 'n' Roll', the Zeppelin number, and it may well be released on the Lemmy Goes to the Pub label when we're all dead!

Later on that summer, I made an appearance on this horrible TV show called *Club X*. The segment we did was great, though. It was all about black leather jackets, and I wrote a song for it, which was named, cryptically enough, 'Black Leather Jacket'. We whipped out a scratch recording of the song for playback on the show. I played bass on the tape, but on camera I played piano. The sax player we had laid down three tracks, so he brought in two of his friends to mime the other parts. Phil Campbell was on guitar and Philthy on drums, and Fast Eddie was on my bass, which was stolen the night of the filming. I never did find out who took it, although there were several leading suspects. Aren't there always?

I also played on a Nina Hagen record some time around here. I'd met her at a festival and I've always liked her. She's a crazy woman, just great – besides which she's very pretty. Anyhow, she asked me to play on her record and I didn't happen to be doing anything that day so I said yes. I've appeared on a lot of different people's albums – I have some free time, why not?

Motörhead was also spending time in the studio, working up songs for a new record. It was at that studio that I found Wurzel feeding his dog with a spoon. I walked downstairs one day and there he was, on his hands and knees.

'What are you doing, Wurz?' I asked.

'She's upset,' he said. 'She thinks I'm leaving her.'

'Why would she think that?'

'She saw me packing my case.'

'Wurzel,' I said, 'dogs don't have the concept of suitcase. They don't know about packing clothes for trips. Dogs don't wear clothes!'

'Well, she thinks I'm leaving.'

There was no talking to him. He called her Toots because she had a white line up her nose and she taught Wurzel to fetch sticks. He'd go outside with the dog and we'd sit and watch them. He'd throw a stick and the dog would look at him until finally he'd go and get the stick and throw it again. Actually, that dog was pretty smart.

Anyway, when we weren't watching Toots teaching Wurzel tricks, we recorded demos of 'No Voices in the Sky', 'Goin' to Brazil' and 'Shut You Down'. These all ended up on *1916*, but by then we knew that whatever we did for a new album, it wasn't going to be on GWR. We'd been very wary of Doug Smith for the past year or so. Our attorney, Alex Grower, was looking closely at him around this time, and it became clear that Doug and his wife, Eve, were not people who had the band's best interests at heart.

So we spent several months extricating ourselves from Douglas's management and finding someone new. Wurzel brought this guy, Phil Carson, round to my house one day and we took him on as manager for the next couple of years. He used to be involved (if that's the word I want) with Peter Grant and Led Zeppelin, and he managed Robert Plant for a while after that. Phil's barmy like me, but with more string and/or discipline, as we say in the trade! I really liked him and still do. Phil would get us signed to Sony – after fifteen years, Motörhead's first truly major American record deal. We went quite far with that; not anywhere near far enough (what else is new?), but that story's for another chapter. In fact, it's the one coming up next.

CHAPTER ELEVEN

angel city

T he real big news of 1990, as far as I was concerned, was that
I moved to America. I'd started planning it in 1989, but a
few months later, when it finally happened, it happened in a
flash – one moment I was in London and the next I was living in
West Hollywood, down the street from the Rainbow and the
Sunset Strip. The Rainbow, for the few who don't know, is the
oldest rock 'n' roll bar in Hollywood, and my home away from
home – actually, it's only two blocks from my home!

But quite a lot went on before that. I played a bit part in
another Comic Strip special, *South Atlantic Raiders*. It was a
parody on the Falklands War and I was supposed to be some sort
of sergeant. Basically it just involved me speaking a few lines in
a terrible Spanish accent and then falling forward on to a noisome
mattress! Typecasting?! I was also cast as a river taxi driver in a
movie called *Hardware*. That was a tedious experience. The
director thought he was some Gothic artiste, and it was really a

fucking pain in the ass. We were standing around all day and they made the terrible mistake of giving me the whisky early – I was supposed to have a bottle, but they handed it over when I got there. So by the time they got around to my scenes, I was thoroughly wrecked and tired and emotional. I got paid up front, which was all right, but filming, like I've said, is just a fucking bore. On a more entertaining note, Mick Green – the guitarist for one of my favourite bands of the sixties and seventies, the Pirates – asked me if I wanted to do some recording with him, and of course, I said yes. We did 'Blue Suede Shoes', which wound up on some NME benefit album of Elvis covers. We were listed as Lemmy and the Upsetters. The song was later released as a single, and the flipside was a song Mick and I wrote together called 'Paradise'. I enjoyed working with Mick – he's one of my heroes. People don't know about it today, but back in the early sixties, he was legendary, right alongside Clapton and Jeff Beck. It's just that Mick was the one who didn't get lucky.

And, of course, I couldn't let too much time go by before getting Motörhead back on the road. During one of the British dates, some kid spat at me and this big gob of mucus landed on my guitar. I really hate that shit, so I walked to the front of the stage and said, 'See this?' and I took the gob of spit and smeared it in my hair – 'I'm going to wash my hair tonight, but tomorrow, you'll still be an asshole!' That got a huge crowd response, and even got written up, but actually I pinched that line from Winston Churchill. He was at a dinner party and a woman said to him, 'You, sir, are drunk.' 'Yes, madam,' he replied, 'and you are ugly, but tomorrow *I* shall be sober.' Ain't that a beauty? Who says history's dull?

It was after a tour through Europe that I moved. Phil Carson set it all up. His people found the apartment and I went over at the beginning of June. The rest of the band stayed in England, but my living on another continent didn't really affect things. It wasn't like we were hanging out with each other constantly – I mean, when you've been on a bus with somebody for six months, you don't want to be around them on your time off. It was right about that time, though, that Wurzel started to hate America. Maybe it was some form of jealousy – I really don't know. Living here wasn't that big a change for me as I'd been coming to the States for so long anyway. I just didn't realize the amount of corruption in the government, the extent to which the rot had set in, but that's the same with any country, really. And it's a lot more overtly racist here than it is in England – back home, they're far sneakier about it. But I can get groceries delivered to my door, and there's a lot more emphasis here on giving the customer what he wants, not what you think he needs. The only real trouble I had with adjusting to America was the sense of humour gap. The British have a very black sense of humour, see. It's very vicious and Americans just don't get it. I practically destroyed my entire social life within two weeks of coming over here. I'd say something that I thought was hilarious and I'd get these horrified responses – 'How could you say that!' They were outraged and hurt and all kinds of shit. Jesus, it's not necessary to be that hurt! Cripples are funny – I'm sorry, it's not my fault! I'm just an observer here.

Another thing people don't understand is my collection of Nazi memorabilia, which really kicked in when I moved here. World War II artifacts have been around ever since I can remember – after all, I was born the year the war ended, and people were always bringing home souvenirs and shit. I had one dagger when I came over here, and two medals, maybe a flag and an iron cross, and that was all. And like with any hobby, the more you get into it the more interesting it gets, if it has any depth to it. So now I have a huge collection of stuff from wartime Germany – daggers, medals, flags, you name it. I like having all this stuff around because it's a reminder of what happened, and that it's in the past (for the most part – Nazism still exists, but at the margins). I don't understand people who believe that if you ignore something, it'll go away. That's completely wrong – if it's ignored, it gathers strength. Europe ignored Hitler for twenty years. We could have beaten him in 1936: the French army could have chased him out of the Rhineland and he would have been done. His people would have been toppled from power. But the French ran away – again – and let him in. As a result, he slaughtered a quarter of the world! And he was a non-smoker, non-drinker, vegetarian, smart suit, short hair, well turned-out. Would have been served in any restaurant in America, unlike Jesse Owens, the hero of the 1936 Olympics.

Jesse Owens came home, covered in glory and eight medals after showing Hitler the benefits of democracy and a multi-racial society, and they wouldn't serve him dinner in a restaurant in his own town. What the fuck is that? That kind of double standard is what really pisses me off. Do you know that there are still clubs in England and America where Jews aren't allowed? This is a country of denial. Look at the model airplane industry – they won't put a swastika on the model of a Messerschmitt 109, and that was the national insignia of Germany at the time. So does that mean that in the future, there will be no white stars on the side of a fucking Mustang kit because somebody in the planning room believes it's a symbol of American imperialism? Are any Jews less dead because they won't allow a swastika on a plastic model airplane? No! And let's not even get into what so-called Americans did to the real Americans – the Indians. As you can probably tell, I've had my share of arguments over all this. Apparently people don't like the truth, but I do like it; I like it because it upsets a lot of people. If you show them enough times that their arguments are bullshit, then maybe just once, one of them will say, 'Oh! Wait a minute – I was wrong.' I live for that happening. Rare, I assure you.

Anyhow, let's get back to business, meaning the nasty business of the record industry. That was one of the main reasons I moved to Los Angeles – to be near our record company. We'd had a meeting with Jerry Greenberg, the head of WTG, in London, and he was most interested in us and very supportive. But I immediately thought to myself, 'I've got to be on the spot.' I couldn't be in England with Motörhead on an American label because it had never worked before. And this was the first time we'd actually been signed to make a record – each time before, the American corporation was just picking up a record we'd made for a British company. So it was even more important for me to keep an eye on things.

From the start I knew my suspicions were justified. The first thing the record company did when I arrived was to give me a brunch at their offices – brunch! I mean, what the fuck is *brunch*? Can't they spell lunch, do they have a problem with the letter 'l'? And do you know what this big deal, welcome-aboard *brunch* consisted of? Take-out Chinese food in foil pans – 'You want some more sweet and sour pork, Lemmy? Great to have you over here, man! Motörhead has always been one of my favorite bands!' Ha! None of them had ever heard a fucking thing we did, except for the week before when they had to cram. It's such shit, and so obvious, yet they thought I couldn't see them for what they really were. Nearly everyone there was some old industry executive shoved into a new position at a new label. I didn't see anybody new and vibrant about.

That said, I do want to mention that Jerry Greenberg was great, as was his assistant, Leslie Holly. Leslie used to let us use the office phone to call around for gigs and new management. We couldn't have afforded all those transatlantic phone calls on our own, so that really saved our butts. What we didn't realize at the time was that we were being taken for a ride – and so was Jerry Greenberg! All I can figure in retrospect is that Sony must have been using WTG as a tax write-off, because those fucking executives seemed to do everything they could to guarantee that WTG – and, as a result, anything Motörhead did for them – would lose money. But let's face it, when have record labels *not* been manned by a bunch of idiots? Like the old CD long box affair during our time with Sony. They were having huge fights over the long box – it was one of the most inconvenient forms of packaging anyone ever came up with, and there were people at Sony losing their *jobs* over the loss of the fucking long box! That alone says a lot about what's wrong with the industry. Fuck it – call me old-fashioned, but I've always preferred vinyl over CDs anyhow.

Record company stupidity (and Chinese take-out brunches) aside, people did take note of my move to Los Angeles. There was a real buzz going on for us when we got signed to WTG and when I moved over here. I was on the cover of *BAM* and getting all these invites from people. It was great, being big news again for a while. And we were about to live up to all this hype and attention (brief as it was) by making one of the best records of our career.

But before we even got in the studio we had a record coming out, totally against our wishes. Our former manager, Doug Smith, released that live recording of our tenth birthday party show. We had told Douglas back in 1986 that the video of the show was enough and we didn't want it out, so he'd been sitting on it ever since. Once we were away from him, though, he did what he wanted with it. It was purely a cash-in thing, of course. We slapped an injunction on him to keep him from releasing it (actually Wurzel was the one who took action in England, as I was already living in the States), and that kept it at bay for a while. But we gave up in the end; it was just too much work. And besides, like I mentioned, we were working on a new record, so we were quite busy.

Of course, being Motörhead, it couldn't possibly go off without a hitch. The first thing we had to overcome was the album's original producer, Ed Stasium. We recorded four songs with him before we decided he had to go. See, he overstepped his mark. One day we were listening to a mix of 'Going to Brazil', and I said, 'Turn up them four tracks there.' He did and there were all these claves and fucking tambourines that he'd put on – he must have gone in after our session and added all that junk. He certainly didn't do it while we were there! That was very strange, and so we fired him. After that, we got Pete Solley, who was great.

Several of the songs on *1916* – 'Love Me Forever' and '1916', for example – were very different from anything we'd done before, but it's not like we were *trying* to change; we just did. Things started to change when I came to the States to live, and we just sort of continued on from there. But quite a lot of *1916* was exactly what our fans had come to expect from us, only better, of course. Take 'I'm So Bad' – it's a loud rock 'n' roll song with absurd lyrics, just typical Motörhead. What's really strange, though, is that some woman from the *Melody Maker* said that the lyrics are sexist! I don't know where she got that. 'I make love to mountain lions/ Sleep on red-hot branding irons/ When I walk the roadway shakes/ Bed's a mess of rattlesnakes': *you* tell *me* how that could lead to the oppression of women! Then there's my usual Chuck Berry fixation in 'Going to Brazil'. 'Ramones', the fastest (and shortest) song on the album, actually started off as a slow number. Then at one point I said, 'Let's play it a bit faster,' and it sounded just like the Ramones, so that's how that came about. And although 'Angel City' was about living here in LA, I wrote the lyrics before I moved. 'I'm gonna live in LA, drinkin' all day/ Lay by the pool and let the record company pay –': that's really not too far from the truth! 'I'm gonna kick ass, I'm gonna spit broken glass/ I'm gonna shoot out all of your lights': it was one of them songs where I cracked myself up writing it. I was all by myself, laughing outrageously. And we put some saxophone on it – that was something new.

But what really surprised people (in a positive manner, I hasten to add) were some of the other tracks. 'Nightmare/The Dreamtime' and '1916' both relied heavily on keyboards, which was very different for Motörhead – or any heavy band in 1990. In fact, '1916' also had cello and no guitars whatsoever. I wrote the words before I wrote the music. It's about the Battle of the Somme in World War I, but I've had people come up to me and say, 'Isn't it about the Irish Rebellion?' because that was in 1916 as well. (The Irish are always singing about 1916, and the great Post Office massacre and all that.) But it happened that I was in England, watching a programme about World War I and I had a brainstorm when they got to the Battle of the Somme. Nineteen thousand Englishmen were killed before noon, a whole generation destroyed, in *three hours* – think about that! It was just terrible – there were three or four towns in northern Lancashire and south Yorkshire where that whole generation of men were completely wiped out. And those towns are still suffering from it because they never were able to build their population up again. Places like Accrington, in Lancashire, were fucking destroyed. They brought five old guys back to the battlefield in this TV special. One guy, who was about ninety, said, 'They told us to walk, not run, and we walked across and all the lads around me laid down. I thought there might have been an order from the rear that I hadn't heard. And then I realized they were all dead.' It's a case of the English killing more Englishmen than the Germans. Hindenberg, who later became president of Germany, said, 'They were lions led by donkeys.' So I wrote a song about it. But I do have a lot of ambivalence about that tune. This kid wrote to me and said he played it for his grandfather, who was there, and the old man cried all the way through it. That's a very great compliment, but I'm not sure I like the guy feeling that bad for my gratification. It's an amazing thing to have happen, though, to reach back over all those years and touch somebody like that.

We were quite happy with the recording of *1916*. The artwork, of course, was another matter, but that's because the record label was sticking its grimy hands in it. Whenever that happens you can pretty much guarantee that things are going to get fucked up. Bronze did the same thing with *Overkill*. We were all gathered in the conference room, the tables were removed and there was this easel sitting there with an overhead light shining on it. They pulled off the cloth, gave it the grand unveiling, and there it was – a motorcycle engine block with a woman's nude torso coming out of it. She was sprayed red and the background was blue. It was just pathetic. And the company man says, 'There you are! So what do you think?' I picked it up and said, 'That's your best shot, is it?' and I threw it out the window. I think he figured out I wasn't too pleased! If you look at the cover of *Overkill*, you'll notice there's no engine or naked woman to be found, just one of Joe Petagno's classic renderings. Anyhow, we had much the same problem with *1916*. They brought in five sketches, all of them atrocious. So we sent them all back, amongst much moaning and groaning and temper tantrums from the art department – you'd think we were dealing with a bunch of nine-year-olds! Sony ended up farming it out to somebody else, which was fine with us. And in spite of our efforts, they still screwed it up – you'll find all the flags of Europe on the cover of *1916 except* for France. And the whole point of the title song is that it's about a battle that was fought in France! But what can you do? Even so, I think it's one of our best sleeves, and one of our best albums overall.

Although *1916* wasn't released until the beginning of 1991, the first single, 'One to Sing the Blues', came out a few weeks earlier – on my birthday, as a matter of fact (that's really a great song – maybe we'll put it back in the set one of these days). In February, the usual happened – we went out on the road and did a bunch of TV and radio shows. Phil Taylor's mother died just as we were beginning our tour through Great Britain. She had cancer, and we sent him home to see her. He was able to spend some time with her before the end. We all loved Ma Taylor and her death really hurt Phil. I don't know if that's the reason he gave up on the music – probably not – but it certainly didn't do him any good.

Opening for us throughout Great Britain were the Almighty and an American girl group, the Cycle Sluts, who came with us through Europe, too. The Cycle Sluts were something else! They were pretty much a novelty act, with funny lyrics. I think they were doing it for a laugh and the chance to travel around the world. They were nice girls, and I enjoyed having them around. I had a terrible crush on one of them for the whole European tour, but I never got her. Typical.

There were only a couple of troublesome points on that tour. While we were in Britain, I got the gastric flu and we had to reschedule four dates. I was really sick and spent four days in a hotel, just throwing up. It came out of me like a thunderbolt. We'd be in the van and one minute I was all right and the next minute I was heaving out the window – 'Stop the van!' (Those viral things are gonna keep getting stronger, 'cause every five years a new strain comes out that they didn't plan on, and someday one of those bugs is gonna kill half the planet.)

The other trouble concerned that other deadly virus known as our record label. They sent a camera crew on the road with us and spent five days in Germany shooting a video, *Everything Louder Than Everything Else*, then tried to stick us with the $9000 bill! Of course, we never paid, and a couple of years later, we were dropped, so they had to eat it – bad luck, guys, back to the drawing board! Tax loss anyway, right?

Overall, the songs from *1916* went down pretty well. We set keyboards off to the side. For a while, Phil Campbell was playing them on 'Angel City', but he got very stroppy and we had to stop him doing them after a bit. We'd wind up with horns and no guitars. Phil would have had to have been an octopus to make it work – he is some sort of amphibian, but definitely not an octopus! So our guitar roadie Jamie did the keyboards until we phased them out. We never did play '1916' live; it's too iffy, because you have to have silence for it, and you're not gonna get it with our audience. Any mixed reactions we had in England didn't have anything to do with our music – a few of our English fans seemed to be a bit upset that I'd moved to the States. It was like I deserted them or some such shit. Since half the band – Wurzel and Phil Campbell – were still living in Britain, they couldn't quite hate us, and they couldn't completely love us either. (Philthy had come to the States, too, with me, but he had the wrong visa in his passport and they sent him back! Another Motörhead foul-up.) They didn't really know what to do with us. The main trouble was that we didn't totally sell out the venues, so all the English promoters stopped booking us, except in London, for the next five years. They were the only country in all of Europe – the whole *world*, actually! – that wouldn't underwrite our shows and guarantee the money. And we certainly couldn't afford to put up the cash – it would have amounted to something like £100,000 to tour our own country! I certainly didn't have that kind of money, and if I had, I would have spent it on something else. We finally got to go back to tour England in 1997, and it thoroughly amused me to see that we sold out everywhere we played.

In May, before we went to Japan, we made an appearance on the *David Letterman Show*. Actually it was only me and Phil

Campbell; Wurzel didn't want to do it and I don't remember where Phil Taylor was. They only wanted two of us anyway because we had to play with the show's band. We didn't perform a song from the new record, though – it was Chuck Berry's 'Let It Rock'. And we never did meet David Letterman; in fact, he got the name of our album wrong. He called it *Motörhead*! But we did see a lot of Paul Schaffer, the band leader – he was great. All in all, though, the *David Letterman* experience was not that impressive. They gave me a hard time about my cigarettes – 'Pardon me, but you can't smoke in here.' 'Why not?' 'It fogs up the camera lenses.' Stupid excuse No. 1,869, you know?

By the time we went to Japan we had changed managers, again. Phil Carson was offered a job at Victor Records, and I can't blame him for taking it. So we went with Sharon Osbourne – Ozzy's wife – but that only lasted for a few weeks. I'd been asking her to work with us for ages because I knew she was a great manager, but as it turned out, she wasn't for us. It did not go at all well. Our trip to Japan was the clincher. We wanted to take our tour manager with us, 'cause he knew us, but she insisted on sending hers, this guy named Alan Perman (he's dead now, and no, we didn't kill him – although I would have liked to). Alan destroyed our career with Sharon. He claimed we wrecked a hotel and all kinds of shit, and we didn't do anything! *Nothing*. What he did was give all the float money to Phil Campbell, which was a completely idiotic thing to do. Shows you what kind of a tour manager he was. And then he tried to cover himself by saying he had to pay for us wrecking this hotel. We did none of the stuff that he said we did. We weren't exactly angels but this was just one of those times we were actually innocent! (And I'd like 3,426 other cases to be taken into consideration!) It was unbelievable, a complete fabrication. And then he came back and dumped the whole crew at the Hyatt in LA, found our regular tour manager Hobbs' room, gave him $300 and left. What's Hobbs going to do with $300 and six crew in the Hyatt House? And the band hadn't been paid yet, either.

This was all very bad news, but unfortunately Sharon believed Alan's lies and thought *we* were the bad news! Once we were back in the States, it was a foregone conclusion. We were already judged and sentenced. Sharon dropped us three days before the start of our American tour because of Alan – he was her boy, see, so she had to stick up for him. And Sony got infected by all of this, too, and were running around in a panic – 'Oh, we can't ever send you to Japan again!' They'd rather take anybody else's word, even an asshole of a tour manager, than ours. Jesus. We even arranged for the on-the-spot guy from Sony in Japan to phone them up and tell them the truth and still they wouldn't believe it. Someone from Japan came down to our Irvine Meadows show later in the year and told our record company how great we were and it still didn't fly! That's how much credibility we've got. We've got this reputation – which we don't deserve, mostly – that we're bad people and we're not professional. At this point in my career, why would I even care about trashing a hotel room? It'd make more sense for me to go and trash my own apartment – it'd be cheaper!

Anyhow, in between the Japan fiasco and touring America – which went better, even if we didn't have management – we went through Australia for our second, and probably last, time. That was a disaster. I walked off stage at one show because, once again, some kids were spitting on me. I don't like being spat on (and really, who does? Even the punk bands in the seventies didn't like it!). Call me old-fashioned if you like, but I won't put up with it. I told them, like I always tell such crowds, 'If you carry on doing that, I'm leaving, and I won't be coming back. So if you see anybody doing this, cripple him because he just stopped your show.' Usually it works, but it didn't on the Gold Coast. It was really a shame, because I don't like walking off stage, but I will not be fucking spat on! Incidentally, one of the reasons I won't put up with it is this: Joe Strummer of the Clash was singing once and one of these dickheads spat right down his throat! Not only was it nauseating, boy and girls, no – wait – he got *hepatitis*! Nice, huh? Not *me*, sweetheart!

Anyhow, on to Sony's brilliant Operation Rock 'n' Roll tour. They had five heavy bands from various Sony labels do a tour together. The line-up was Alice Cooper, Judas Priest, us, Metal Church and Dangerous Toys. The Metal Church and Dangerous Toys guys were the best company – you never saw Alice (he was generally on his bus watching Japanese splatter movies) or anyone in Judas Priest, but I'd always run into some of the guys from the other bands somewhere. Usually at a strip club. Every city we went to, we'd all go down to the local strip club, and there they'd be. Nowadays, I'm the only one in our band that goes out – the others have become responsible citizens (well, not Phil Campbell).

Anyhow, the record label sent us all off in this blaze of manufactured glory. Things were a bit rough for us at the start, since we didn't have a manager, but Hobbs picked up the slack wonderfully. Leslie Holly at WTG lent us a hand as well, and I'll be forever grateful to the two of them. Then the other bands' crews pitched in, too – they'd finish their meals early and come out and do our shows, and for nothing! That was really nice of them. We stole nearly every show on that tour, but you don't have to take my word for it. Track down any of the reviews, and you'll have proof enough. The *LA Times*, for example, called us 'the tangy mustard in a bland noise sandwich', which I thought was odd, but nice! We were getting our pictures in the paper and Alice and Judas Priest weren't. But some nights, when a band had to be bumped off the bill, guess who wound up the loser? If you've hung in with me till now, I think you know the answer. To be fair, we did cost more than the bottom two bands, and Metal Church did get bumped off of some dates, too. Dangerous Toys stayed on because they were the apple of Sony's eye at the time. The singer had red hair and sang with a falsetto, just like Axl Rose, so you figure out their motives. We ended up being cut out of six or seven dates. In North Carolina, when we got scratched, we went down to South Carolina with Metal Church and did our own gig. The problem was nobody was fighting for us, since we didn't have a manager. If we had the manager we have now, believe me, we would have been on every fucking night of that tour!

Unfortunately, we missed the last four gigs of that tour, and amazingly enough, it wasn't Sony's fault! There was an accident backstage in Boston and I broke my ribs. See, I was climbing all over this bird at the side of the stage – she was really keen and I was really keen. 'Do you want another drink?' I said, and she said, 'Yeah.' So I reached over for my drink and fell over my own equipment and cracked two ribs. It only took me about a week to heal, just long enough to miss the end of the tour.

We found another manager finally on that Operation Rock 'n' Roll tour – Doug Banker. He'd worked with Ted Nugent, and he had also created some gambling system that got him banned from Las Vegas. But anyway, he came up to us at one of the shows, and we decided to work with him. When he started off, he seemed quite good, but then it began to degenerate. I think part of it was that he lived in Detroit and we really needed to have somebody right there on hand, not halfway across the continent. Plus he still had things going with Ted Nugent in some form or another. I'm not quite sure what happened, really. The bottom line is he just didn't get into it enough, and with Motörhead, you've got to be all or nothing. Either do it completely or don't bother, 'cause it's a hard fight for us, and we need someone who's gonna fight full-time. I don't think Doug Banker realized that, and that he would have to put up with too much shit – record label shit, accusations regarding incidents we weren't guilty of, etc. I admit we're a fucking tough band to work with! But it took Doug, and us, a few months to realize how transitory our working relationship was going to be.

In the months after the Operation Rock 'n' Roll tour, things were looking up, which was a change – things hadn't looked up for Motörhead in about a decade! We had all those great reviews, our new management, which hadn't yet had time to sour, and *1916* got nominated for a Grammy. To be honest, I was quite surprised when I got word of it. (If I'd known what an anti-climax the ceremony was going to be, I probably would have just said 'Fuck off!' and left it at that!) I was beginning to do quite nicely financially, after more than a quarter of a century in the music business. A good portion of this was thanks to the Ozzy Osbourne album, *No More Tears*. That record sold millions, and I wrote the lyrics to four songs on it (I've since written more, and a couple appear on *Ozzmosis*). That was one of the easiest gigs I ever had – Sharon rang me up and said, 'I'll give you X amount of money to write some songs for Ozzy,' and I said, 'All right – you got a pen?' I wrote six or seven sets of words, and he ended up using four of them for the songs 'Desire', 'I Don't Want to Change the World', 'Hellraiser' and 'Mama I'm Coming Home'. I made more money out of writing those four songs for Ozzy than I made out of fifteen years of Motörhead – ludicrous, isn't it! I'd like to mention that I'm available for more songwriting if anybody is interested. Quite reasonable rates – just the mortgage on your first-born child!

By the time 1992 had begun, we were working on songs for the next Motörhead record, which came to be known as *March or Die*. The Grammy ceremony happened during this period. Doug Banker and his wife attended along with me. His wife was sitting in between me and him, but when they were announcing the candidates for 'Best Metal Performance', he switched seats very quickly, just in case, so he could get on camera. That was funny as shit! Metallica won that night, of course – they'd sold something around four million albums, while we'd racked up about 30,000 so it wasn't even a competition. But the acknowledgment was nice. If only for length of service we should get a fucking medal from the music business. All we ever got from Sony were headaches (and I have more to tell, so hang on to your corsets!). *1916* was our most critically acclaimed record, as far as the mainstream went – it got a great review in *Rolling Stone*, and an A+ in *Entertainment Weekly* (actually, the woman who helped me write this book wrote the *Entertainment Weekly* review – but that was long before she met us!). So in that way, it was a success. And we made a success of our months on the road – we got the audience off its ass, we got the crew off their asses, we got the promoters off their asses and we got our managers off their asses (or off *ours*!). The only thing we weren't successful at was getting the record company off its ass! We thought maybe we'd be able to accomplish that with *March or Die* . . . Ha! Fooled again!

There were other problems too, that were becoming glaringly apparent when we were getting ready to make *March or Die*. The biggest one was Phil Taylor – when he came back to the band in 1987, things started off okay, but they gradually got worse. For a long time we were trying to convince ourselves that Phil was all right, but he really wasn't. In '84 he left because he idolized Thin

Lizzy, and thought that with Robbo, he could do the best for himself musically. He began to look down on what Motörhead did. And of course, when he came back, other than the fact that we were better, Motörhead was basically very similar to when he left. So there was something missing in his drumming when he returned. 'Eat the Rich' wasn't a particularly well-played track, as far as drums went. And after *Orgasmatron*, *Rock 'n' Roll* was pretty feeble for drums. He would start tracks out at one pace and then end up at another. It was really fraught, because you'd go on stage not knowing what was going to happen. And you couldn't discuss anything with him 'cause he'd just go nuts. Once Phil Campbell said to him, 'You played like a cunt tonight,' and he went fucking nuclear – but of course, Philthy always hurts himself when he goes nuclear. He was losing it off stage, too. There was the time he tried to climb out of his room through the bathroom mirror at the Park Sunset, thinking it was a window. He rang me up saying, 'It's time for soundcheck and I can't get out of my room!' and this was at five o'clock in the morning! It was great timing because I was just about to climb over on this woman. So, as you can imagine, I was pretty pissed off. But I told the chick, 'Stay there, hold that thought,' and went downstairs. Sure enough, his door was jammed, and as we were both trying to push it – me outside, Phil in – the LAPD came up behind me with a fucking huge pistol. There I was, dressed in underpants and a kimono and the cop's got me against the wall, patting me down – procedure run amok! Then he started asking me questions, like, 'Is he dangerous in there?'

'Oh yeah, yeah,' I said. 'He's pretty dangerous – mostly to himself. I wouldn't worry about it.'

Then the cop wanted to know, 'Has he got any weapons?'

'Oh, he uses anything, furniture, walls. Anything.'

The cops couldn't get in through the door either, so they went in through the window and burst the door out with a puncher. And Phil was sitting there, covered in cuts and bruises, trying to climb through the bathroom mirror. Didn't he notice somebody who looked just like him coming through from the opposite direction? You'd think he'd get out of the way, wouldn't you?

Shit like that was happening a lot. Maybe we could have handled these incidents, but the fact that he couldn't keep time was just too much. He was really bad in the end – on *1916* we had to put him on a metronome to do 'Goin' to Brazil'! Then he was supposed to get together with Wurzel and Phil Campbell in London to work on the songs for *March or Die* (I was in LA at the time, furiously writing more lyrics), and it was a disaster. They played for half an hour and Phil Campbell turned around to Phil Taylor and said, 'You don't know these fucking things, do you?'

'No, I don't,' he replied.

'How come? We've been practising them at home, me and Wurzel – why don't you know them?'

'My Walkman broke at Christmas.'

Good excuse, eh? And this was weeks and weeks after the holidays! So that was pretty bad news, and by March, when we played at a Randy Rhodes tribute concert at Irvine Meadows, it was worse. By then we knew we had to fire him; we'd started recording the new album and it wasn't working out at all. But while it was necessary, I'll always feel bad about the way I fired him – I did it on the phone and it wasn't right. I shouldn't have done it that way but I just couldn't face another fit. We had warned him three times in the past two years to get his act together, and Phil had been in the band long enough to know when he was fucking up. But it didn't seem to bother him and finally he had to go. Tommy Aldrich did most of the drums on *March or Die*, except for 'Ain't No Nice Guy', which Phil did, and 'Hellraiser', which was done by our new drummer, Mikkey Dee.

I'd known Mikkey for many years. Motörhead did a tour with Mercyful Fate when Brian Robertson was in our band and Mikkey (who is Swedish) was their drummer. In fact, I'd asked him to join the band once before, around the time Pete Gill joined up, but he was just joining Dokken at the time so he couldn't do it. This time, I cornered him at the Rainbow – he was living in LA at the time – and he was free. So we had him down and tried him out. The first thing Mikkey did with us was 'Hellraiser' and he was very good immediately. It was obvious that it was going to work. We did two songs with him in the studio – 'Hellraiser' and 'Hell on Earth' (one of Motörhead's eternally amazing lost tracks) – and then we immediately went out on the road with Ozzy. It was trial by fire time for Mikkey and he was scared shitless, but he performed miraculously. It was funny, really, because the rest of the band had their doubts about him. After all, here was Mikkey with his big, blond hair, and he's good-looking and he knows it. So there were a lot of snide 'big hair' comments going on, and all this shit about glam-rock sissies. But it only took Mikkey one show to shut them all up. It was zippo time – not a word after that. Everyone was going, 'Jesus Christ!' and I was laughing, saying, 'Yeah? Wasn't it you guys that were going on about sissies and glam rock just an hour earlier?' Mikkey, I have to say, is the best drummer I've ever played with (having said that, I want to add that Phil Taylor was excellent in his day, too).

Between being such a great drummer and having that mass of big, blond hair, Mikkey is an absolute wonder, as far as attitude goes. He's even more arrogant than me and that's saying something! But he's got a sense of humour about himself, which makes it all right – I mean, if he didn't have a sense of humour about himself, he'd be unbearable. But he's so flash that it sends me into fucking fits. He knows what he's doing the whole time – he'll be doing a number on a bunch of birds and then he'll catch my eye and we'll just laugh. Occasionally, however, he'll have a false sense of security. One time we were in a whorehouse in France, on a boat, for some reason – there were all these little floating brothels. Mikkey, Phil, a couple of lads from the crew and myself were there because there was nowhere else to go, basically, and we had thought it was a strip bar but it turned out to be a whorehouse – doesn't make much difference in France. They only had champagne, and I didn't have anything to drink but the other guys did. At the end of the night we got a bill for something like 200,000 fucking francs! So Mikkey went completely apeshit, screaming, 'I'm not going to fucking pay them!' with this thick Swedish accent that comes out when he's pissed off. They called the cops immediately, and the French cops hate Englishmen even more than they hate other Frenchmen. So the CRS (the riot police) came in and they had guns, and Mikkey's shouting, 'Why are you here? It's a fucking whorehouse! You're fuckin' part of this clip joint! You fuckin' French cunt!' and all this shit. And this cop has his pistol pulled and Mikkey was tearing open his shirt and yelling, 'Go on! Shoot me!' And we kept telling him, 'Don't do that, mate, 'cause he will shoot you. He wants to shoot you.' Finally we were able to drag him out. He kicked the police car and the cops were right behind him, but he got away with it all – they probably didn't want anything to do with a loony like him. And that champagne couldn't have been very good because after four drinks, Mikkey's usually on one knee.

Generally we don't have any trouble with Mikkey at all. He's really part of the band – not like Brian Robertson pretending to be some kind of guest star – and he wants to be involved in everything, which is very good. Sometimes, though, he'll come on the bus in the middle of the night when everybody's sleeping and blast the stereo. Me and Phil usually get bunks as far away from the front lounge as possible! But that's a very small price to pay for what we get having Mikkey in the band.

Anyway, I need to backtrack a bit and talk about the making of *March or Die* because quite a lot went on during that time in addition to our changing drummers. For one thing, Los Angeles had a riot after the Rodney King verdict. We were at the Music Grinder, which was in the east part of Hollywood – right on Hollywood Boulevard, in fact – recording 'Hellraiser' rather appropriately. I came out from doing my vocal and there was a TV in the lounge showing a burning house. And I looked out the window and saw the very same house from the other side! It was right down the street! Everything was on fire, people were running around – it was complete mayhem. Mikkey was there and he was screaming, 'My car! My car's outside!' and the guy from the studio came in and said, 'We've got to cut it a bit short today, boys.' As you can tell, we weren't terribly concerned with the historical significance of this event. We went home – there was a curfew, it turned out, for about four days – and it was like driving through a battlezone. The rioters, I heard later, got as far as the Beverly Center but not all the way to Beverly Hills, which, if you ask me, would have been the logical place to go if you're downtrodden. You know, kill the aristos and all that. But no – they attacked each other, which I thought was really stupid. Black people were attacking Koreans; where the fuck did that come from? I don't care how lippy the Koreans are in their stores – you don't have to go to that store, then, do you? Take your business somewhere else! And then they burned their own corner stores; that's really smart, isn't it? And on top of that, the whole thing was being taped by the news crews and the police helicopters and these rioters were waving into the cameras, going, 'Hi! I'm looting!' I mean, your number one rule about looting is *not to be seen doing it*, right? Those people wanted to be media personalities even more than they wanted to be free. Fucking idiots – they deserved to go to jail, if you ask me!

We also got a new manager, Todd Singerman. As far as Motörhead goes, *that* had some historical significance. I don't remember how we were introduced, but Todd just showed up at my house one day. He wouldn't leave until I said he could manage us. I don't even know how he got to Motörhead because he had never heard of us before. 'I want to be your manager,' he told me and I said, 'But you haven't had any experience.' 'Don't worry,' he said, 'I used to work for a Congressman.' He was fucking fixated! I'm not kidding: he was around every fucking day, ringing the doorbell – 'Hi, it's Todd!' and I was like, 'Oh, fuck!' But he was chauffeuring me around and taking me to parties and different things – you know, showing how useful he was. Finally he wore me down. Doug Banker wasn't working out and I knew we needed another guy, so I said to the rest of the band, 'Look, we need a new manager,' and they were game because they'd been after me to get rid of Doug Banker for a while. And I told them, 'I've got this guy called Todd Singerman. I think he'd be good.' Wurzel was suspicious; after Doug Smith, he never trusted anyone. Life can do that to you, you know. But Todd came around and talked his way into the job. He worked hard to get the job, and now that he has it, he has to work even harder! Any time he complains about being snowed under, I just tell him, 'Look, you fuckin' volunteered for the job, man. Too bad!' And he does an excellent job. Todd's a fighter, and we need someone like that. He's persistent, too – something I learned about him early on!

Somewhere in the midst of all of this (and there's even more to come!), *March or Die* got made. We used Pete Solley again, but – as often happens with our producers – he wasn't as good the second time around. I think the title track to the album was the sticking point, 'cause he had his version of 'March or Die' and that was it. I wanted a few things changed and he didn't help me at all. He just sat there, put his feet up on a chair and let the engineer work on it. I thought that was a bit crappy. That's why 'March or Die' didn't work. It should have: it was a tremendous track, and I have a couple of takes of it on tape that are much better than the version on the album. Other tracks are quite good, like 'Stand' and 'You Better Run'. The record label wanted us to cover a standard and it was Phil Campbell, I believe, who came up with the idea of doing Ted Nugent's 'Cat Scratch Fever'. Frankly, I like our version of it better than Nugent's – his is very thin, if you ask me. Ours knocked his out of the fucking loop – of course, nobody remembers ours. Overall, I think *March or Die* is underrated. I bet you think I'm going to put a good portion of the blame for that on the record company, and you're right.

WTG was dying as we were making this record. Every time we came by their offices there were fewer and fewer people there, and by the time the album was released, only Jerry Greenberg and Leslie Holly were left. But the biggest indication about where we stood with our parent company, Sony, came when we released *March or Die*'s single, 'Ain't No Nice Guy'. That track had everything going for it: it was a great song, to begin with, and since it was a ballad it had serious radio potential.

Then I wound up having Ozzy sing on the track along with me. Initially, he wanted the song for himself, but I wouldn't give it to him (maybe I should have let him have it – more people would have heard it), so I had him come in and put vocals on. And Slash from Guns N' Roses contributed the guitar solo; he came in one day, had a few drinks and laid down a couple of guitar tracks. Incidentally, I like Slash quite a bit. Guns N' Roses may have had a nasty reputation but he's a very nice, very genuine guy. Anyhow, we had this great song featuring two of the biggest performers in heavy rock. Jerry at WTG knew it was a great song. There was no way it could lose – that is, unless our record company tried to purposely sabotage it. And that is exactly what happened. It was a band's worst nightmare.

'Ain't No Nice Guy' was actually a radio hit, but that was completely down to us, without any help from Sony, or its marketing department at Epic. We asked them to get it on AOR (album-oriented rock radio) and they wouldn't do it. They said, 'We asked AOR and they wouldn't play it.' That, we knew, was a blatant lie because our management got it on; one of our own men, Rob Jones, and another guy we hired made all the calls to the radio stations. With two phones, we got eighty-two AOR stations in two months. And all these stations told us that Sony had never pushed it – these people had never even heard of the track until we told them about it! 'Ain't No Nice Guy' wound up No. 10 in the radio charts, and Sony didn't make call one – imagine what would have happened if they'd given it just the slightest amount of effort! But no: they actually tried to *stop* it from being played. One of the label's radio guys called up a station in Kansas City and said, 'I heard you're playing "Ain't No Nice Guy". I wish you wouldn't. We didn't give it to you.' What a fucking asshole! Here they had a hit song and they were going around trying to kill it! Our manager Todd rang this goon and totally lost it with him.

'I've been kissing your ass for a year and a half to try to make you do your job,' he told the jerk. 'I've done *my* job and the only person who hasn't is you! If that record isn't back on rotation by ten-thirty tonight, I've got some cousins in South Central who'll make sure you don't write any more rejection slips for anybody!'

Of course, we were back on the air an hour later, but isn't it sad that they make you go to that level? They give you no recourse: if you're nice to them, they think you're a pushover and ride all over you; if you're an asshole, at least you're dealing with them on terms they can understand but more likely than not you will be fired, which is eventually what happened to us. But being an asshole seems to be the only thing that will get a reaction out of these bloody suits.

Since we didn't get any help from the record company at radio (to put it very mildly!), it won't surprise you to learn that they also held us up at MTV. Here we were with this No. 10 song on rock radio and all we needed was about fifteen grand or so to shoot a video but they wouldn't let us have it. So we took about $8000 of our own money and made our own – Ozzy and Slash, nice guys that they are, even came down and appeared in it. Although the video's a bit jumbled, it didn't turn out too badly. But MTV didn't play it for a while because Sony took three weeks to sign the release!

Let's talk about another thing we did that Sony wouldn't do for us: we got on the *Tonight Show*, and we were the first heavy rock band to appear on that show, ever. It was our manager, again, along with our independently hired publicist, Annette Minolfo, who used their connections to get us on. Of course, the day we were taping, the record company sent a couple of corporate types to keep an eye on us, but that didn't disguise the fact that they'd done nothing to get us on. In fact, they had told us it couldn't be done!

I really enjoyed being on the *Tonight Show*. Jay Leno was really a gentleman, much nicer than David Letterman, whom we never even met when we did his show. Jay came up to the dressing room two hours before the show and asked us, 'Have you got everything you need?' He didn't have to do that. During rehearsal, people were running around, panicking over the usual nonsense – 'You can't have it that loud! It vibrates the cameras!' So I said, 'How did they shoot all those train crashes then?' It's bullshit. Nothing shakes those fucking cameras! They were saying the same thing at the BBC twenty years ago, and it was lies then, too! But the actual show was a lot of fun. After our first number, I had to give five bucks to Branford Marsalis, who was the *Tonight Show* band leader at the time. Todd had introduced me to him at a club in Hollywood one night, when he'd just started with Jay and the *Tonight Show*. I said to him, 'You should have us on the show,' and he said, 'Yeah, we will.' Ha! 'I bet you five bucks you don't.' He said, 'Okay,' and we *did* get on. The other guests included that kid, Neil Patrick Harris, from the TV series called *Doogie Howser* and character actress Edie McClure – she was a great girl. I had fun talking with Jay and joking around with Edie, we played two numbers and overall, it was a very good show – no thanks to Sony!

A couple of weeks prior to our *Tonight Show* appearance, we also played three West Coast dates on the Metallica/Guns N' Roses stadium tour. I'm not sure how we got on; it was probably Metallica's work. They're the only band who have ever acknowledged their debt to us. Those three stadium dates went well, especially the latter two. We got all the PA and were treated with a decent amount of respect, which is as it should be.

Speaking of respect, I suppose this is as good a time as any to get back to the ugly business with Sony, where we had no respect whatsoever. I can only conclude that WTG was used as a tax loss for Sony because of their attitude towards us. It seemed as if they did nothing at all to help us, and everything to damage the sales potential of our records, especially *March or Die*. When that album came out and only Jerry and his assistant were left, we knew that WTG was on its way out, but we figured that Sony would put us on one of their other labels, probably Epic, because that's who was doing our marketing. That's the sort of thing that usually happens, and with the Grammy nomination and the great reviews we'd got for *1916* – and on *March or Die*, for that matter – it only made sense. But no, they dropped us, and to be perfectly honest, I think they did us a favour. Those Neanderthal corporate executives at Sony are all stupid, ignorant, fucking elitist twats. And that's not sour grapes because I felt that way long before they dropped us! They've got no idea about music at all. They sell millions of records, but wouldn't you if you had the Michael Jackson catalogue and Mariah Carey? Believe me, Mariah Carey is far better off without Tommy Mottola! Mottola was the one who wouldn't even acknowledge me at his own fucking Grammy party. Fuck him and fuck the rest of them. They're the most inept bunch of motherfuckers I've ever seen in my life. Oh, yes.

We did some headlining dates in Argentina and Brazil and then – before having to regroup and think about getting a new record company – we attended the CMJ convention in New York. CMJ is a college music trade paper and it holds a convention every year. Several organizations have these music conferences and I've been to quite a few of them. They're odd affairs: there are generally a bunch of minor executives slapping each other on the back and spending their expense accounts at the bar, but there are also a lot of younger people, not much more than fans, who are just starting their careers in the music business (poor souls!). And of course the corporate suits have a few artists they're trying to parade around. I was there, but nobody was *parading* me around – nobody dared! Wurzel and I were on a panel – those things are such jokes! Nothing meaningful ever gets said. At this particular one some woman metal singer who called herself the Great Kat wasted everyone's time babbling on and on about how wonderful she was! Wurzel, meanwhile, was taking a piss in a bottle behind the tablecloth. But I do remember that particular year's convention fondly because Wurzel and I ran into a man I very much admire – guitarist Leslie West.

Leslie West is great, a complete maniac with these mad fucking psycho eyes. I introduced him to Wurzel, and he gave Wurzel this look and said, 'Tell me, is that a name your mother heard of, or was it given to you later?'

Wurzel, who was a bit unnerved by Leslie's mad stare, replied, 'L-later, in school.'

'Tell me, Wurzel, tell me the truth – do you take drugs?'

'Y-yes, I do.'

'Step this way.'

So they disappeared into the men's room, both of them in one stall, which is not an easy thing to do, considering Leslie's size. West dropped the cocaine on his shoe and he said, 'I don't want you to think the wrong thing of me, Wurzel, but you're going to have to go down on me now!' So Wurzel had to get down and snort it off his boot!

Leslie West didn't have much patience with this convention. 'I can't stay here, Lemmy,' he told me. 'All these people are fucking peasants.'

'I know that!' I said. 'I'm trying to get out of here myself.'

'Well, I'm leaving,' he said. 'It grieves me, Lemmy, to leave you alone here, but I'm going.' And he went out to his car and took off. I can't say I blame him. They never did shit for him, any of his record labels. There's a guy who should be number one, but he's been ignored for years by the 'hit machine'.

Anyhow, by the end of the year we were without a label once

again, but we were much better off, if you ask me. After hearing one too many lies from the powers that be at Sony, I finally asked one guy there, 'Why didn't you tell us the truth?'

And this was his response, absolutely verbatim: 'That's not the way this business works.'

Can you imagine somebody saying that! How could you be so dishonourable? People like that should be hung by their balls from a burning piece of wood. But after almost thirty years in the music business, I should have figured it out. I've always said that good business is theft – if you've had a good business day, you've stolen somebody's money. These people treat music purely as a commodity, like selling cans of beans. Most of the people that promote bands have not even heard the bands they promote. They just got a name that came up in the shuffle. Nobody seems to believe in the music any more. The industry's building all the time, but they're killing the music. They're trying to, anyway, but I won't let them as long as I'm alive. Fuck 'em, you know. They are disgraceful, stupid, arrogant, forgettable bastards – that's right, forgettable, because people are gonna remember me, but the suits will be forgotten. Fuck 'em. Who are they? Somebody who worked for Sony? Ha! You'll have to do better than *that*!

CHAPTER TWELVE

we are motörhead

As you can probably tell, I wasn't exactly distressed at being dropped by Sony. We'd been in worse situations. Things like that don't bother me at all – you just have to keep going and everything will sort itself out. It always does. You can't run around panicking and giving up; you've got to have the strength of your convictions; you've got to know that somebody out there is going to recognize you as worthwhile and that you'll still be in the picture. If you look like you're beaten, then who's going to come forward?

So we carried on throughout the last days of the Sony débâcle like we always do – we played some gigs. Not long before we got dropped we did about five dates with Ozzy Osbourne and Alice in Chains. Ozzy was doing one of his so-called 'farewell' tours –

like he's ever really going to retire! He'd fucking go nuts if he retired! Ozzy is one of the most charismatic performers in the world; that's what he does. Take that away from him and he'd go completely crazy. If he could see himself the way everybody else does, he'd never go on about retiring ever again. He *will* have to retire one day, I suppose, but not until he can't walk any more. But anyway, we only played a few of those 'retirement' shows and then got thrown off the bill because we did the Guns N' Roses/Metallica dates on our days off. That wasn't very rock 'n' roll, if you ask me, but since we were playing third, under Alice in Chains, I didn't really care.

We also did some recording. We had a couple of songs on the soundtrack to Clive Barker's *Hellraiser III: Hell on Earth* – 'Hellraiser' (perhaps not surprisingly) and 'Hell on Earth', which were recorded in the same session. In addition to those, we recorded 'Born to Raise Hell', on which I shared vocals with Ice T and Whitfield Crane, the singer from Ugly Kid Joe (he's a nice guy . . . *now* he's a nice guy! Hi, Whit!). The latter song was a last-minute thing – it played over the end credits, and didn't appear on the soundtrack album. We actually did a video for 'Hellraiser', but Sony, of course, didn't pay for it – I think it was the movie company's doing. So as you can see, our career wasn't at all dependent on anything Sony did (and thank God for that!).

Later we did some shows in Argentina and Brazil, with Alice in Chains opening for us. Some of those South American countries are virtually lawless, and you really have to watch your ass there. One year when we were down to do some shows in Brazil, we got invited to the President's son's house, and the cops tried to railroad us on the way. That's a great source of income for them, to arrest people like us and then ransom us for a lot of money. And of course, all rock bands are hugely wealthy – ha, ha! This particular time, we were playing with Iron Maiden and Skid Row, and after we finished, we walked up to the parking lot, and all these security guys were standing around the van we were supposed to use to get to the hotel, and one of them was inside fooling around with one of the seats. He came out looking really shifty and I thought, 'Fuck that!' So I went over to my guys and I said, 'Nobody gets in the fucking van!' and I insisted that we get another one. The guy tried to tell me, 'Oh, there are no other vans,' and I said, 'Then we'll stay here the fucking night. I'm sleeping in the dressing room. Okay?' Another van was somehow found, and we dropped off the people who were staying in the hotel and headed for the President's son's house. About ten yards up the promenade, what do you know but we had a cop on our tail. The guy got us all out and went straight for that seat. There was nothing there, of course, and he didn't know what to do! He asked us some lame questions – 'How old are these girls?' and all that – but he was screwed and he knew it. Then we had to wait (he said the van was 'overcrowded') until they brought us *another* van and I thought it was going to be the same scam again. I went walking off down the promenade to the hotel, with Todd following me – I don't see why you should willingly put your head on the block! But the van came driving past and there weren't any cops following them and they said, 'Get in.' So we got in and finally arrived at the President's son's house. That was something else altogether! You get up there and all these soldiers suddenly walk out of the woods with their guns at the ready, asking for the secret password and all that. We had clearance so we were let in without any more hassle. We had an all right time but there weren't enough girls there, if you ask me. Phil Campbell was running around drunk with the President's son and all these large security guys, they ended up being a great bunch – not that you'd form a long-lasting friendship or anything.

We did the States again, too, this time with Black Sabbath. The peculiar thing about touring with them was that every day they had a nap in the afternoon; everything shut down, it had to all go dark in the dressing room and three of them sat side-by-side on the couch, nodded off like little rabbits. Bobby Rondinelli, actually, didn't *want* a nap, but he was out there with Geezer and Tony! It was kind of boring for us in Milwaukee because we shared the dressing room with them – it was all one big room, divided up by a curtain. So all the lights were out and we had to sit in darkness for an hour. It was very fucking strange. Even if Motörhead's around until 2035, I don't think we'll ever be ready for naptime. That said, I do have to say that Black Sabbath delivered every night. They were consistently good all through the tour.

The year ended on sort of a sour note. We were supposed to tour England but as I've already mentioned, it got cancelled because the promoters wouldn't guarantee the money and we sure weren't going to fund it ourselves – you know the story. We did go right through Europe, though, and did very well, as always.

See, we're the only consistent factor in the whole scheme: we always show up and play our stuff, we're always on time, and we're always pretty reasonable (well, mostly). If the promoters did their job half as well as we do ours, we'd all be happy.

We spent a week early in 1993 playing a few low-key shows at this place in Anaheim called California Dreams that doesn't exist any more, and figuring out what to do about a record deal. We had to have a deal, of course, and we ended up getting one with a German company, ZYX, which was a fucking disaster. But they offered us more money than anyone else – they offered us stupid money, up front – so we took it. And we were fucking broke: that's what you do when you're skint, you take the money. It did start off looking good, I have to admit. For one thing, Germany had been our best market for years, so it made sense to sign with a German label. And they made all kinds of promises and they flew across the Atlantic all the time to see us. Since ZYX was primarily a dance label (that should have tipped us off right there), they said we could do the distribution and have our own subsidiary label and all that. But in the end they insisted on doing it all themselves, which was a complete nightmare. They didn't know anything about American marketing. Plus the guy that runs the place is the one who started the company back in 1926 or whatever. He was so fucking old he spit Noah's Ark and all decisions had to run by him. I don't recall how many times Todd went across the Atlantic to deal with them, but it was more than they did coming to see us! Todd had only been managing us for a little over a year during all this and those months were really a baptism of fire for him. However, he rose to the occasion remarkably well.

Anyhow, we had no clue about what we'd gotten ourselves into, and we just went along making an album, like we always do. This was the first time Mikkey was in with us from the start and he turned out to be even better than we expected. He was very involved in the songwriting process for this album, which came to be called *Bastards*. Phil Taylor hadn't been interested in the writing process for a very long time before we fired him. And Mikkey also came through when we got in the studio. He banged out the drum tracks in record time. He was amazing, and has continued to be amazing to this day . . . not to mention amusing!

We also got a new producer for this album. For the better part of our careers, it seemed like Motörhead changed producers every other album – Jimmy Miller did two, as did Vic Maile and Peter Solley. They never seemed to be any good for more than that. I think we wear them out! I don't remember the name of the other guy we were looking at for the new record, but it was between him and Howard Benson and we went with Howard. Howard certainly earned the gig: he was keen and he came to all the rehearsals (though I have to say it was the last time he did *that*!). Howard was there, Howard was gonna do this record whatever fucking happened. He just came and hung around until we said yes. That's really what he did – in the end, we just said, 'Fuck it, let's let him do it!' He really wanted this album and we gave it to him and amazingly enough, he stayed with us for the four albums. I don't know how he managed to break the two-album barrier but he did and we were generally pretty happy with him in spite of some of his weird habits (I'll get into those later, but don't hold your breath – they aren't that exciting). He did a great job on *Bastards* – I think it's one of the best albums Motörhead has made so far. Every song on it is strong. 'Death or Glory' and 'I Am the Sword' are probably my favourites, along with 'Lost in the Ozone'. Then there's 'Don't Let Daddy Kiss Me', which is about child abuse. I wrote that one on my own and I'd had it for three years in my pocket. I offered it to everybody – Lita Ford, Joan Jett – 'cause I thought a girl should sing it but no one ever took it up. They would hear the song and say, 'I love it! I must sing it, you've got to let me have that song!' and then three weeks later, the manager would call and say, 'No.' So I wound up singing it myself.

We really enjoyed making *Bastards*. Although he was with us for the next album, *Sacrifice*, I really consider it Wurzel's last Motörhead record, because it was the last one where he was really there in spirit. And we had fun showing Howard how to work with us. He gets really girly in the studio and it's a simple thing to get him upset. He'll start going on – 'Don't insult me, man!' and all – and I'll just say, 'It's impossible to insult you, Howard. Why should I bother? You're doing that all by yourself.' Once he was wearing a shirt that had, I don't know, the number 36 or something on it, and Phil said, 'Is that shirt foreign, Howard?' He said, 'No, why?' And Phil replied, 'I've never seen "cunt" spelled like that before.' We got him *twice* with that and finally he started freaking out – 'Why did you hire me, then, if you don't like me!' And Phil said, 'Well, you were the only one in our price range.'

Despite this Howard really liked being our producer. He certainly won't stand to have anyone else talking shit about us, that's for sure (I think he's probably had to defend us at some length at one time or another). We did argue quite a bit while we were in the studio, though, me and him. Early on in our working relationship, there was one day where I'd been waiting around to do some vocals for endless hours while he was going over some guitar part or something. So I finally got a hamburger and I was just starting to eat it when he said, 'Right! Vocals!' 'Oh, you cunt!' I said. 'Why don't you let me eat my fucking hamburger?' But no – 'Come on, come on, we're on a deadline!' Howard being a bitch in the studio, you know. So I did the logical thing; I shoved the burger's contents into the mixing board. I figured it was fair. Howard's eating habits, incidentally, leave quite a bit to be desired – he eats all these terrible vegetarian things, fruit and nuts. That shit's not healthy! Human beings are carnivores – just look at our teeth! Our digestive systems are not made to handle vegetarian food. It makes you fart all the time, and you get intestinal flora. Vegetarianism is unrealistic – that's why cows have four stomachs and we have one. Think about it. (Hi, Howard!) And don't forget – Hitler was a vegetarian!

The whole time we were working with ZYX, recording the album was the only thing that went smoothly. But when we're in the studio that's generally the way things go anyway. Mikkey, when he first began recording with us, was surprised at the way we do everything off the cuff. He was used to people like Don Dokken, who work on the same record for three years and have everything planned out beforehand. I can't stand working that way. We go in with nothing and just hammer it out. It costs less that way, and obviously it works. If it didn't we'd do it another way. Anyhow, the record was great but the problem was you couldn't find it anywhere. You could find it in Germany – it's a German label, and that's the only market they know. Everywhere else it was terrible. It took a while, but they finally got it in Japan. In the US nobody even knew we had a record out. We toured a lot behind it anyway – we figured that if you can't get the record, then we'd better get out there and play it for you! But really, the whole situation was tragic.

Bastards was one of the very best albums we ever did and it just vanished completely. It's just so disappointing, when you pull out all the stops for an album and you're really thrilled with it and nobody else cares, especially not your own record company. We couldn't even get ZYX to pay for promotional copies. Our publicist, Annette Minolfo, asked for 200 CDs to give to DJs and press and they said no, it was too expensive. Too expensive?! They just gave us half a million dollars advance to make the fucking thing and now it's too expensive to promote it with 200 fucking CDs! Somebody's got to have his head up his ass, right? One thing I have to say about *Bastards*, though: at least it was on the radio, which is more than anyone could say for *1916* or *March or Die*. That's because we actually sent them the record ourselves. Simple, really.

Anyhow, after we finished making *Bastards*, we went through both North America and Europe twice, the usual sort of thing. We had some fun in Montreal with Mikkey. There were two guys backstage – transvestites. They were dressed to the nines and they wanted to have their picture taken with us. As you know, I don't care about a person's sexual predilections, much less how they dress, and Phil's the same way (Phil dresses up like that himself half the time – why do you think he's called 'Stiletto Heels' on *Bastards*?). But Mikkey's another story altogether – for all his pretty-boy looks, he hates that sort of thing. So we told the guys, 'Yeah,' but waited until the last minute before informing Mikkey. Then it was, 'Mikkey! Come and take a picture with these chicks!' And he comes running out, 'Hi, girls!' and all that. Stopped him in his tracks. It was really funny, 'cause one guy's skirt had no back and his ass cheeks were sticking out. But we had the picture taken anyway, and Mikkey was muttering, 'Fucking queers,' under his breath. And on top of that, we went out to some club on the bus, and Mikkey went somewhere else, then came back to the club. He didn't know that after the rock show it turned into a gay disco! He got out of the taxi in a 20° below blizzard, and there was no bus. The only warm place was the disco, so he had to go in. He was stuck there for two hours with all the transvestites asking him, 'Where do you get your hair done?' I would have paid a hundred bucks to see that – it must have been fucking fantastic! Ho, ho, *ho*!

One of the treks through the US was our second time out with Black Sabbath, and everything was going great until we were headed for Los Angeles and I got some horrible flu bug. Mikkey and Wurzel both had it in Denver. It started to hit me in the morning as the bus arrived in LA. I got this feeling like I had to lie down, then I realized I was terribly ill. It was the most virulent shit I've ever had. We were supposed to play the Universal Amphitheater that night, but Todd told me flat out we weren't going on – 'Lie back down. You're not going anywhere.' It was good of Black Sabbath to keep us on the tour after that, really, because for all they knew, I was malingering. Whenever I get sick, everybody always says I'm overdoing the drugs again, but I was really ill! I was up in a couple of days anyway – that's how those flu bugs are. But of all places, it had to be LA.

We also played in Argentina, in front of 50,000 people (we try to do South America every year if we can – depends on whether or not the armies are on the streets!). It was at a football field, with the Ramones, and I have to admit we stole the show from them, even though they are huge down there. I mean, most of the crowd was wearing Motörhead shirts and all 50,000 of them seemed to be stomping for us. You just couldn't follow us that night. I don't care who it was – I don't think the Beatles could have followed us that night. That's what makes all the other shit unimportant!

Between Japan and Europe, we had a few days off, so our manager Todd, our drum roadie Pap and I went to Thailand. It was a very interesting trip, indeed, because life apparently means absolutely nothing there – if you pay $600, you and a group of people can see a chick get fucked, beat up and shot. They buy these girls off their penniless families in the interior, who need the money to feed their ten other kids. This sort of attraction (?!) is how businessmen get their kicks down there. We didn't see anything like that, of course, but we did go to this club where there were about eleven girls on stage. They all looked about sixteen and all of them were the most beautiful women you've ever seen – terrific, large breasts, long legs and those Oriental faces. Any one of them was a guy's dream come true in about six different ways. But what they were doing was so weird! They weren't exactly stripping, because they were pretty much naked already, with just this cummerbund-type thing around the middle. But one would squat down and she was firing a peashooter out of her crotch and bursting balloons. Another one was in a sling and the other girls were swinging her at yet another girl with a dildo – she got knocked off the table twice. Another shoved a block of razorblades up there, and pulled them out on a string. The whole thing was a very strange experience. Erotic it wasn't!

Eventually we all came back home and once again we were without a record company in the States. I don't recall how we parted ways with ZYX. I think we just left them and went to CBH, the head of which, Rainer Hansel, has been our German promoter for years. So that got us settled as far as Germany was concerned, but as for the States, we had nothing. Mikkey was in a panic, but then he always is. He sees his paycheck flying away over the horizon. It is fair, because he's got a family to support, and so does Phil. I don't, but still, I can never be bothered with all these panics people seem to like having. Everybody thinks it shows that they care if they panic all the fucking time, but it's not true. You miss a lot of details when you panic. Eventually we did get a deal in the States, but by the time that came about we had already recorded our next album, *Sacrifice*. We had record deals in Germany and Japan, two big markets for us, and *they* wanted an album, so we had to keep going.

Sacrifice is one of my favourite records of ours, especially considering the difficulties that were going on behind it. Howard was producing us again, but he'd also just gotten an A&R gig with a label called Giant. So his mind was in at least two or three different places, and half the time the engineer, Ryan Dorn, was holding it all together, following the direction Howard gave him. And it was becoming clearer every day that Wurzel was on his way out of the band. He wouldn't extend himself at all, and usually just sat there while we were writing songs, with his guitar across his knees. When we stopped playing, he stopped playing and when we started again, he would too. The whole thing with him seemed like it happened overnight, but of course it had been building up for a long time. It was very difficult for me because for years he was my best friend in the band and then he became this person I didn't know and hated me, and that can break your heart, you know?

Still, we went in the studio with some great songs – we wrote 'Sex and Death' in ten minutes on the last day of rehearsal. I changed the lyrics once we were recording, but that's always the way it goes. I altered 'Another Time' out of all recognition and I had three sets of lyrics for 'Make 'Em Blind'. That's what's fun about making a record – you go in with one thing and come out with something completely different. I added a part in 'Out of the Sun' – I had to because it only had two and a half verses, and who can sing half a fucking verse? But when Mikkey and Phil and Wurzel were rehearsing it, they weren't thinking of that, since they aren't singers. Fuckin' musicians! So one day when nobody else was around except for Jamie, my guitar roadie, I added a piece on my own. I played bass and Jamie played guitar and we tacked it in there secretly – complete subterfuge. Then I gave the others a tape of it – Wurzel played it in the rental car and when he heard it he nearly drove off the road! Sometimes in the studio something practically comes out of thin air – 'Make 'Em Blind' was like that. We improvised a lot of that in the studio, and Phil did this brilliant solo in one take. It sounds like it's being played backwards, but he played it forward and he fell over halfway through it – right over the couch, flat on his back with the fucking guitar, laughing uproariously. We didn't even need to think about doing it again – it was great.

Sacrifice also has a lot more nonsense on it than most of the albums before it; the lyrics don't mean anything you can really get a hold of. But they convey the mood all right, especially the title track and 'Out of the Sun'. 'Dog Face Boy' was about Phil Campbell – I only decided it was about him after I'd written it, though. 'Poor boy out your mind again/ Jet plane outside looking for another friend' – as soon as Phil gets off that plane, *boom*! He's gone. Most people are still in their shower after the ride to the hotel, but he's already got the hired car and has been in two bars looking for fun. One time he came to LA and he grabbed the rental, which had zero miles on it at the airport. He showed up the next day and it had over 200 miles – he was driving to Sunset and Vine streets in Hollywood and he wound up in Pomona! That was miraculous. After that he got a map of LA and now he knows the city quite well – he could probably get a job here as a tour guide.

It wasn't long after we finished the record that we lost Wurzel. I had already talked him back into the band three times. I'd go to him, 'Why don't you hang in there, it might get better,' etc. We kept trying to find out what his problem was so we could address it, but he could never come up with anything. Things would bother him but he'd keep quiet until he had worked himself into a frenzy, so you could never see it building up. For example, he'd begin carrying on, like, saying to me, 'You get all the publicity!' And I'd tell him, 'But Wurzel, you stopped doing publicity. You and me were the top names in the band for years and then you suddenly stopped doing press, so your name is gone. Besides, I've been in the band nine years longer than you and people still remember me from Hawkwind. You haven't done any publicity for five years and you've just been sitting at home with your wife and dog, so how do you expect anybody would hear about you?' And of course nobody wants to be told that! But all the same, that was the reason. It's not my fault. Wurzel's attitude just went straight downhill and you can't go on being defeatist. It finally got to him.

It was an English TV show that apparently was the last straw, as far as Wurzel was concerned. It was called *Don't Forget Your*

Toothbrush, and although the show itself was awful – basically it was just a game show hosted by some horribly bouncy ex-DJ wearing silly clothes and a sillier haircut, and people would win travel packages – the music was great. Jools Holland, who used to be in Squeeze, was the band leader; he plays incredible piano and sounds like Ray Charles when he sings. Anyhow, he had this set-up where the featured artist did two songs with the studio band backing him up. So I went on and we did 'Ace of Spades' – with a four-piece brass section! – and 'Good Golly Miss Molly'. It was the first time I'd ever done 'Ace of Spades' without the rest of Motörhead, and because I did that, Wurzel blew up. Jem, his wife, was phoning the TV station while I was there, saying that Wurzel should be on instead of me! Christ. Then I got this fax from Wurzel saying all sorts of terrible things. He accused me and Todd of stealing his money – like I need Wurzel's money (as I've stated before, I make more money off of royalties 'cause I get paid from the back catalogue). And he was convinced people were going around and plotting behind his back – I mean, how senseless is that? Wurzel told the others he'd left the band. He didn't tell me, which was especially hard since, like I said, we were best friends in the band for a very long time. But the end was a nasty episode. I just hated it and I was glad when it was over. Somebody told me he came to one of our gigs in Brixton after he'd left and apparently he stood there through the whole show, crying while he was watching us. People always love telling you bad news, don't they? That was a terribly sad thing to hear.

With Wurzel gone, Mikkey and I figured we needed to get

somebody else. But then Phil said, 'I'd like to try it on my own.' So we decided to carry on as a three-piece and see how it went, and it turned out to be amazing. It used to be that Wurzel was always the energetic one on stage. He was the one who did all the leaping around. But the first night we played without him, there I was singing and minding my own business and this *thing* zoomed past me . . . and it was Phil! I couldn't believe it because he'd never moved a muscle on stage before that. He really tried hard and played his ass off. He really came through, but perhaps I shouldn't sound so surprised. It's true that he's a very strange person, but he's also a natural when it comes to playing guitar. Phil can be in any sort of condition and he'll still play you a good solo. He just does it instinctively – Brian Robertson was the same way. Phil just picks up a guitar and it practically becomes part of his body. The fact that he's determined to be a little pervert just makes life on the road all the more interesting!

To be honest, I'm glad we're a three-piece again. For one thing, it saved us the trouble of finding another guitar player! But also, as I've said before, when there are two guitars, you can never get things worked out completely because somebody won't agree with it. With one guitar player the bass can do anything. In the early days, I used to play all kinds of weird shit behind Eddie and it would work. So things are a lot freer now with this line-up, and everybody seems to know where they stand, which is a plus. Also, we get more money!

Anyhow, *Sacrifice* had been finished for just a few months when we had a new American label, CMC, ready to release it.

CMC hired us off our German label, CBH. That was our first offer in the US in years, and they showed a lot of faith in us from the start because they shipped the album before we had even signed the contract! We're with them to this day, and five albums later, I can still say they've done pretty well by us. Tom Lipsky, who owns the label, believes in what he's doing. His people put their money where their mouths are – they're honest (surprise and shock!) and I like that. We had a solid first year between CBH and CMC. We played nineteen dates in Germany and all over Europe and people were actually bringing us the *new* record to auto-graph! That was a change – usually the fans would be holding records from three years ago. But CBH really got the record out there, and CMC did their best for us too.

As always, we toured America. You've gotten the idea, I'm sure, that the road is my natural habitat, but there are still some things about it that annoy the fuck out of me. One is the patron-izing attitude some of these record company publicity people have towards the band. They actually take you by the arm and try to rush you around – I hate that! I'm not a dummy and I'm not a fucking commodity. Some people just insult your intelligence, and when you react they call you troublesome. You get a bad name for asserting your intelligence and independence. I'll give you an example. While we were in Canada this chick had all this shit set up for us to do – Much Music, the Canadian version of MTV, and all that. But we were incredibly depressed that day. None of us wanted to go on stage because the monitor system was so horrible. We hadn't been able to hear each other play for the last eight gigs, and I was talking about just dropping the tour and going home – 'Fuck this. This music is my life and I can't play it properly because it sounds like shit on stage. How is the audience going to enjoy it if I'm not enjoying it?' (It sounds stupid, I know, but it's quite real, I assure you!) And while we were having this crisis, she was hovering around us, saying, 'Much Music is outside.' I told her I couldn't do it – I was too depressed. And I was! I couldn't have gone on TV with the attitude of, 'Hey, everything's wonderful!' because it wasn't. I said, 'Can't we tape it after the show?' And she said, 'No, no! It has to be done now because after six o'clock they have to pay extra for the camera.' What the fuck does that matter? *Pay more for the camera!* Jesus. So anyway, the other two trooped off and did it, and she wrote this letter saying that we were troublesome and arrogant bastards. The thing that got me the most was she claimed I insulted her sexually! Do you know what I said? I said, 'You're the best-looking representative we've had from a record company in years.' That was *it*! If telling someone they're looking good is harassment, then the world has truly gone out of its fucking mind.

As you can tell, a lot happened to us in 1995. Plus I turned fifty at the end of the year. Todd wanted to do something big, so he threw me a semi-surprise party at the Whiskey – he actually told me about it the day before, the swine. The night of this big event, there were lines around the block and it was fucking packed once you got inside. The people who couldn't show up wished me happy birthday on video (Dee Schneider took up about half the tape!). To be really honest, although I appreciate all the effort everyone put into it, a gathering like this is not my idea of a good time. It's just that I hate being *that* much of the centre of attention. Not all my own guests were able to get in because of the fucking fire marshals and I never did get a chance to relax with the ones that *did* get in. Let's face it, with something like this relaxing isn't on the agenda! I was being pulled left and right, to and fro, fore and aft. Nevertheless, it was a really nice thing for everyone to do, and the evening had some real high-lights. Metallica flew down and performed some of the more obscure Motörhead songs – that was a great tribute. Metallica is one of the few bands that has consistently given us credit, and I hold them in high regard for that.

Somewhere in the midst of all the touring we were doing, we got to work on our next record, titled (inappropriately enough) *Overnight Sensation.* We spent four weeks writing it and four weeks in the studio and then we did some European festivals, and when we came back we were in the studio another month or so. It generally takes us about three months to do a record, and this one was no different – it's just that those three months were a little spread out! We hired Howard again as producer, but Duane Barron came in and did a lot of work under Howard's direction. Then Howard came in at the mix and sorted it all out. Duane was all right – you could tell he liked guitar!

Actually, this was our first official album as a three-piece since *Another Perfect Day* with Robbo. If you're wondering what that was like – it went the same as a four-piece except one guy wasn't there! Or the same as the Everly Brothers plus one. It was a bit more fraught, but that was just because Phil, being the only guitarist, felt that there was a lot riding on his shoulders (which there was). So he was under some added pressure, but he proved himself well. *Overnight Sensation* is a great album for him. Mikkey was his usual perfect self – he always finishes his drum tracks well ahead of schedule. This time around he did them in one day. And why spend any more time than you have to? People think that the longer you take for an album the better it's gonna be, and that's not true. Look at Jeff Beck, Clapton and Page – they played a lot of their early classic work in one take. They had no choice! In those days, you had to do the best solo you had in about fifteen to twenty seconds. You had to make your point quick! None of this Jerry Garcia nonsense. Jeff Beck made his name in eighteen seconds on 'Shapes of Things'! The sixties were a great time for breeding excellent musicians, far better than now. And speaking of less time making better albums – our back catalogue proves that loud and clear.

Overnight Sensation was also our first official record for CMC – *Sacrifice* was already partly here in the States on import before they got it. But the label really proved itself with *Overnight Sensation* – it was the best-distributed record we'd had for ages. They worked out a deal with BMG, which helped. I do have to say, though, that sometimes I worry about CMC's business sense. Like I've said before, good business is theft, and since CMC has been nothing but straightforward with us, that makes them bad businessmen by definition! But I think I can deal with that.

We had some interesting experiences while touring for that record. We went back to Hungary, which had changed a lot since we'd last been there. Before it was like Russia, very oppressive, but now it's more like Germany. And speaking of Russia, we went there for the first time and played four shows. Russia is a very strange country, unlike anything else I've ever seen. I went to eastern Europe before the wall came down and after it came down: I've played in East Germany, Hungary of course, and Czechoslovakia and none of them was anything like Russia. People in America who haven't been there really have no clue about it. It's insane. There's security everywhere, nine deep around everything. It seems like everybody's an ex-soldier. I guess that's because when the Soviet Union collapsed, half the police force collapsed with it – they didn't need that many anymore, so most of them became 'security', which means 'private army'! Those of them who aren't driving cabs in LA, that is! Having all that security around was stifling. And as for the free market, it's mainly casinos because the only way they can get any foreign currency is by the gaming in the casinos. So those are everywhere, but the country's still starving to death. The gigs, however, were incredible. Every one of them was sold out, and the audiences went fucking crazy! That part I liked (but then, it's always the best part of touring – that and getting laid after the gig).

Of course, there were a few nightmares since the promoters hadn't been promoting for very long. For example, we were going from Moscow to Rostov, which is a long fucking ride.

They told us to show up at this address at such-and-such an hour, and we drove out of Moscow. We kept going and it was getting darker and darker until there was something like one street lamp every half mile and finally we turned off the road and stopped by this tall hedge. As our eyes got used to the dark, we could see armed guards in sentry boxes at each side of a gate. This guy ordered us to pull over, so we did and he and the promoter began arguing in Russian. It was spooky. Then these two fucking great trucks suddenly whoomed in. They were army trucks – except they weren't being driven by soldiers – but anyhow they got waved straight through. We finally figured out the place was some sort of Russian air force base doing a bit of 'import-export' on the side! The promoter came back and told us, 'We can't go in yet. The general is about to visit.' So we had to sit around until this big, fucking staff car with a flag on it appeared. This guy in a little coat and cap got out, went in and came back out – he was probably just collecting his cut. Finally we got waved in. There were soldiers all over the place, chattering like mad – Russians are like Italians that way, they'll go on for half an hour. After all of this, they got us to the plane and Phil saw it first. He came back to the car and said, 'I'm not flying in that.'

'Don't be such a sissy,' I said, and got out of the car myself to see what the matter was. Then *I* came back and said, 'I'm not flying in that!' It was some sort of two-motor 1957 Ilyushin Bomber or a transport plane, completely gutted inside. The passenger lounge was at the back part of the cargo hold and it was nothing but some garden furniture! Plus the fucking thing wasn't pressurized – totally open to the elements. So we said we wouldn't go, but we sent the crew in it. Hey, it gives them a good story to tell later on. Keeps them happy, relating their tales of woe.

Tony, our light guy, almost got mugged by a couple of policemen once we did get to Rostov. We had a great show, then we all went to this café. All the crew were wearing these hats with the Soviet badge on the front – those big fur hats they're making for tourists now. So it was like being surrounded by fucking munchkins. And Tony was talking away at these people and he and another roadie, Dave Road Warrior, went off with these two supposed cops to 'find some girls'. But they put them in separate cars, which was somewhat suspicious and after about ten minutes, Dave noticed the other car wasn't behind him. He said, 'Fuck this,' and just got out and walked back. And then Tony went off at the people he was with until they turned around and took him back – the British Embassy was mentioned along with various threats. Dave walked back. I'm sure if they'd ever gotten to the place, it would have been about twenty-five miles outside of town with one girl and six geezers with blackjacks, ready to beat them senseless and steal all their money.

I would have loved to have gone over there when it was still the Soviet Union so I could compare it to what it's like now. Really, it's misery over there for most of the locals. We went to St Petersburg, which is fantastic – *Dr Zhivago*, the Winter Palace and all that history. So, romantic dummy that I am, I thought,

'Right, let's take the train back to Moscow! It'll be a Russian experience.' Well, it certainly was a Russian experience. The guy told us, 'No problem, we have booked the train.' So we get to the station and there's a great, long train there. We get on and I go to the compartment with my ticket number on it, open the door and there's a woman with two kids in there! So I say to the conductor, 'There must be some mistake.'

'No, no – ' He shows me the ticket and she's got her name on it, too. What they do is they book you and they throw the peasants out – she and her kids got tossed off the train. I said, 'Hey, man, you can't do that!' And they said, 'Do you want to share your compartment with them all the way to Moscow?' I had to admit, 'Now that you mention it, I don't.' But obviously nothing has really changed since the tsars' days – the guys at the top do anything they want and everybody else pays for it. It's always been that way in Russia. Fucking Lenin, for all his blather, changed nothing for the peasant.

Touring was going particularly well for us – in fact, there were some countries like Argentina and Japan, where they put us in bigger venues. And it was around this time that the English promoters discovered that yes, they could turn a nice profit with Motörhead shows. Our three-piece line-up was performing excellently, so we thought it was high time we made another live record. We did, eventually, but first we made another studio record, *Snake Bite Love*. It came out quite nicely, even though we recorded it all over the place instead of doing it all at just one or two studios. I also improved my Risk game – Howard Benson, who produced again, had it on his computer, so I played it whenever I wasn't recording. With *Snake Bite Love*, and *We Are Motörhead*, the record we just finished, I really feel that this line-up has come into its own in the studio. We like recording – I like it more now than I ever have before. With Mikkey and with one guitar player who, like Phil, is a natural, it's really easy. The prima donna scenes have gone way down in number. We all have the occasional one, but not often. We're all very professional (we should be after all these years!), so it's a simple process.

Snake Bite Love came together like our albums usually do – six weeks before we recorded it, we didn't even have one song. But when it came time, we put it together very quickly. Unfortunately, I was sick for some of the rehearsals, and when you leave two guys together who aren't singers, you end up with some weird arrangements. So a couple of songs, 'Desperate for You' and 'Night Side', have odd structures. It's really tricky getting it all to sort of fit together. And of course a lot of things can get changed around in the studio. The title track started life as a completely different song. Mikkey put the drum track on with a totally different set of chords. Then he went back to Sweden and Phil came in one day and said, 'I'm sick of this one. I don't like it already.' And I said, 'Yeah, you're right.' So he went in and came up with a completely new riff and the whole thing changed! That album is also a prime example of me writing the words at the last minute – you know, lazy son of a bitch one more time, right? But we got it done, and I think it's a very good album. The only problem any of us have with it is Mikkey hates the title. Homophobe that he is, he thinks it's gay. He called me from Sweden – 'I don't like this "Love" in the title. Don't want the "Love". *Bite the Snake* or something like that would be all right.' 'Ah, fuck off Mikkey,' I said. 'What's the matter with you?' Then he called me up again! 'Hey, Lemmy, about this title . . .' But I had to let him have his say.

So while we were on tour for *Snake Bite Love*, we finally got around to making the live record, which turned out to be a double album – we decided to get the whole gig in for once. There wasn't enough room on the previous ones for the whole gig – they were made back in the days of vinyl, see. There was some debate about what to include, like whether we should do 'Overkill' again – after all, it had been on the other live records. But then, this was a different line-up, so we figured it was valid. Besides, our fans are diehard archivists, many of them, and they love shit like that. I know a couple of them who've got five different versions of most of our albums from all over the world – a Japanese copy, Argentinian, German, etc. They're never going to play them, though, or even take them out of their wrappers. It's rather odd, if you ask me – why collect them if you're not gonna play them? But then, I collect knives and I'm not going to stab anybody, so I'm one to talk!

Incidentally, I have to say that some of the Japanese translations of my lyrics are incredible. On our first record, one song has the lyric, 'We came across a bad vibe/ Naked, grinding fear'. Their version of it was, 'We came across a pipeline and they kept trying to interfere' – fantastic! It's better than the original! It's wonderful stuff, like fucking Shakespeare. Almost.

Anyhow, we're nearly at the end of this resumé and still I digress. The live album: we recorded it during May, 1998 in Hamburg, Germany, at The Docks (a club, not a wharf!), and I'm proud to say it is completely overdub free (in fact, I said it on the liner notes). We chose Germany because the Germans have been such loyal fans of ours. They always rescued our ass when we were going down for the third time. They stuck with us, and we knew Hamburg would be a great audience. It's like Liverpool – a seafaring town, and you know where you are with a sailor! The record's called *Everything Louder Than Everyone Else* and was released in spring of 1999.

Our last album of the twentieth century, *We Are Motörhead*, opened up the new millennium for us. We went on the usual year-long tour, which was uneventful – or, rather, no more eventful than usual, other than touring Ireland, which we hadn't done in many years – until the end. We went back to Russia and our schedule was brutal – two eighteen-hour drives back-to-back and no days off for about a week. Then it took us forever to get out of Russia to Poland. We didn't get to Warsaw until eleven o'clock at night – our crew were loading into the venue at one in the morning! But the audience stuck around because it was the first time we'd been there. Then we had to drive all the way down to Austria . . . finally I collapsed. Touring is second nature for me, but a person's body can only take so much. It was the end of the tour anyway, so it didn't really matter.

After taking a month off, we began working on the new album, *Hammered*. Phil and Mikkey flew out to LA on 10 September

2001 – the best possible time anyone could have scheduled a plane flight considering what happened the next day! The guys wouldn't have been in danger, of course – the flight was non-stop from England to Los Angeles – but who knows when they would have arrived in town?

I suppose I should have my say about the terrorist attacks. I don't suppose it'll be a popular point of view, but they need to be put into some sort of perspective. They *were* a horrible tragedy, but also what happened in New York and Washington is the same thing that England and America did to Berlin every day for three years during World War II – and Germany did the same thing to England. And it happened in every other city in Germany and lots of cities in France and Poland, too. But most Americans don't think about that. They think everything starts and finishes with America. It is the first time this has ever happened to America, so you would expect them to overreact a bit. So let's not panic too much – it can be got over. *Anything* can be got over.

But back to *Hammered*. We recorded it in the Hollywood Hills at Chuck Reid's house (he was doing rap stuff before, and I think he's still getting over it!), with Thom Pannunzio producing. It was released in April of 2002. Within a month it had already sold more than the last two records combined and the tour has started off great. We're getting more money, we're getting in bigger places, so we're in excellent shape.

Things have been pretty good for me, and for Motörhead, over the past several years. I bet you thought I was going to say 'so I can't complain' but you should know me better than that by now!

There will always be a few things eating away at me. If you've gotten this far with the book, you may have noticed that over the past twenty-five or so years, Motörhead have made quite a few albums. So one thing that will always puzzle me are those people who, for some bizarre reason, think our career ended with *Ace of Spades*. Since I've moved to America, we've made our best records ever. They far surpass the ones that everybody remembers. Anyone I've played our latest records to has been astounded. But most people seem to have gone deaf, as far as we're concerned, somewhere around 1979 or 1980. 'Yo, dude, "Ace of Spades",' – that's the famous cry that has come to plague me. Occasionally I get really pissed off. It'd be nice if instead I heard someone say, 'Have you got anything new out? I'd like to hear it.' That would be much better. But no, they come up to me and say, 'You guys were so great!' And I say, 'Yeah? If we were so great, how come you stopped listening to us after 1980?' That's what I don't understand – the usual reply is, 'Oh, I got married.' People are fucking weird.

If you think you're too old for rock 'n' roll, then you are. And it even happens to musicians – you see them on stage and they sound great and everything, but it's almost like you can tell they're looking at their watch. 'Have we finished yet? Let's go back to the wife and poodle.' The reason that rock 'n' roll is such a young thing is . . . because it started with young people, obviously. But then they grew older and their attitude changed – they became more anxious to be accepted by the rank and file. I don't have any trouble with that myself because I know I'm not gonna be accepted by the rank and file, even in rock 'n' roll! So I was an outsider from Day One. But it's all right by me – somebody's gotta do it.

Like I was saying before, we've been making the best records of our career but hardly anybody seems to hear them. I keep waiting for us to be rediscovered, but it hasn't happened quite yet. But as long as I can keep making records and touring, I can soldier on. Not being a huge success doesn't bother me – after all, I have been there and done that. Sometimes people ask, 'What about these bands that you inspired making it over you?' They're not making it over us: they're just making it, and you get inspired by anything you listen to. It doesn't matter. It's just that kids are getting in bands and making it, like they always have. I don't have any problem with that. It's great that we inspired them – it proves we were right!

One thing I am very glad of is that I went through the sixties. People who didn't really don't know what they missed. We pushed a certain consciousness, a way of life and it was exciting – no AIDS, people weren't dying so much from drug abuse and it was truly a time of freedom and change. The only time I've seen any rebellion was in the fifties, sixties and early seventies. The rest of it you can keep. The kids now have attitudes more like the parents we were all trying to fight! They'll probably raise a bunch of fucking freaks. We raised a bunch of estate agents, a bunch of fucking accountants. God knows how we did it. I guess it's because most people give up. As I pointed out earlier, a lot of people say, 'I used to listen to Motörhead,' implying that when you grow up, you can't. Well, I'm glad they say that, man, 'cause I don't want no grown-ups listening to *me*. Grown-ups are the ones who fuck everything up. Since I was about twenty-five, nothing changed, except I got smarter and wiser and things have an effect on you. But I never thought I was any older, really. It was just a very long twenty-five! I can't imagine being fifty. If I'd lost all my hair or something, I might believe it, but I haven't.

I lost my father a couple of years ago – rather careless of me, don't you think? Actually, I lost both of them, my biological father and my stepfather. They died within seven months of each other. It was kind of sudden. You would think they had conspired just to piss us off! My stepfather, who saved us from the difficulties put on us by my real father, left me debts, and my real father left me money, so there you go. I didn't like either one of them, actually, and as far as I'm concerned, my biological dad will always be an asshole – he left a young girl on her own to bring up a child and she had her mother living with us as well! Fuck this 'Don't speak ill of the dead' shit! People don't become better when they're dead; you just talk about them as if they are. But it's not true! People are still assholes, they're just *dead* assholes!

Anyhow, I'm very much alive, and this is certainly not the last you will be hearing from me!

CHAPTER THIRTEEN

brave new world

What did I tell you?

Hello and welcome to the end of the book. As we are well past the deadline, I'll keep it short (about five foot two).

In my life so far, I have discovered that there are really only two kinds of people: those who are for you, and those who are against you. Learn to recognize them, for they are often and easily mistaken for each other.

Also, it seems that our brave new world is becoming less tolerant, spiritual and educated than it ever was when I was young; of course we are all susceptible to the 'good old days' syndrome, but this is not an example of it . . . Inherited hatred (i.e. hatred your parents schooled you in) is not only stupid, it is destructive –

why make your only driving force hate? Seems *really* fucking dumb to me.

Finally (and this is good advice), buy our albums. You won't be sorry!

Love,

Lem

VS

September, 2002

'He was just true to school and had more integrity in one finger than most rock and rollers.'

Slash, Guns N' Roses

'Lemmy was not only that kind of whiskey-drinking rock 'n' roll star, but he had the biggest heart and set such a great example because he was so kind to everyone . . .' Dave Grohl

EPILOGUE

It isn't easy. How could it be? Lemmy was nine feet of Kevlar-covered raw steel, with a quadruple dose of 'fuck you' coarsing through his veins. A universal presence. A tribal leader. Look, he was going to outlast us all: me, you, towns, cities and civilizations. We used to laugh that when all was gone, when the world was levelled by whatever will reset the clock to zero, there would be giant cockroaches and Lemmy (who would most probably be riding one to some untapped underground oasis of liquor and smokes). His dying on 28 December 2015 was not part of the plan, regardless of health issues, regardless of anything. It just wasn't part of the deal.

Yet here I am, entrusted to write an epilogue for his excellent autobiography, *White Line Fever* (penned with the wonderful Janiss Garza), requested to update you, dear reader, as to what has been going on in 'Lemmy Land' since 2002, when the book ends.

Why me? Back in 1982, I wrote to Lemmy asking if he would do an interview for my school magazine *Hollyvine* (four pieces of highly unremarkable, photocopied A4 paper stapled together, not what would be considered a major PR coup). Lemmy not only granted fifteen-year-old-me the interview, he met me at the studio door with a pint of vodka and orange, ushered me to a chair in front of the control desk, showed me where the volume button was and blasted the *Another Perfect Day* album which Motörhead were completing. He also let me hang around for the entire night. It wasn't too much longer before I would meet him again, this time at the Dalymount Festival in Dublin. I had managed to bluff my way into an internship with *Sounds* magazine (at that time a giant music weekly) and had further managed to wangle a feature assignment. It was an unashamed, passionate, fan-boy rant about why the *Another Perfect Day* album deserved far more respect than it was getting from fans and critics alike. Lemmy had greatly appreciated this spirited, teenage defence of his work, thus I found myself backstage and grabbed in a headlock, my nose squarely planted in his armpit – Lemm was wearing a sleeveless shirt. It was the unique, unforgettable scent of a free-wheeling lifestyle that has remained ingrained in my consciousness to this day. He also robustly thanked me, which was like getting a nod from God. These two experiences thoroughly beggared my teenage belief, and gave me a platform of confidence which helped support a move to the US barely four years later.

If it hadn't been for Mister Ian 'Lemmy' Kilmister, I would not have gone on to be a writer for over three decades, and enjoy a career that has seen me scribble for the likes of *Sounds* magazine, *Kerrang!* and the *San Francisco Chronicle*, among many others, before landing a wonderful position as Metallica's staff scribe for their *So What!* publication in the late 1990s. It was also to be the beginning of a friendship, and working relationship, which continued until the very end of Lemm's life and never wavered.

It should, of course, be him doing this final piece of writing in his book. I've checked my phone a few times to make sure he hasn't sent me a text reminding me of that fact. But obviously, since I accepted the (impossible) task, there haven't been any.

But please *know* that *every* word I write will be written as if Lemmy himself were not only reading it, but offering his own comments.

I hope both you, and he, approve.

Steffan Chirazi
April 2016

Thanks to Robert Kiewit for his invaluable eye. *He'd* be happy it was looking (and maybe even the other one was too!).

THE FINAL SUCCESSFUL YEARS

When Lemmy wrote the last chapter in this book in September 2002 (which was indeed short, about five foot two – hey, that's his joke!), he lamented a world that was becoming dumber, less educated and more hate-driven, all things Lemmy refused to tolerate. He was not to know that the ensuing decade-plus would finally reveal a world outside Motörhead's immediate fan base that was not only ready to hear what he had been saying for the better part of forty years, but to start appreciating him as a mould-breaking icon. He probably broke some other serious moulds too, spore-ish little things that would've been of great interest to the medical community, hiding under piles of stuff in the uniquely cluttered Harratt Street apartment, but enough digression!

Back in the early 2000s, Lemmy was as robustly disgusted about the state of the world as ever, 'Brave New World' from the 2002's *Hammered* album growling, 'So this is the beginning, as the new century dawns/ The world's a better place for you and me . . . Living in a constant state of dull frustrated rage/ The innocent shot daily in the street'. Yet far from sounding like an angry old man, by remaining true to himself as he always had, Lemmy was about to become cooler than ever (something, it must be made clear, he did not give one shit about). As Motörhead continued to tour in support of *Hammered* through 2003 (including a six-week tour of the US with Iron Maiden and Dio), new free-range youths were starting to find the band thanks to their work with Triple H and the WWE, and 'Ace of Spades' being on Tony Hawk's PlayStation game *Pro Skater 3*. At the same time, the 'arties' and 'musical literati' were finally starting to peer in his direction.

In February 2004, Motörhead were invited to play the Royal Opera House in London as part of a promotional initiative called 'Visit London's One Amazing Week', to encourage tourism to the capital city, marking the first time a band of their immense sonic proportions had nearly shattered the glass. The message was clear: Motörhead were about to enjoy new cultural relevance, and suddenly, a wider audience became interested in the history of this 'Lemmy', the man who was in the first British band to play behind the Iron Curtain, the man who had roadied for Hendrix, the man who had helped propel extreme psychedelic rock into British brains and the man who had created the loudest rock 'n' roll group in history. Lemmy's rich way with words was also receiving overdue, wider attention. British national newspaper the *Guardian* published a major feature on him in 2004, with the *Independent* and others following suit in 2005.

Lemmy was also starting to more vigorously explore his own musical roots. Having participated on an Elvis tribute album in 2000 – Swing Cats' *A Special Tribute to Elvis* – with guitarist Danny B. Harvey and drummer Slim Jim Phantom (ex-the Stray Cats), the trio found an effortlessness in their work together that convinced them a side project was well worth their time. The Head Cat was not simply a tribute to heroes such as Buddy Holly, Eddie Cochran and Johnny Cash, it was an avenue of expression that gave Lemmy enormous happiness. Far from interfering with Motörhead, there is a strong argument for stating that it helped the band continue their resurgence, as Lemmy was able to switch gears and drop into a sound which was part of his DNA but which was never going to have prominent expression in Motörhead's heavier music (as heard on 2011's *Walk The Walk . . . Talk The Talk*).

This was also the time when Lemmy started to do some solo recordings with the objective of one day releasing a solo album. Focusing strictly on music and styles he liked, collaborations took place between Lemmy and Dave Grohl, the Reverend Horton Heat, the Damned, Joan Jett and Skew Siskin. It would end up being a project pursued at some leisure, it must be said, but Lemmy enjoyed doing it and had planned to bring it to full, final fruition.

Now that he was having some fun exploring with the side-projects, Lemmy's focus on the next few Motörhead albums was sharper than ever. *Inferno*, released in 2004, was every bit as explosive as you'd hope, producer Cameron Webb giving the band a new edge and proving more than able to handle their sarcastic Englishisms, yet the album also delivered a wonderful rock 'n' roll moment with the acoustic 'Whorehouse Blues', Lemmy taking up harmonica duties. Dave Grohl's Probot project, featuring the unfeasibly wonderful 'Shake Your Blood' collaboration with Lemmy, was also released. Lemmy also found time to exercise some of that deep well of humour, with Motörhead reworking their song 'You'd Better Run' to 'You'd Better Swim' for the *SpongeBob SquarePants* movie soundtrack.

In 2005, Motörhead finally won a richly deserved Grammy, albeit for their cover of Metallica's 'Whiplash', and the Motörenaissance was clicking into top gear by the time 2006's *Kiss of Death* was entering the German Top 5. The following year, Motörhead blitzed the Royal Festival Hall in London after being invited by alternative superstar Jarvis Cocker (from Pulp) to the Meltdown Festival. Traditionally curated by figures of great artistic respect (Nick Cave, Laurie Anderson, David Byrne and David Bowie were among previous curators), Cocker's choice of Motörhead to open the festival was rich proof that they had broken into the rare air of artistically venerated, and universally appreciated, bad-asses.

In 2006, Lemmy and the Head Cat saw 2000's *Lemmy, Slim Jim & Danny B*, re-released as *Fool's Paradise*, which caught the ear of writer and filmmaker Wes Orshoski. Together with film-making partner Greg Olliver, Orshoski pitched the idea of creating a documentary on Lemmy. With the proviso that the film would embrace his entirety as a human being and not simply dwell on the 'easier' topics (which happily dovetailed with what the young filmmakers wanted to do), work began in 2007. The film would take three years to complete, but when it was finally released, *Lemmy* the movie (complete with the tagline '49% Motherfucker, 51% Son of a Bitch') received widespread praise and catapulted Lemmy yet further into the platinum-plated cultural icon arena he deserved to be in.

The albums and tours were continual as Lemmy did what he loved the most and lived in the bus lounge for months at a time. *Motörizer* (2008) was a teeth-smasher, the breakneck 'Rock Out' showing Lemmy wasn't about to go easy on the ear, and even slower, bluesier fare like 'One Short Life' was swaddled in thick and heavy aural gravy. *The Wörld Is Yours* (2010) continued in the same vein, with Lemmy showing some of his strongest lyrics yet on the likes of 'Brotherhood of Man' ('Blood on all our hands, we cannot hope to wash them clean/ History is mystery, do you know what it means?/ Slaughter, kill and fighting still, and murdered where we stand/ Our legacy is lunacy, brotherhood of man'). A thirty-fifth anniversary tour saw shows in New York, Manchester, UK and Santiago, Chile, which were recorded and released in 2011 as *The Wörld Is Ours, Volume 1: Everywhere Further than Everyplace Else* (Volume 2, *Anyplace Crazy as Anywhere Else*, was recorded at Wacken and released in 2012).

The pace of life was as it always had been, and Lemmy continued to barrel through it with consummate ease. *Perhaps* it was getting a *little* calmer backstage. Over the last few years, Lemmy had come to appreciate even more the peaceful environs of his dressing room, where he could quietly continue to devour books on all manner of subjects, play games on his iPad and sometimes play some tunes. His room continued to be a place where friends would drop in for a chat, a shot or few of bourbon and some rich discussion. A visit to Lemmy was always like visiting a rare, unique jewel; he was a man who steadfastly refused to be anybody's fool, who robustly rejected the idea that *he* should change in order to be more 'popular' and a man whose gold-plated integrity and avuncular warmth continued to inspire (and re-inspire) all visitors.

The darkest spot of these years came in 2011 when Michael 'Wurzel' Burston died on 9 July of heart disease at sixty-one years old. In recent years there had been a mending of fences, and his passing hit Lemmy hard. Like the passing of Ronnie James Dio a year earlier, Girlschool's Kelly Johnson in 2007 and Michelle Meldrum in 2008, it was a reminder to Lemmy that no one got out of this alive, and that some were rudely taken far earlier than seemed fair.

In February 2012, on the *Gigantour* tour with Megadeth, Motörhead were forced to cancel their last four shows due to Lemmy suffering from upper-respiratory issues and laryngitis, but apart from this isolated setback their roadwork continued untroubled, including the US *Mayhem* ampitheatre tour with Slayer and Slipknot. Lemmy even got the chance to meet, and pay tribute to, one of his biggest idols, Chuck Berry, at an all-star tribute show for Berry in Cleveland, Ohio. But as another successful Motöryear drew to a close, matters were about to change significantly. Lemmy had, it must be said, stampeded through life as healthy as a herd of wildebeest sweeping majestically across the plain. No major worries and no scares, which, given the 'all-in' freedom with which he had imbibed, placed him firmly in the 'science-wants-a-look' category. So when his health *did* finally present a challenge, it was blunt, indignant and scary.

(Fighting) 'Til the End

It was Lemmy's heart that first started to loudly voice its discontent, appearing suddenly to be furiously overworked and out of rhythm, which (in turn) taxed his whole system. So in early 2013, Lemmy went into hospital to get a defibrillator. With this being his first serious health condition, Lemmy was feeling a new emotion – vulnerability. But with a strong network of support around him, as well as a few close friends stopping by to help reassure him that he was still Lemmy and no stinkin' defibrillator was gonna hold him back, he made his way back to fitness.

If asked in interviews, Lemmy would tell people he'd had 'heart problems' but he was absolutely *not* about to put the full scope of his personal health into the public arena, chiefly because he did not want people endlessly saying things like 'get better' and doling out what he would've considered uncomfortable levels of sympathy. 'Not worth fussing about' would perhaps be the best way to phrase his thoughts, and he also had little interest in physically showing a depleted self to the fans. Remember, this is a man who always took great pride in his appearance, who was still absolutely committed to his hand-made cowboy boots, tight black jeans and black shirts.

However, even Lemmy knew deep down that you can only play poker at the reaper's table for so long before your bluff starts to get called. Ute Kromrey, Motörhead's European media and marketing maestro, was starting to take on a role as Lemmy's 'nurse' on European tours, working with Lemmy's personal assistants to make sure his increasing daily health matters were taken care of.

The pattern would appear to be that after a bout of health work, Lemmy would roar back into things at full tilt, but there was a slow, steady erosion of his system that was frankly unremarkable given the decades of freewheeling living it had supported. Probably the biggest contributor to this erosion was the further development of Type II diabetes, a real hammer blow for someone who sipped Jack Daniels and Coke like water (in fact, far more than he ever drank H_2O) as well as a diet that was not especially 'low-carb'. It was suggested to him that he start using Diet Coke instead of Coke, and he scoffed at the idea, steadfastly refusing to do so and quickly spotting it whenever an assistant tried to substitute it. Another problem was that whenever Lemmy *did* embark upon a healthy dietary path, it would be carried to the sort of extreme which became counter-productive. Blueberries were once suggested as a fine alternative food to graze on, but Lemmy would end up eating punnets of the buggers in a day, thus undoing their benefits! Rome, so someone whispered once, was not built in a day.

Lemmy continued to make some lifestyle changes, sitting on a LifeCycle bike for twenty to thirty minutes a day and starting to cut down the amount of Jack and Coke he drank, as well as the number of ciggies he smoked. His legs and feet became further issues, numbness and pain each taking their toll with increasing regularity (he would not, however, hear of ditching his famous cowboy boots for flat-soled affairs). The heart also continued to be an issue, and as Lemmy's system compensated for problems related to both that and the diabetes, there was nothing left in the tank to deal with relatively straightforward healing. A fall resulted in bruising of the hip, which in turn came to be termed a 'severe haematoma' (in layman's terms, a large bruise) and led him to be ordered off the road by the doctor for immediate rest, to allow the hip to heal.

A return to the European festival run went well, and with dates placed only around weekends, there were always several days off between shows. On the one hand, this was a good thing, Lemmy having plenty of time between performances to rest. However, increasingly, there was the underlying feeling that perhaps there was a little too long between shows if Lemmy was going to be out there at all. Where we might think rest and relaxation, the truth is that for a musician, days off are simply days spent sitting in a hotel, days where the playing hands can get soft without regular shows.

In June, it became obvious that Lemmy had not rested sufficiently back at the start of the year and now his doctors were unequivocally telling him to stop, go home and recuperate properly. Begrudgingly, he agreed to throw in the towel on the rest of the summer 2013 dates, saying, 'I'd like to thank everyone who wished me well; it was a tough decision for me as I don't like to disappoint the fans, especially in times where the economy is bad and people spent their money to see us.'

Rest up he did, yet the situation wore on, and he decided that he wanted to try and play the Wacken Open Air Festival on 2 August. Currently in its thirty-second year and recognized as one of the biggest metal festivals in the world, Wacken annually sells every one of its 80,000 tickets within weeks of its on-sale date, regardless of the headline acts. This enormous celebration of rock and metal culture has consistently attracted the likes of Iron Maiden, Ozzy Osbourne, Judas Priest, Deep Purple and Saxon, yet for many, Motörhead were the talisman whenever they played. Opinions around Lemmy's health were firmly split but, regardless, arrangements were made to do the show. It was as if Lemmy himself needed to see and feel, once and for all, that this was a very real issue that would require lifestyle modification from here on out. And Lemmy needed to hear it definitively from the most important person involved – himself.

The weather in Wacken that day was unfeasibly hot, high nineties with no sign of dropping and a wretchedly high level of humidity. Lemmy stayed in his heavily air-conditioned dressing room/cabin as he always did, reading a little bit, entertaining the odd old friend who ambled by and ghosted in, his tour assistant Ian Gainer keeping a close eye. It is true to say he didn't look as strong as, say, a decade earlier, but Lemmy nonetheless looked like he was ready to test his maker, ignoring much of the quiet concern from both the crew and Ulrike Rudolph, the UDR label boss who had been a loyal friend and integral part of the Motörhead family for over two decades.

But again, *Lemmy needed to know*, plus there was his underlying belief that he felt so bad about being forced to cancel the summer tour that this simply *had* to be done, both for the fans and the Wacken festival itself (one Lemmy always loved). 'I've been ill recently and I've come onstage to play some rock 'n' roll and fuck myself some more!' he roared at the audience, before launching into 'I Know How to Die' and striding into 'Damage Case'. No one on either side of the stage barrier found the oppressive heat easy, and added to his own condition, the gig was turning into a marathon for Lemmy.

Never one to do what he was told, as 'The Chase Is Better than the Catch' ended, Lemmy decided for himself it was time to stop. A combination of overwhelming fatigue and a genuine fear he was pushing himself beyond safe limits were the critical factors in his decision. He made his way back to the dressing room, where he gathered himself slowly. Of course, given the nature of the moment, cell-phones and websites were exploding with speculation as to the state of his mortal coil. Truth be told, Lemmy had pushed himself to a limit and received the answer that perhaps even he hadn't believed until that moment. His life would have to change if he wanted to continue not just playing, but living. However, he did not suffer a collapse, a failure or a systemic breakdown that evening; he simply pushed himself to the red line and stopped. Despite the heart, despite the heat and despite the powerlessness he felt after '. . . Catch', Lemmy *still* retained control of the moment. He also had his answer.

On returning to the US, he agreed that it was time to throw himself as fully into lifestyle modification as he feasibly could without feeling that he was giving life up. He would still need to take speed in order to maintain his day, but it was another white substance that was proving most dangerous to him – sugar – as well as carbohydrates in general. His meals were prepared under the jurisdiction of both his doctors and his loyal girlfriend Cheryl (a trained chef). He continued to get on a LifeCycle every day to keep things moving, he switched from Jack and Coke to vodka and orange juice (the sugar in orange juice notwithstanding!), and he started to get more sleep and general rest. It was obvious to all, including the man himself, that Lemmy was dealing with ailments and certainly paying back some of the tax on decades of no-sleep-no-compromise living. However, he was determined to continue. As much as he might be heard complaining about things on occasion, his overall, consistently expressed sentiment revolved around what else would he do if not play? What else would he do if not make music? What else would he do if not tour?

Lemmy also carried deep inside him the 'team' angle. Motörhead had always been both a team and family to Lemmy and, as the patriarch, he simply could not bear to consider letting them down. Guilt had already taken an ugly toll on his spirits with the date cancellations of 2013, and however much those around him tried to let him know there was nothing to feel guilty for, Lemmy (being Lemmy) always carried some of it. Most of all, Lemmy did not want the fans to feel let down. It was quite a dilemma. Showing weakness was absolutely not on the cards, yet stopping altogether due to health issues was also not an option. And so whilst the adjustments Lemmy made to his life might not have been as drastic as perhaps what was considered necessary at the time, for him they were enormous. Amidst all of this came one more major change in Lemmy's life – his departure from the Harratt Street apartment to a larger, brand new and squeaky clean condo a stone's throw away. A 'fresh' start indeed.

With Cheryl caring for him, Lemmy recuperated and regenerated as best he could. The *Aftershock* album, recorded at the beginning of the year and intended for a summer release, came out in October 2013 to strong reviews. Their first album in three years, *Aftershock* was pure, unadulterated and defiant Motörhead music to the core, unashamedly rocking blues influences as always, with Lemmy conjuring even more impossibly eloquent yet imperiously angry lyrics ('Silence when you speak to me'!). The album entered the US Billboard charts at No. 22, and the traditional winter tour of Europe beckoned. However, Lemmy's health continued to present complications as both he and doctors battled an equilibrium between his diabetes, heart condition and a sustainable lifestyle. The tour was rescheduled for early 2014, but still his body refused to cooperate and the band were forced to cancel the dates altogether.

An invitation to play the prestigious Coachella Valley Music and Arts Festival in Indio, California in April had been accepted, two shows on two weekends in front of the ultimate American hipster audience, so everything was channelled to see if Lemmy would be able to make them. In terms of Motörhead's US reputation, landing a slot at Coachella was a huge affair. A cross-genre cornucopia of both the hottest acts in music and those considered worthy of eternal veneration, Motörhead's Coachella gigs saw them on the same bill as artists like Outkast, Lorde and Beck, further solidifying their cultural immortality with both critics and non-fans. Warm-up shows the previous week in San Francisco and a real confidence-booster at Club Nokia in LA left Lemmy feeling ready to saddle up again, and besides Coachella, the band headed to Europe for their almost annually anticipated summer festival appearances, before returning to inaugurate the first Motörhead Motörboat cruise ('The Loudest Boat in the World').

It has been suggested in some quarters that Lemmy was pushed beyond his will to do things. Such thoughts are simply an insult to the man. *Anyone* who believes Lemmy didn't do what he wanted clearly has no firm grasp on who he was. *Of course* he considered others, and there is little doubt that he felt guilty about cancelling shows. And *of course* he was tired more easily, not as strong as before and often needed to rest heavily between shows (Lemmy was finally getting fully acquainted with the word 'sleep', one which had certainly not featured heavily in the vocabulary of his life prior). However, quite simply, this was what Lemmy did. This was his life. This was his chosen path, and whether driven by instinct, desire or (as is most likely) a firm mixture of both, Lemmy was always going to play as much as damn possible. It had not escaped him that Motörhead's cultural renaissance saw them enjoying their greatest success for decades, that venues were increasing in size and selling out, and he for one wanted to enjoy it as much as he could. Perhaps the one thing that caused him problems was that he had gone from a towering figure of strength to someone whose health was a main point of conversation. Lemmy never had any time for sympathy directed towards him, and despite his overall appreciation of people's good wishes, it would undoubtedly have stung him to have been on the receiving end of 'get well soon' sentiments so often.

November 2014 saw Motörhead do a smaller-than-usual European tour with friends the Damned and Skew Siskin, after which the band took five weeks off before getting together in 2015 to make a new album. The writing and recording was not a fun time for the band. Producer Cameron Webb insisted that the majority of work be done live in the studio, and this meant all the band together and recording in the same room. This was new and somewhat uneasy territory that initially led to discomfort amongst the group. Yet *Bad Magic* was Motörhead's best album in a decade, and both critics and fans raced to give it accolades, Lemmy's opening battle cry of 'Victory or Die!' announcing their loudest work for a decade with a vitriolic vigour that showed him as angry as ever. Lemmy's ability to articulate social and societal concerns was razor sharp ('Look around and see the soldiers, see them marching off to war/ Take a careful look as they swing by/ They're all heroes but they don't know what they're fighting for/ That's the spirit victory or die') and as a whole, the album's lyrics were imbued with defiance and contempt for the system, liars, cheats and bastards. By hitting the Top 5 of virtually every European country (Lemmy particularly appreciated the No. 1 slot in Germany), and achieving a Top 40 place in the US charts, the album, which had caused so much stress being made, was proving its point.

With the fortieth anniversary plans being discussed, Lemmy pondered several suggestions, including resurrecting 1982's *Iron Fist* tour stage (which was lowered from the venue ceiling where it was rigged by four enormous chains, with lights underneath its front edge) and flying the famous, hugely popular and newly updated 'Bomber' lighting rig one more time. The Bomber won, although unlike the late seventies when the original rig made its debut, Lemmy was not about to perch himself on the Bomber's nose as it ducked and weaved around the stage.

Although he was certainly thinner than usual, Lemmy's eyes still packed a sparkle and his tongue remained sharply engaged with that clever, sarcastic wit. Like anyone staring down seventy, he was most certainly imperious and somewhat withering when it came to evaluating certain 'advances' in modern life. Even though he used an iPhone and iPad, Lemmy had little time for extolling virtues of the internet, and almost seemed resigned to the fact that overall, appreciation of craftsmanship and quality had been shoved aside by the incessant pace of the modern world. Visitors to the condo would sometimes find themselves looking at, say, a WWII dagger, with Lemmy waxing lyrical about the craftsmanship involved in both the manufacture and engraving on the piece. Decidedly NOT made in Hong Kong! And he still always had time for a great voice and genuine music to his ears, with Skew Siskin, Skunk Anansie, Evanescence and others all getting played whenever guests were around, and he continued to keep an eye and ear open for young road warriors. It *is* fair to observe that Lemmy's overall sense of road gusto was waning, yet stopping was illogical, as touring was what he did. Lemmy was doing his bit to keep the train rolling. Onstage, he had started to wear very stylish white leather creepers, while offstage he had really cut down even more on his smoking and drinking, and wasn't going out nearly as much as he used to.

The year 2015 was going well as Motörhead approached 26 June and their early evening Glastonbury Festival spot behind the Libertines and Florence & the Machine on the Pyramid Stage. It was, for many reasons, a definitive moment in Motörhead's history. Having spent their early career as a band, lifestyle and attitude of many (and not just a genre), here they were in their fortieth year coming back to claim their rightful throne as a pioneering institution within British rock 'n' roll history. With their performance broadcast live by the BBC, and the band stalking through a thundering, raucous and particularly bone-rattling performance, Lemmy's already considerable legend got perhaps its greatest British mainstream exposure yet. The *Daily Telegraph* observed that Motörhead were 'a perfect fit, the kind of band that sound better in the mud and rain', whilst the *The Times* proclaimed that 'early Friday evening at Glastonbury 2015 belonged to Motörhead' and 'it was refreshing to have an alternative to all that peace, love and sustainable living'. However, it was the *NME* (not especially known as friends of Motörhead over the years) who perhaps put it best when they roared, 'Ian "Lemmy" Kilmister strides on, chakras defiantly unaligned and looking, as always, cool as all mirror-shaded, wart-faced, hairy fuck.' The respect was also blooming back in the US. In August, Motörhead were officially honoured by the LA City Council for their fortieth anniversary, something Lemmy was very proud of given his twenty-five years as a resident.

Things were, however, gradually getting harder.

General wear, tear and fatigue had got their claws into him, and Lemmy would quietly ponder the irony of a band enjoying one of their greatest eras of popularity only for his health to increasingly interfere. Still, he soldiered on, the rest of the year's summer festivals going well, before the fall US tour. This proved to be an uphill struggle, with Lemmy cutting short shows in Salt Lake City and Austin due to respiratory issues related to altitude sickness, and the Denver show being cancelled altogether. Still, after some rest, Lemmy rebounded strongly to finish off the dates and also spend a week on the Motörboat cruise out of Miami.

Perhaps because of his own radiant self-belief and strength, everyone from band to management to loved ones and friends simply thought Lemmy's recurring health issues were down to a combination of manageable ailments and good ol'-fashioned age. Questions were asked and doctors consulted, but Lemmy was keen to see how the autumn European tour went.

The tour started well, with both Phil Campbell and Mikkey Dee feeling the shows were as strong as ever and that, save the occasional forgotten lyric (which happens to many musicians who refuse a video prompter), Lemmy was performing well. Cheryl was on the road, as was Ute, so Lemmy was well attended to. All was going fine, when on 11 November Lemmy received word of Phil 'Philthy Animal' Taylor's death. It was a hammer blow. Taylor had been struggling for some months, and only days earlier, Lemmy had spoken with him on the phone. Yet despite knowing how ill he had been, Taylor's passing was deeply upsetting, the death of a former band mate and old pal surely bringing his own increasingly fragile health into sharper focus.

The European tour was not only sold out but was taking place in some of Motörhead's largest venues in years, and the band went on to play two sold-out shows in Munich which were recorded for future release (the plan had been to also record two sold-out shows at the London Apollo, aka Hammersmith Odeon, in January 2016). There was even time to cancel a couple of shows and play them at the end of the leg – this time nothing to do with Lemmy's health!

Meanwhile, in LA, the decision had been made some time back to throw a seventieth birthday bash at the Whiskey-A-Go-Go on 13 December. Friends would gather for the event and enjoy rock 'n' roll music reflecting Lemmy's tastes, from musicians such as Matt Sorum, Slash, Rob Trujillo, Slim Jim Phantom, Danny B. Harvey, Whitfield Crane, Scott Ian, Sebastian Bach, Steve Vai, Billy Idol, Chris Jericho, Bob Kulick, Billy Duffy, Steve Jones, Zakk Wylde and son Paul.

For many who had not seen Lemmy for a couple of months, his gauntness was a shock to the eyes. He looked worn out, very tired, very slow, and his speech seemed a little harder than usual to decipher. There again, this was a nearly seventy-year-old man who had, only forty-eight hours prior, returned from a full European tour! The party went well, but Lemmy sat and watched it all from the balcony, not getting up to jam with anyone, prefer-ring to listen to the music and also read a book.

Lemmy agreed to go to the hospital two days later, as he was still not feeling anywhere close to recovered. More tests were done, as well as a CAT scan of the brain. The tragic results came through quickly. It was all beyond fathomable. Lemmy had an aggressive and terminal cancer. The darkest of undetected pas-sengers had hidden amidst other ailments, somehow evading detection despite all the medical attention Lemmy had been receiving. It was everywhere – in his brain, his neck, his body. The prognosis was that he would have somewhere between two to six months. There was no coming back. No one close to the man was sure what to do. In the early afternoon of 26 December, his management team (Todd Singerman, Shelly Berggren, Dixon Matthews) and his physician went to the condo, where Cheryl and Paul were already with him.

Always a brave and practical man, Lemmy took the news far better than expected, a minor (understandable) grumble about the short amount of time left, but otherwise an unbelievably measured acceptance of the situation. Lemmy was asked what he wanted to do with regards to letting people know. Did he want to at all? Should only a few people be told? Would he want to see people? Lemmy was comfortable with people being told he had cancer, he said there was no reason to hide it from anyone, that if a few close friends wanted to visit, sure, why not? Slowly, the horrible task of sharing the information was carried out. Only a month earlier, the recipients of this grim news had been receiving calls inviting them to Lemmy's seventieth birthday bash at the Whiskey-A-Go-Go in Hollywood. Now they were gently being advised to make plans to come and say goodbye in the coming weeks.

If the terminal cancer results had been an enormous shock, the news which broke just two days later, on the afternoon of 28 December, was unequivocally heartbreaking. One of Lemmy's old friends, Mikeal Maglieri, from the Rainbow Bar and Grill, had been visiting. Lemmy had finished playing his favourite video game, Megatouch (brought from the Rainbow to the condo), and had gone to lie down for a rest when he just . . . went . . . away. It had only been seventeen days since Lemmy had walked offstage at the Max-Schmeling-Halle in Berlin.

Within hours the tragic news was viral. Every major news network from Fox News, CNN and CBS in the US, to the BBC and ITV in the UK, were running reports, and the internet simply blew up. Hundreds upon hundreds of people descended upon Lemmy's home-from-home, the Rainbow, and in the next seventy-two hours reporting became even more intense, as the world's press carried a steady stream of obituaries, tributes and mournful headlines. Perhaps the most fitting was French daily *Libération*'s coarse, yet perfect, front page – 'FUCK!', one Lemmy would've surely chuckled at.

His peers were quick to offer tributes. Ozzy Osbourne was one of the first to express his deep sadness. 'Lost one of my best friends, Lemmy, today. He will be sadly missed. He was a warrior and a legend.' Metallica also paid tribute: 'Lemmy, you are one of the primary reasons this band exists. We're forever grateful for all of your inspiration.' Alice Cooper, Queen's Brian May, Gene Simmons from Kiss, Iron Maiden, Nikki Sixx of Mötley Crüe, Judas Priest and so many others also took to social media to express their condolences. In the coming days, so many memories and thoughts were shared that they all became a blur.

The memorial that took place on 9 January 2016 was not an easy thing to plan. Lemmy was not, to put it mildly, a fan of churches, so the venue had to be flexible. Having moved to LA all those years ago, and spent the subsequent years extolling the virtues of his chosen home, that was the city in which Lemmy wanted to be laid to rest, and Forest Lawn Cemetery in the Hollywood Hills (where Ronnie James Dio was buried) was the best choice. Furthermore, with millions of fans in mourning, it needed to be decided what Lemmy would have wanted from such an 'event', if anything at all? A celebration of his life as much as possible. A memorial. And a touch of 'party' too; Jack Daniels shots were served to all who attended (there was enough for seconds) and the Bonzo Dog Band played gleefully over the PA as those who had come to both pay their respects, and celebrate his life, filed in. At the front of the chapel, amidst the flowers, were Lemmy's amp stacks, urn (a wonderful piece of work styled after one of Lemmy's famous hats), boots, booze, Motörhead photos and a bass sitting at the front of the chapel. The decision was made to stream the memorial free via YouTube, allowing hundreds of thousands to gather in their respective localities and hear the tributes and stories told by guests.

Lemmy would've been quietly proud to see how many of his

peers and pals came to offer their thoughts. Ozzy Osbourne, Lars Ulrich, Dave Grohl, Slash, Rob Trujillo, Rob Halford, Triple H, Dee Snider, Geezer Butler, Gene Simmons, Jerry Cantrell, Mike Inez, Whit Crane, Slim Jim, Scott Ian, Duff McKagen, Nik Turner – the list of fellow musicians and entertainers who attended was enormous, with many more sending their respects. Mikkey Dee shared some personal thoughts, whilst Phil Campbell was too ill to travel but made sure to send a suitably 'Lemmy-humoured' flower arrangement! For the packed chapel it was tough yet cathartic to hear members of Lemmy's Motörfamily speak, like Roger De Souza, Ian Gainer, Ute Kromrey and Dixon, while son Paul delivered a stirring eulogy. The final word belonged to Lemmy himself – one of his assistants, Steve Luna, hitting one of his Rickenbacker 4001s and turning up the volume to recreate the 'end of show' feedback, before the memorial concluded back at the Rainbow. There, friends, family and fans talked and laughed and cried and drank, but the truth is that beneath it all was utter disbelief. Lemmy was not simply an artist, not just a musician, he was a lifestyle and an adjective in his own right, the quintessential forerunner of loud, fast, free and truly liberated living, the sort of person who appealed across genres, genders, cultures, professions and continents. The void his passing had left was simply too big for his family, friends and fans to process.

In the days, weeks and months which have followed, everyone who loved Lemmy has said the same thing: 'It doesn't feel real. It remains an abstract.'

But even though Lemmy . . .

A man of almost indecent decency

A man of tremendous wit and wisdom

A man of words and beautiful language

A man of integrity

A man of honour

A man of himself and a man of the people

A man of warmth and a good man

A man who once tried a year or so without facial hair after 1969 and realized it didn't work

A man whose legs didn't see sunshine until 1992

A man who once stored a gig plate of cheesy scallops in a bus bin and retrieved it twelve hours later for breakfast

A man who could tell you everything about the SS *Titanic* – *everything*!

A man who for decades watched a telly with a few large bullet holes in its speaker grille (well, they *looked* like bullet holes but he hates guns, so who knows?)

A man who enjoyed assembling those little toys inside Kinder eggs

A man whose knowledge of world history would shame most professors

A man who loved Spike Milligan, Harry Secombe, Peter Sellers and *Monty Python*

A man who, for all his grumbles about mankind's problems, ALWAYS had time for everyone

A man who did not tolerate bastards or weasels

A man who loved and appreciated women

A man who could write a wonderful lyric

A man who could play a beautiful bass

A man who changed the rules in all the right ways

A man who was a lifestyle and made it OK for *you* to live *yours* without judgement

A man who was totemic for so many, a hero . . .

. . . has left the building, Ian Fraser 'Lemmy' Kilmister remains a legend. Born to lose, he lived to win, and he continues with his legacy to make sure that many, many more do exactly the same, whatever their chosen path might be. So please … raise a glass and turn the bastard UP! He would expect nothing else.

INDEX

acid (LSD) 57, 58–9, 69, 73, 82, 83, 84, 90, 94
acupucture 135
Adverts, The 119
album covers 81, 230–1
Aldridge, Tommy 148
Alice Cooper 90, 204, 205–6, 236, 237
Alice in Chains 257, 258
Alice, Nina C. 160
Allen, Ronald 200
Almighty, The 232
Amen Corner 57
Amon Duul II 89
Anderson, Dave 71
Andromeda 30
Araya, Tom 211–12
Arnold, P. P. 60
Artwoods, The 26

Bad News 199
Baker, Ginger 26, 57
Bandwagon Heavy Metal Soundhouse, London 133
Banker, Doug 238, 239–40, 247

Barker, Clive 258
Barrett, Syd 57
Barron, Duane 276
Beach Boys, The 25, 42
    'Here Today' (from Pet Sounds) 42
Beatles, The 23, 27–30
    Sergeant Pepper 57
Beck, Jeff 126, 207, 222, 277
Beirut, Lebanon 64
belladonna (atropine sulphate) 65–6
Bender, Ariel (Luther Grosvenor) 108–9
Benllech, Anglesey 8
Bennett, Susan (Sue) 63–4
Benson, Howard 262–3, 263–4, 269, 276, 281–2
Berry, Chuck 34, 116
    'Louie Louie' 116, 121
Bidmead, Guy 187, 203, 211
Biff (Saxon singer) 135
Big Three, The, 30
    'Zip-A-Dee-Doo-Dah' 24

Bill Haley and the Comets 12
 'Razzle *Dazzle*' 12
 'Rock Around the Clock' 12, 15
 'See You Later Alligator' 12
 'Skinny Minnie' 42
Birds, The 24–5, 27, 55, 102
Black Sabbath 100, 266, 267
 .naps 260
Blackpool Tower 53–4
Blue, Vicki 128
Blue Oyster Cult 101, 122, 151
Bolton, Roger 121
Bolton Wanderers 7
Bond, Graham 26, 56–7
Bonzo Dog Doodah Band 78, 115
Boone, Pat 211
Bosnia 50
Bowie, David 91
Boys Don't Cry, 'I Wanna Be a
 Cowboy' 198
Bradford City Football Stadium Fire
 Disaster Fund 187
Brock, Dave 72–3, 74, 78, 83, 88, 95,
 170
Bron, Gerry 115–16, 178
Bron, Lillian, 115–16
Bronze Records 115–16, 121, 123,
 133, 135, 167, 178, 191, 230
Brown, Dez 105
Brown, James 34
Bruce, Jack 56–7
Bubbles, Barney 81
Burnett, Johnny
 'Train Kept A-Rollin'' 113
Burns, John 112
Burslem, Stoke-on-Trent 5
Burston, Mick 'Wurzel' 132, 176,
 180, 182, 187, 191, 199, 201,
 215, 216–17, 233, 243, 263, 302
 CMJ convention 253–4
 evening of terror 208
 joins Motörhead 171, 172–3,
 174–5
 kidney stones 184
 leaves Motörhead 269, 271–2
 personal problems 203
 Toots (dog) 218–19
Byrds, The 24

Calvert, Bob 76–80, 84, 148
 *Captain Lockhead and the
 Starfighters* 78
Campbell, Phil 158, 176, 180, 184,
 201, 202, 206, 212, 218,
 232–3, 242, 248, 260, 263,
 266, 279, 282, 284–5
 attempts to quit Motörhead 213–15
 breaks ankle in fight 207
 David Letterman Show 233–4
 and Fat-O-Gram 194
 hospitalised by 'brown speed'
 216–17
 joins Motoörhead 171–2, 174–5
 manic behaviour on tour 270–1
 new-found energy on stage 273
 playing on *Overnight Sensation*
 277
Captain Sensible 119
Carey, Mariah 4, 253
Carroll, Ted 112, 113
Carson, Phil 220, 223, 234
Cavern club, Liverpool 28, 29
CBH, German record label 268,
 274

CBS 46

Chesters, Neville 55

Chiswick Records 112, 113, 115, 141

Churchill, Winston 222–3

Ciggy (Cyril, drummer with Rocking Vicars) 39–41, 42–3, 46, 48–9

Clapton, Eric 24, 113, 207, 208–9, 222, 277

    Clarke, Eddie 109–12, 120, 122, 127, 129, 130–1, 134, 138, 139, 156, 157, 184, 187, 218

    berates Lemmy's drinking, 135–6

    excessive salad 147–8

    fights 110–11

    joins Motörhead 109

    leaves Motörhead 161–2, 178

    reluctantant singer 132

    solo for 'Capricorn' 125

    on *TisWas* 140

Clary, Julian 210–11

Clash, The 118, 236

Clooney, Rosemary 12

CMC, American record label 273–4, 277

CMJ convention, New York 253–4

cocaine 44–5, 83, 93, 94, 107, 254

Cochran, Eddie 14

Cocker, Joe 57

Colwyn Bay 20, 26

Comic Strip team 199, 221

Conwy, N. Wales 17, 31

Corsaro, Jason 194, 195

Count Bishops, The 114

Coverdale, David 145

Crane, Whitfield 258

Cream 57

Crest Hotel, Edinburgh 127

Cycle Sluts, The 232

Daily Mirror 27

Damned, The 116–17, 118–20, 157, 199

    'Ballroom Blitz' 120

    'I Just Can't Be Happy Today' 120

    'Over the Top' 120

Dangerous Toys 236, 237

Dave Road Warrior 280

Davidson, Leo 'Angry Faces' 61

Decca in Finland 46

Decline of Western Civilization, Part II: The Metal Years, 210

Dee, Mikkey 246, 264–5, 268, 284–5

    homophobia 266, 282–3

    joins Motörhead 243–5

    miraculous playing 243–4, 262

Deejays (Sundowners), The 31, 32

Deep Purple 26

D'Elia, Roger 60–1

Dettmar, Del 72, 91

Dexedrine 59, 60, 82

Dick, Will Reid 156, 161

Dikmik (Hawkwind musician) 69–70, 71–2, 82–3, 88–9, 92–3

Docks, The, Hamburg 284

Doctor Hook 99

Dokken 243, 265

Donovan 'Season of the Witch' 61

Dorn, Ryan 269

Downey, Brian 175, 202

Downlines Sect, The 26

Drifter 212

Drug Store, Chelsea 66

Dufort, Denise 127, 140, 144
Duke, Phil 61
Dylan, Bob 22

Eat the Rich 199–201
Eddy, Duane 31
Edmunds, Dave 101–2
Eire Apparent, The 57
Eko guitars 32–3
Electric Ballroom, London 119
Electric Garden, London 58
Electric Light Orchestra, The 91
Elsmore, Andy 155
Emerson, Keith 57
Emil Ford and the Checkmates 13
  'What Do You Want to Make
      Those Eyes at Me For' 13
Eno, Brian 78
Entertainment Weekly 240
Epstein, Brian 28, 29, 30
Escape Studio, Kent, 112–13
Eurythmics, The 133
Everly Brothers 102,

Feeney, Harry (Reverend Black) 37,
    38, 47–8
Fender guitars 25, 28, 32, 38
Finland 37, 50, 128–31, 176–7,
    211
Florida 147
Flowers of Romance, The 117
Foghat 56
Ford, Lita 181, 209, 263
Four Pennies, The 102
Fox, Lucas 97, 98, 103–4, 187
Fox, Samantha 186
Foxton, Bruce 117–18

Frankie Goes To Hollywood 185, 186
  'Relax' with Lemmy 185
Fryer, Fritz 102

Garcia, Gerry 277
Gardner, Kim 25
Gerry and the Pacemakers 30, 186–7
Giant, record label 269
Gibson guitars 28, 33, 34, 38
Gill, Pete 134–5, 177, 180, 243
  born-again jogger 175
  comes out 176
  fired from Motörhead 201–2
  joins Motörhead 175
  waves dick around 175–6
Gilligan, Dave 'Giggles' 126
Girl Guides 10, 11–12,
Girlschool 126–8, 145, 161, 178,
    187, 209
  'Bomber' (cover) 144
  'Emergency' 144
  'Please Don't Touch' (cover)
      144
  'Take It All Away' 126
  The St Valentine's Day Massacre
      EP (with Motörhead) 144
  TisWas (TV show) 140
Glitter, Gary 185
Gloucester Road flat, London 70
Glyn, (Glun), bass player 33–34
Gopal, Sam 60–2
Gorham, Scott 163
Grammy Awards 3
Grant, Peter 220
Grease Band, The 57
Greek Street Chinese food store,
    Soho 46–7

Green, Mick 24, 199, 222
Greenberg, Jerry 225, 226, 248, 249
Greenslade 99
Greenslade, Dave 99
Griffiths, Brian 'Griff' 30
Groves, Brian 32
Grower, Alex 219
Guns N' Roses 249, 252, 258
Gustafson, Johnny 30
GWR, record label 193, 196–7, 219

Hadwen, Paul 194–5
Hagen, Nina 218
Hallesy, Trevor 123
Hammersmith Odeon, London 101,
    108, 122, 141, 177
Hanneman, Jeff 212
Hansel, Rainer 268
Harley Street doctors 60
Harmony Meteor guitar 33
Harrison, George 28
Hawkwind 69–95, 98, 114, 137, 178
  albums:
    Doremi Fasol Latido 81, 84, 88
    Greasy Truckers 88
    Hall of the Mountain Grill 84,
        88
    Silver Machine 81
    Space Ritual 81, 88, 89, 137
    Warrior on the Edge of Time 80,
        84, 88
  American tour (1973) 89–91
  dancers (Renee, Stacia, Toni) 75,
      80, 85
  gigs:
    anti-heroin 190
    Glasgow University 76

Hayden Planetarium, New York
    90
  Isle of Wight Festival 70
  Olympia, Paris 89
  Roundhouse 82–4, 86, 88
  Tower Theater, Philadephia 89
  Wembley Stadium 77
  personnel see Anderson, Dave;
      Brock, Dave; Calvert, Bob;
      Dettmar, Del;
  Dikmik; House, Simon; King, Simon;
      Lloyd Langton, Huw; Ollis,
      Terry;
  Powell, Alan ; Rudolph, Paul; Turner,
      Nik;
  songs:
    'Kings of Speed' 84
    'Lost Johnny' 84
    'Motörhead' 84, 91, 99
    'Night of the Hawks' 169
    'Power Cut' 88
    'Silver Machine' 82, 84, 198
    'The Watcher' 84, 88
    'You Shouldn't Do That' 72, 82
Heaton Moor Road flat, Stockport
    20–21, 22–23
Heckstall-Smith, Dick 26
Hellraiser III: Hell On Earth 258,
    262–3
Hell's Angels 166–7
Hendrix, Jimi 35, 55–6, 57, 60
heroin 62–3, 64, 104, 217
Hindenburg 230
Hitler, Adolf 212, 224, 264
Hobbs (tour manager) 235, 237
Hofner guitars 28, 30, 50
Holdon, Gary 187

Holland, Eddie 'Leaving Here' 102
Holland, Jools 272
Hollies, The 48
Holly, Buddy 13–14
   'Peggy Sue' 13
Holly, Leslie 226, 237, 248
Hollywood 14
Hopf bass guitar 72
House, Simon 91
Howard, Jo 208
Howe, Ashley 123
Hughes, Maldwyn 31
Hutchinson, Johnny 30
Hynde, Chrissie 107

Ice T 258
Ikettes, The 60
Ilyushin Bomber 279–80
Ireland 142–3
Iron Maiden 150, 259

Jackson, Michael 253
   'Thriller' video 180
Jackson's Studios, Rickmansworth
   137, 144
Jagger, Mick 29, 64
Jam, The 117
James, Brian 119
Japan 164–5
Japanese translations of lyrics 283–4
Jelly Roll Morton 79
Jett, Joan 209, 263
Jimi Hendrix Experience 55–6
John the Bog 84–5, 86
Johnny Kidd and the Pirates 24, 222
Johnson, Holly 185, 186
Johnson, Kelly 126, 127–8

Jones, Steve 117
Judas Priest 236, 237

Keen, Speedy 112, 115
Ken (bass player with Rocking
   Vicars) 39
Kennington, Frank 106–7
Kilmister, Ian Fraser (Lemmy)
  bands:
    DeeJays (Sundowners), The 31,
     32
    early bands 30–5
    Hawkwind 69–95, 99
    Head Cat, The 299, 300
    Motörhead 98–290
    Motown Sect, The 33, 34–5
    Opal Butterfly 66–7
    P. P. Arnold 60
    Rainmakers, The 33
    Rocking Vicars, The 35–51
    Sam Gopal 60–2
    Sapphires The, 31
  begins playing bass 71–2
  benefit record 'You'll Never Walk
    Alone' 186–7
  cancer diagnosis and death 316–17
  drugs 19–20, 44–5, 57–60, 64–6,
    82–3, 84–8, 90
    busted in Canada 93–4
    toxic blood 103
  fiftieth birthday party 275–6
  film, TV and videos:
    Club X 218
    David Letterman Show 233–4
    *The Decline of Western
     Civilization, Part II: The
     Metal Years*, 210

Doctor and the Medics video
    199
Don't Forget Your Toothbrush
    271–2
Eat the Rich 199–201
Hardware 221–2
Lemmy 300–301
South Atlantic Raiders 221
TV show with Julian Clary
    210–11
TV show with Kirsty MacColl
    185
video for Pat Boone 211
gelignite incident 8–9
Girl Guides 10, 11–12
girlfriends:
    Ann 11
    Anne-Marie 43–4
    Cathy 20–1
    Debbie 141–2
    Katie 188
    Naughty Wendy 217
    Sue 63–4
    Tracy 44–5
as guest artist:
    with Duff McKagen's band
        187–8
    gig and recording with The
        Damned 119–20
    with Hawkwind 179, 190, 198
    on Nina Hagen record 218
    with Nolan Sisters 151–2
    'Relax' with Frankie Goes To
        Hollywood 185
guitars 14–15, 38, 72, 91
    first guitars 30–1, 32–3
health problems 303–317

International Lemmy Day 204
jail 93–4, 130
'Male Sex Object' competition,
    comes second 145
memorial 318–19
moves to America 221, 223
Nazi memorabilia 224
producer on Ramones song 187
razorblade incident onstage
    215–16
recording with Mick Green 222
    'Blue Suede Shoes' 222
    'Paradise' 222
relatives:
    death of father and stepfather
        288
    George Willis (stepfather) 7–8
    mother 1, 2, 5–6, 7, 8
    Patricia Willis (stepsister) 8
    Paul (son) 44–6
    relationship with father 1–3
    Sean (son) 21
    Tony Willis (stepbrother) 8
sets bed on fire 181
songs for other artists:
    Girlschool ('Head Over Heels')
        209
    Lita Ford ('Can't Catch Me')
        209
    Ozzy Osbourne albums *No More
        Tears* and *Ozzmosis* 239
school 6–7
    expelled 15–17
seventieth birthday party 315–16
sexual education 9–12, 15
stewardess incident 3–4
Stones party at the Savoy 208–9

Kilmister, Ian Fraser (Lemmy) – *cont*
  Thailand trip 267–8
  UFO sighting 49–50
  views on:
    American double standards 224–5
    band wives 157–8
    British humour in America 223
    'drug war' 190–1
    fans and rock stardom 253–5
    heroin 62–3, 132
    Japan 164–5
    Los Angeles riots 245–7
    Motörhead's recent recordings 286–7
    relationships 139
    rock 'n' roll 286–7
    September 11 attacks 285
    sex 23, 152–3
    Sony 4, 226–7, 249–50, 252–3, 255
    spitting at performers 222, 236
    staying young 179
    vegetarianism 264
  work at Hotpoint factory 17–18, 32
  work at riding school 10, 11
King, Simon 66, 76, 78, 88, 92
Kinks 'Dandy' 46
Kohoutek comet 90

LA Times 237
Laswell, Bill 194, 195
Led Zeppelin 91, 102, 220
Lee, Tommy 11–12
Lem Club, Italy 89
Lemmy *see* Kilmister, Ian Fraser

Lennon, John 28, 29, 57
Leno, Jay 251
Letterman, David 234, 251
Lillywhite, Steve 208
Lipsky, Tom 274
Little Richard 13, 98
  'Long Tall Sally' 168
Liverpool 23, 28
Ljubljana, Slovenia 50
Llandudno 26, 31
Lloyd Langton, Huw 70–1
London 53–4, 55, 64, 98
  60s culture 56–61
Lord, Jon 25–6, 27
Los Angeles 3, 90–1
Love Pirates of Doom 199
Love Sculpture 'Sabre Dance' 101
Lynne, Jeff 102
Lynott, Phil 187

MacColl, Kirsty 185, 208
Maile, Vic 137, 138, 144, 187, 203, 211, 262
Major, Ray 67
Manchester 20, 23, 32, 33, 35, 37, 43–4, 102
Mandrax 59–60, 82–3
marijuana (dope) 19, 57–8, 88, 151
Marquee club, London 112, 114, 117–18
Marsalis, Branford 251
Matlock, Glen 117
Mayall, John 113
MC5 98
McAuliffe, Kim 127
McCartney, Paul 28
McDaniels, Pete 25

McKagen, Duff 187
McKenzie, Ali 25
Megadeth 197
Melody Maker 130, 171, 228
Mercyful Fate 181, 243
Mercury, record label 149
Merseybeat 23
Merseybeats, The 23, 30, 55
mescaline 74, 83
Metal Church 236, 237
Metallica 181, 240, 252, 258, 276
Methedrine 61
Metropolis (film) 125
Middle Earth, London 58
Miller, Frankie 201
Miller, Jimmy 122, 123–4, 125, 131,
    132, 262
Ming (friend) 19, 20–1
Minolfo, Annette 251, 265
Mitchell, Mitch 56
Mitchell, Graham 189
Mods 25
Montenegro 50
Moody, Micky 152
Moon, Keith 39–40
Moorcock, Michael 77, 80–1
    Hawkmoon books 80
Moors Murderers, The 107
Morris, Steve (Moggsy) 39, 40
Moscow 278–9, 281
Motörhead 3, 31, 72, 73, 78, 81, 97,
    98–290
    albums:
        1916 219, 228–30, 232–3, 242,
            252
        Ace of Spades 132–3, 136–9,
            145, 149, 154, 286, 288

Aftershock 309
Another Perfect Day 162,
    167–8, 193–4, 276
Bad Magic 311
Bastards 195, 262–3, 265,
    266
Bomber 124, 131–3, 134, 135
*Everything Louder Than
    Everyone Else* 283, 284
Hammered 284, 285
Inferno 299–300
Iron Fist 137, 156
Kiss of Death 300
March or Die 239, 240, 242,
    243, 245, 248, 252
Motörhead 113
Motörizer 301
No Remorse 178, 183, 184, 194,
    203
No Sleep At All 211
No Sleep 'Til Hammersmith
    145–6, 155,156
On Parole 105–6, 113
Orgasmatron 182, 193–7, 199
Overkill 123, 124, 132, 134,
    145, 154, 230
Overnight Sensation 276–7
Rock 'n' Roll 203–4, 241
Sacrifice 263, 269–70, 273, 277
Snake Bite Love 281–3
The World Is Yours 301
The World Is Ours 301
We Are Motörhead 282, 284
American fan club 150
artwork on albums 230–1
'Bomber' lighting rig 133–4, 144,
    141, 177–8, 196, 312

Motörhead – *cont*
  Clarendon Hotel Christmas party
    141
  deported from Finland 130–1
  EPs:
    The Beer Drinkers 113, 141
    The Golden Years 135
    The St Valentine's Day Massacre
      (with Girlschool) 144
    Stand By Your Man 167
    with Wendy O. Williams 160–1
  formation 97–9
  gigs:
    debut at Roundhouse, London
      99–100
    Coachella 309–10
    Giants of Rock festival, Finand
      211
    Glastonbury 313
    Hackney Speedway 166–7
    Hammersmith Odeon 101, 141,
      122, 177
    Hammersmith ten-year
      anniversay 187
    Heavy Sound Festival, Belgium
      181
    Kaiser Auditorium, Oakland
      197–8
    Meltdown 300
    Motörboat 310, 314
    Port Vale Football Club 150
    Punkahaarju Festival, Finland
      128–30
    Reading Festival 133
    Rotation Club, Hanover 169
    Royal Festival Hall 300
    Royal Opera House 298
    Stafford Bingley Hall 135–6
    Summernight Festival,
      Nuremberg 151
    TT Motorcycle Race, Isle of
      Man, 181
    Wacken 306–7
    'Wooaarrggh Weekender'
      festival, Norfolk 184
    Wrexham Football Club 165–6
  Grammy nomination 239–40
  Iron Fist rig and staging 156–7, 196
  management:
  see Banker, Doug; Carson, Phil;
      Kennington, Frank;
      Osbourne, Sharon;
    Secunda, Tony; Singerman, Toddd;
      Smith, Douglas
  Orgasmatron Train rig 196
  Overkill backdrop 141
  parachute stunt 150–1
  personnel:
  see Burston, Mick; Campbell, Phil;
      Clarke, Eddie; Dee, Mickkey;
      Gill, Pete; Robertson, Brian;
      Taylor, Phil; Wallis, Larry
  police harassment 159–60
  record deals:
    Bronze Records 115–16, 179,
      180
    CBH 268–9
    Chiswick Records 112, 113, 115
    CMC 273–4
    GWR 193
    Sony debacle 249–50, 252–3,
      255
    Stiff Records 111
    United Artists 101, 105–6, 111

WTG/Sony 220, 225–7, 248–9, 252

ZYX 261–2, 268

songs:

'1916' 228, 230

'Ace of Spades' 138, 149, 154, 168, 272

'Ain't My Crime' 195

'Ain't No Nice Guy' 243, 248, 249–50

'All the Aces' 132

'Angel City' 229, 232

'Another Perfect Day' 169

'Another Time' 269

'Beer Drinkers and Hell Raisers' 113

'Bomber' 132, 168

'Boogie Man' 204

'Born to Lose' 105, 113

'Born to Raise Hell' 258

'Brave New World' 297–8

'Capricorn' 125

'Cat Scratch Fever' 248

'The Chase is Better Than the Catch' 139, 307

'City Kids' 102, 105, 113

'Damage Case' 125, 307

'Dead Men Tell No Tales' 135

'Deaf Forever 196

'Death or Glory' 263

'Desperate for You' 282

'Dog Face Boy' 270

'Dogs' 204

'Don't Let Daddy Kiss Me' 263

'The Dreamtime' 229

'Eat the Rich' 241

'Emergency' 144

'Fools' 105

'Goin' to Brazil' 219, 228, 242

'Hell on Earth' 243, 258

'Hellraiser' 243, 258

'I Am the Sword' 263

'I Know How to Die' 307

'I Won't Pay Your Price' 125

'I'm So Bad' 228

'I'm Your Witchdoctor' 113

'Instro' 113

'Iron Horse' 105, 113

'Jailbait' 139, 191

'Keepers on the Road' 113

'Killed by Death' 179

'Lawman' 132

'Leaving Here' 102, 135, 111

'Locomotive' 179

'Lost in the Ozone' 263

'Lost Johnny' 102, 105, 113

'Louie Louie' 116, 121

'Love Me Forever' 228

'Make 'Em Blind' 269, 270

'March or Die' 248

'Masterplan' 161

'Metropolis' 125

'Motörhead' 102, 113, 144, 168, 187

'Night Side' 282

'Nightmare' 229

'No Class' 125, 161, 191

'No Voices in the Sky' 219

'On Parole' 105, 113

'One Short Life' 301

'One to Sing the Blues' 231

'Out of the Sun' 270

'Overkill' 168, 283

'Please Don't Touch' 144, 145

songs: – *cont*
    'Ramones' 228–9
    'Rock Out' 301
    'Sex and Death' 269
    'Shake Your Blood' 300
    'Shut You Down' 219
    'Snaggletooth' 179
    'Stand' 248
    'Stand By Your Man' 161
    'Steal Your Face' 179
    'Step Down' 132
    'Stiletto Heels' 266
    'Stone Dead Forever' 132
    'Talking Head' 132
    'Tear Ya Down' 116, 125
    'Too Late Too Late' 135
    'Train Kept A-Rollin'' 113
    'Traitor' 204
    'Under the Knife' 179
    'Vibrator' 105, 113
    'Victory or Die' 311
    'The Watcher' 105, 113
    '(We Are) The Road Crew' 138
    'White Line Fever' 111, 113
    'Whorehouse Blues' 300
    'You Better Run' 248
soundtrack and appearance in *Eat the Rich* 199–201
soundtrack for *Hellraiser III: Hell On Earth* 258
ten-year anniversary party 217–18
tours:
    Ace Up Your Sleeve 140–1
    with Alice Cooper 204–6
    Australia and New Zealand 181–2
    Beyond the Threshold of Pain 113
Finland 128–30, 176–7
Gigantour 302
Hungary 182–3, 278
Iron Fist 156–7, 312
It Never Gets Dark 188–90
Japan 164–5, 234
Mayhem 302
Overkill 126
Ozzy 'farewell' tours 257–8
Sony's Operation Rock 'n' Roll 236–8
South America 212–13, 258–60, 267
Russia 278–81, 284
USA, first tour 145–6, 147–51
TV and radio shows:
    BBC 'Peel Sessions' 199
    Extra Celestial Transmission 184–5
    Much Music 274–5
    Rockstage concert 144–5
    Saturday Starship 183–4
    Tonight Show 251–2
    Top of the Pops 120–1, 144
    TisWas 140
videos:
    'Ain't No Nice Guy' 250–1
    The Birthday Party 188
    Everthing Louder Than Everything Else 232
    'Hellraiser' 258
    'Killed By Death' 180
Motown Sect, The 33, 34–5, 37
Mott the Hoople 67, 108
Mottola, Tommy 4, 253
Move, The 57, 107, 108
MTV 165, 166, 180, 184, 191, 250–1

Much Music 274–5
Muggers, The 115
Munroe, Tony 25
Murphy (Murph), Irish folk singer
    53–5
Murray, Mitch 'How Do You Do It'
    30
Mustaine, Dave 197–8

Nazareth 76
Needs, Chris 129
Nelson, Ricky 'Travelin' Man' 31
New Musical Express 107
New Wave of British Heavy Metal
    movement (NWOBHM) 150
Newcastle-under-Lyme 5
Nice, The 57
Nodder (roadie with Rocking Vicars)
    40–1, 49
Nolan Sisters 120, 151–2
    'Don't Do That' 152
Nugent, Ted 238
    'Cat Scratch Fever' 248

Oasis Club, Manchester 37, 38
Ollis, Terry (Boris or Borealis) 75–6
Ono, Yoko 57
Opal Butterfly 66–7, 76
Oriole Records 29
Osbourne, Ozzy 145–6, 150, 239,
    249, 250
    'Blizzard of Oz' tour 146, 148–9
    'farewell' tour 257–8
Osbourne, Sharon 149, 234, 235,
    239
Ovation guitars 91
Owens, Jesse 224

Page, Jimmy 87, 277
Palin, Michael 203–4
Pannunzio, Thom 285
Perman, Alan 234
Persian Risk 171, 180
Pete (bass player with Rocking
    Vicars) 42–3
Pink Fairies, The 74, 95, 98, 102, 199
Pink Floyd 57
Plant, Robert 220
Plasmatics, The 160–1, 191
Platt, Tony 167
Police, The 133
Powell, Alan 92, 97
Powell, Cozy 152
Powell, Nosher 200
Presley, Elvis 13, 28
    'Don't Be Cruel' 13
    'I Beg of You' 13
Preston Dave 62
Pretenders, The 107
Pretty Things, The 34
punk music 117–20
Pye Records 137

Quatermass 30

Radio Caroline 40
Radio City 4
Radio Clyde, Glasgow 159
Radio Luxembourg 12–13
Rainbow 26
Rainbow Bar, Hollywood 221, 317, 319
Rainmakers, The 33
Ramones, The 187, 229, 267
    'Go Home Ann' from *Bonzo Goes
        to Bitburg* 187

Rath, Billy 115
Redding, Noel 55–6
Reid, Chuck 285
Release 65
Reverend Black *see* Feeney, Harry
Rhodes, Randy 148
Richards, Keith 103
Richardson, Peter 200
Richmond, Neil 116
Rickenbacker guitars 28
ring modulator 69, 82
Robertson, Brian (Robbo) 163–4,
    165, 166–9, 178, 187, 201, 243,
    245
  fashion sense 167, 168–9
  fired from Motörhead 169, 173–4
  hated by audiences 168
  joins Motörhead 162
  strange behaviour 165–7
Rock Girls, The (or Rock Birds) 44
rock 'n' roll, birth of 12–14
Rockfield Studios, Monmouth 101
Rocking Vicars, The 35, 37–51
  'Dandy' 46
  east European tour 50
  'It's Alright' 46
  personnel *see* Ciggy; Feeney,
    Harry; Morris, Steve; Pete
Rockpile 101
Rolling Stone 240
Rolling Stones, The 24, 28–9, 207
  Exile on Main Street 122
  Goatshead Soup 122
Rondinelli, Bobby 260
Rory Storm and the Hurricanes
    'Beautiful Dreamer' 24
Rostov, Russia 278, 280

Roundhouse, London 82–4, 86, 88,
    99–100, 119
Roundhouse Studios, London 123
Rudolph, Paul 94–5, 98

Sam Gopal Dream, The 60
  Escalator 61
Sapphires, The 32
Sarzo, Rudy 148
Savoy Brown 56
Saxon 134–5, 175, 180
Scabies, Rat 118–19, 177, 199
Schaffer, Paul 234
Schneider, Dee 166, 191, 275
Sean Head Band 79
Secunda, Tony 107–8, 111, 113, 114,
    115
Sex Pistols, The 117, 118
Shadows, The 31
Shelter Records, San Francisco 115
Sinatra, Frank 12, 152
Singerman, Todd 247, 250, 259,
    261–2, 267, 275
Skew Siskin 160
Skid Row 259
Skidmore, Alan 26
Slade 120
Slash 249, 250
Slayer 211–12
  Smith, Douglas 99, 106, 113–14,
    115, 140, 152, 156, 173, 174,
    188, 193, 196, 215, 219, 227,
    247
Smith, Kevin 33
Solley, Pete 228, 248, 262
Somme, Battle of 229–30
Sony 4, 81, 220, 226, 227, 231, 235,

237, 238, 240, 248, 249–50,
    252–3, 255, 258
Sounds 99, 101, 145
South Atlantic Raiders 221
Speakeasy, London 61, 63, 87, 117–18
    speed (amphetamine sulphate,
        methyl amphetamine
        hydrochloride) 19–20, 64, 70,
        83, 87, 92–3, 94, 103
Speed Queen 160
Spellman, Benny 24
Spheeris, Penelope 210
Spinal Tap 158, 199
Spooky Tooth 108
Squeeze 272
St. Petersburg, Russia 280
Stanshall, Viv 78–80
Starr, Ringo 28
Starfighter (F-104) 78
Stasium, Ed 228
Status Quo 152
Steele, Stewart 33, 34, 35
Steele, Tommy 13
Steeleye Span 107, 108
Stevie (singer with Speed Queen)
    160
Stiff Records 111
Stoke Newington Eight 71
Stray Cats, The 102
Strummer, Joe 118, 236
Sundowners, The 31
Siouxsie and the Banshees 117
Swan Song, record label 102
    Sweet, The'Ballroom Blitz' 120

Talmy, Shel 46–7
Tank 157–8, 178

Tarrant, Chris 140
Taylor, Phil (Philthy) 109–12, 120,
    122, 134, 135–6, 140, 144, 145,
    163, 169, 171, 201, 218, 231,
    233, 244, 262
    accidents and injuries 114, 129,
        142–3, 157, 207
    death 314–15
    drugs bust 151
    excessive salad 147–8
    fights 110–11, 114, 207
    fired from Motörhead 240–3
    hospitalised by 'brown speed'
        216–17
    joins Motörhead 104–5
    leaves Motörhead 173–4, 175
    rejoins Motörhead 202–3
Texas, US 89
Theodorou, Irene (Motorcycle Irene)
    98, 109, 110, 114, 116, 151
Thin Lizzy 162, 163, 164, 173, 175,
    202, 240–1
Thompson, Howard 116
Thunderclap Newman 112
    'Something in the Air' 112
TisWas 140
Titanic 206
Tuinol 60
Turner, Nik 72, 73–5, 78, 87
Turner, Tina 125
    'I'll Be Your Sister' 125
Twink (founder of Pink Fairies) 74,
    78
Twisted Sister 165–6, 181

UFO 98
Ulrich, Lars 149–50, 196

United Artists 101, 105–6, 111, 113
uppers (Blues and Black Beauties)
    59, 83, 84–5
Uriah Heep 115

Valium 77, 79
Vanian, Dave 118, 120
Venet, Jack 43
Ventures, The 31
Vicious, Sid 117–18
Victor Records 234

Wagstaff's, Llandudno 30–1
Wallis, Larry 102, 104, 105, 187
   joins Motörhead 98
   leaves Motörhead 109
Ward, Algy 120, 157
Watson, Robbie 19–20
Wessex Studios, London 116
West, Leslie 254
Whitesnake 26, 152
Who, The 37, 42, 55
   'The Kids Are Alright' 46
Widowmaker 71

Wild Bill Hickock 138
Williams, Wendy O. 160–1, 187,
   191
Willis family *see* under Kilmister, Ian
   Fraser (Lemmy)
Wilson, Harold 108
Wizard Records 107
Wonder, Stevie 90
Wood, Art 26, 27
Wood, Ronnie 24, 25, 26, 27, 208
Wood, Roy 91
WTG, record label 225, 226, 237,
   248, 249, 252
Wyman, Bill 208

Yardbirds, The 34, 209
Young Ones, The 174, 179, 199
Young, Bob 152
Yugoslavia 50

Zig Zag magazine 129
ZYX, German record label 261–2,
   264, 265, 268
ZZ Top 113

Connect with U s

Visit us online at
KensingtonBooks.com
to read more from your favorite authors, see books
by series, view reading group guides, and more.

Join us on social media

for sneak peeks, chances to win books and prize packs,
and to share your thoughts with other readers.

facebook.com/kensingtonpublishing
twitter.com/kensingtonbooks

Tell us what you think!

To share your thoughts, submit a review,
or sign up for our eNewsletters, please visit:
KensingtonBooks.com/TellUs.